Race, Place, Trace

Sung Eun Choi is an Associate Professor of History at Bentley University. She holds a doctorate from the University of California, Los Angeles and was a Fellow at the Institute of Advanced Studies in Nantes, France. She is the author of *Decolonization and the French of Algeria: Bringing the Settler Colony Home* (Palgrave 2016). She has taught at Pomona College and Washington State University.

Gabriel Piterberg specialises on the history of the Ottoman Empire and the Mediterranean in the early modern period, and on modern themes such as colonialism, Zionism, and Palestine/Israel. He has published articles in the *New Left Review* and the *London Review of Books*.

Lynette Russell, AM is one of Australia's leading historians. She has authored or edited fifteen books, and numerous journal collections. She is an Australian Research Council Laureate Fellow and Professor of Indigenous Studies at Monash University, and is the only Australian scholar to be elected to both the Royal Historical Society (London) and the Royal Anthropological Institute (London).

Susan Slyomovics is Distinguished Professor of Anthropology and Near Eastern Languages and Cultures at the University of California, Los Angeles. She is also author of *The Object of Memory: Arab and Jew Narrate the Palestinian Village* and *The Performance of Human Rights in Morocco*, and co-editor of *Women and Power in the Middle East*, all available from the University of Pennsylvania Press.

Lorenzo Veracini is Associate Professor of History at Swinburne University of Technology, Melbourne. His research focuses on the comparative history of colonial systems and settler colonialism as a mode of domination. He has authored *Israel and Settler Society* (2006), *Settler Colonialism: A Theoretical Overview* (2010), *The Settler Colonial Present* (2015), and *The World Turned Inside Out: Settler Colonialism as a Political Idea* (2021). Lorenzo co-edited *The Routledge Handbook of the History of Settler Colonialism* (2016), manages the settler colonial studies blog, and is Founding Editor of *Settler Colonial Studies*.

Race, Place, Trace

Essays in Honour of Patrick Wolfe

Edited by Lorenzo Veracini
and Susan Slyomovics

VERSO
London • New York

Funding for Lorenzo Veracini's visiting professorship at the University of California Los Angeles came from the university's International Institute. UCLA's Center for Near Eastern Studies hosted the "Conference on Race, Indigeneity, and Settler Colonialism" co-organized by Lorenzo Veracini and Susan Slyomovics that convened scholars to honor Patrick Wolfe on March 9–10, 2017. Publication of this volume is supported by a UCLA Faculty Research Grant.

First published by Verso 2022
The collection © Verso 2022
The contributions © The contributors 2022

All rights reserved

The moral rights of the author have been asserted

1 3 5 7 9 10 8 6 4 2

Verso
UK: 6 Meard Street, London W1F 0EG
US: 20 Jay Street, Suite 1010, Brooklyn, NY 11201
versobooks.com

Verso is the imprint of New Left Books

ISBN-13: 978-1-83976-616-9
ISBN-13: 978-1-83976-617-6 (US EBK)
ISBN-13: 978-1-83976-615-2 (UK EBK)

British Library Cataloguing in Publication Data
A catalogue record for this book is available from the British Library

Library of Congress Cataloging-in-Publication Data
A catalog record for this book is available from the Library of Congress

Typeset in Minion Pro by MJ&N Gavan, Truro, Cornwall
Printed and bound by CPI Group (UK) Ltd, Croydon, CR0 4YY

Contents

List of Contributors   ii

Race, Place, Trace: A Preface
   Susan Slyomovics, Lorenzo Veracini   vii

Introduction: Patrick Wolfe's Legacy and Method
   Lorenzo Veracini   1

PART I. *Assimilations*

1 Colonization, Land Registries, and the Torrens Act in French Algeria, 1863–1903   *Sung Eun Choi*   21

2 'False Friends?' On Algeria, the Algerian Jewish Question, and Settler Colonial Studies   *Susan Slyomovics*   55

PART II. *Preaccumulations*

3 Mormonism, Primitive Accumulation, Preaccumulation
   Lorenzo Veracini   93

4 J.G.A. Pocock's Antipodean Gaze from the Standpoint of a Fellow Colonist   *Gabriel Piterberg*   119

Conclusion: 'They Are in Our Town but Not of It' – Patrick Wolfe and Belonging   *Lynette Russell*   165

Race, Place, Trace

A Preface

Susan Slyomovics, Lorenzo Veracini

Patrick Wolfe (1949–2016) spoke to historians, anthropologists, and historians of anthropology. And he spoke to and wrote about Indigenous peoples speaking to their colonizers about colonial territorial expansion and dispossession. He remains the most important theorist of settler colonialism – a form of colonialism premised on land over labour. Responding to the development and widespread adoption of postcolonial theory in the 1990s, Wolfe gave priority to settler colonialism's operation through a *logic* of elimination: the settlers come to stay and to permanently displace the Indigenous collectives and polities. His work also emphasized that the logic of elimination could take many forms – massacres, removal, and assimilation – and that therefore there was a profound continuity linking the histories of dispossession and settlement, the ongoing repression of Indigenous communities, and their agency and resistance. Settler colonialism was a current affair for Patrick Wolfe; understanding and addressing its specific structures of inequality was urgent and necessary. Moreover, his comparative analysis linked together disparate settler societies in North America, Australasia, South Africa, Israel/Palestine, Brazil, India, and more.

Throughout his academic career, Patrick Wolfe wrote and lectured widely without a stable university position. He conducted his writing life balanced on the cusp of two technologies. He tapped away on his computer, diligently assuring his machine's uncompromised state by refusing physical connection to the internet – what hackers call a 'secure air-gap'. At the same time, he maintained boxes of three-by-five notecards, each white paper square handwritten with its respective bibliographical citation alphabetized. Nonetheless, both alternative systems of scholarly storage and production were incinerated in the 2009 bushfires that destroyed his home near Healesville in Victoria, Australia. Eventually, Patrick managed to reconstitute the manuscript of *Traces of History: Elementary Structures of Race*. There was, however, no way to salvage many of the missing footnotes, which brings to mind the following observation from historian Anthony Grafton:

> Like the toilet, the footnote enables one to deal with ugly tasks in private; like the toilet, it is tucked genteelly away – often, in recent years, not even at the bottom of the page but at the end of the book. Out of sight, and even out of mind, seems exactly where so banal a device belongs. The footnote's ubiquity makes it invisible ... Like a sewer, the footnote is essential to civilized historical life; like a sewer, it seems a poor subject for civil conversation, and attracts attention, for the most part, when it malfunctions.[1]

While environmental disaster forced Wolfe to go to print with minimal footnotes, there are echoes of an earlier, more famous writing feat by Erich Auerbach. An Ashkenazi Jew like Wolfe (who was also of Irish origins), Auerbach fled Nazi-dominated Europe to Istanbul where he produced without a single footnote his masterpiece, *Mimesis: The Representation of Reality in Western Literature*.[2] According to an interview with Leo Spitzer – another Jewish scholar, who had preceded Auerbach in flight to Istanbul – the scholar who is bookless, beset by conflagrations from humans and nature, makes a virtue of having no footnotes:

---

1 Anthony Grafton, 'The Footnote from De Thou to Ranke', *History and Theory*, 33: 4, 1994, 54–5.

2 Erich Auerbach, *Mimesis: The Representation of Reality in Western Literature*, Princeton: Princeton University Press, 2003 [1953].

Unfortunately there were almost no books. I finally asked the dean about this shortage. He replied simply, 'We don't bother with books. They burn'. I later realized that there was some justice in his view, for most Istanbul buildings were wooden and the fire department was hopelessly disorganized.[3]

Wolfe both acknowledged and lamented to us this sparse use of footnotes. And yet, important conversations with predecessors and contemporaries appear sometimes as traces in his work: conversations with Marx, Mannoni, Du Bois, Fanon, Stuart Hall, Cedric Robinson; and with the Aboriginal scholars and militants he encountered in Melbourne and elsewhere in Australia, including Gary Foley and Tony Birch. These conversations enabled him to magisterially connect race and place, and place making and racializations. The traces he followed in the historical record are mirrored by other traces in his work.

In contrast, the essays brought together in this volume in his honour are weighted down with almost 400 footnotes. We took sanitation and plumbing seriously. The collection opens with an introductory chapter by Lorenzo Veracini dedicated to Wolfe's impact and method. A much-reduced version of this essay was published in *Aboriginal History* in 2016, but for this Introduction it has been extended and now discusses recent critiques of his work.[4] The following two chapters form Part One of this volume and address the ways in which Wolfe's work on the settler-colonial 'assimilation' of land and people enables a novel interpretation of all historical sites of settler-colonial expansion; they focus on French Algeria, which was a settler colony he did not write about. For Sung Eun Choi, Wolfe's approaches to racial difference can be applied to the 'Muslim' indigenes of French Algeria and the ways in which they were encoded as untrustworthy and underdeveloped with regard to land rights in colonial legal taxonomies. In Chapter 2, Susan Slyomovics explores the rare instance of imperial extension of French citizenship to Algerian Jews, an entire native community in a settler-colonial setting. Part Two addresses another category productively employed by Wolfe: 'preaccumulation'.[5] Although Wolfe developed preaccumulation in the context of

---

3 'Leo Spitzer', *The Johns Hopkins Magazine*, 1952, 26.
4 Lorenzo Veracini, 'Patrick Wolfe's Dialectics', *Aboriginal History*, 40: 1, 2016, 249–60.
5 Patrick Wolfe, 'Purchase by Other Means: The Palestine Nakba and

his study of the Zionist colonization of Palestine, in his chapter Lorenzo Veracini engages with it as it applies to the development of Mormon colonialism. Preaccumulation, Veracini argues, enables an understanding of all settler-colonial projects that do not emanate from a specific colonizing polity, instances Wolfe defined as a 'diffused metropole'.[6] In Chapter 4, Gabriel Piterberg offers a comparative essay involving three sites of settler-colonial expansion pursued by diasporic collectives: Aotearoa/New Zealand, Argentina, and Israel/Palestine. Finally, in her concluding chapter Lynette Russell returns to Wolfe's work and the specific location of his militant and interdisciplinary scholarship. This contribution by a prominent Australian Aboriginal public intellectual also offers a rebuttal to recent accusations that Wolfe both neglected Indigenous perspectives and the efficacy of Indigenous resistances.

Each of the chapters collected here engages with a different aspect of Wolfe's work. As they emanate from quite distinct disciplinary backgrounds, these essays deal with an extraordinary variety of sites and themes. Some of us work in Indigenous studies, others as historians and anthropologists doing social history and ethnographic fieldwork, and some of us focus on theory. We believe that this volume illustrates how seminal his contribution was and is, and that there is a lot at stake – that thinking of settler colonialism as a specific mode of domination, and of race and colonialism in innovative and currently relevant (and indeed Marxist) ways, remains important. There are three core reasons why we feel it is especially important to develop the field of thinking inaugurated by Wolfe and to engage with audiences beyond restricted scholarly circles while offering engaged social and historical analysis: first, because the demand for Indigenous sovereignty has been crucial to recent struggles against neoliberal attacks in the settler societies; second, because a critique of settler colonialism and its logic of elimination has supported important struggles against environmental devastation (arguably a manifestation of such a logic); and third, because the ability to think race in ways that are not disconnected from other struggles is now more needed than ever. Racial capitalism and settler colonialism are as imbricated now as they always have been, and keeping both in mind at the same time

---

Zionism's Conquest of Economics', *Settler Colonial Studies*, 2: 1, 2012, 133–71. See also Patrick Wolfe, 'Recuperating Binarism: A Heretical Introduction', *Settler Colonial Studies*, 3: 3–4, 2013, 257–79, at 266.

6   Wolfe, 'Purchase by Other Means', 136.

highlights the need to establish and nurture solidarities that reach across established divides.

These are all issues that are crucial both to current movements and struggles and to scholarly debate. Introducing *Without Guarantees*, the editors of a collection dedicated to Stuart Hall's work and legacy noted that 'cultural studies has been subjected to much abuse lately', but added that their intention was to offer 'some implicit and explicit reflections' on what cultural studies 'can be and what it might become'.[7] In a similar vein, we think of this collection of essays as a preliminary statement about what settler colonial studies can be and what it might become. While we maintain that the struggle for a decolonizing dispensation will benefit all – Indigenous and non-Indigenous individuals and collectives alike – we are aware that political projects of Indigenous resurgence do not need it and that a demand for substantive sovereignty must be suspicious of official processes of repressive recognition. While settler colonial studies offers a valuable decolonial rhetoric for Indigenous collectives facing a denial of recognition (what Wolfe called 'repressive authenticity'),[8] it is largely irrelevant for Indigenous collectives that are pursuing what Audra Simpson has called 'refusal'.[9] An uneven geography of Indigenous engagement with settler colonial studies and recent critiques of this analytic demonstrate this variability.[10] But Indigenous resurgence,

---

7   Paul Gilroy, Lawrence Grossberg, Angela McRobbie, 'Preface', in Paul Gilroy, Lawrence Grossberg, Angela McRobbie (eds), *Without Guarantees: In Honour of Stuart Hall*, London: Verso, 2000, ix.

8   Patrick Wolfe, *Settler Colonialism and the Transformation of Anthropology*, London: Cassell, 1999.

9   Audra Simpson, *Mohawk Interruptus: Political Life Across the Borders of Settler States*, Durham: Duke University Press, 2014.

10   See, for example, Elizabeth Strakosch, Alissa Macoun, 'The Vanishing Endpoint of Settler Colonialism', *Arena Journal*, 37/38, 2012, 40–62; Corey Snelgrove, Rita Kaur Dhamoon, and Jeff Corntassel, 'Unsettling Settler Colonialism: The Discourse and Politics of Settlers, and Solidarity with Indigenous Nations', *Decolonization: Indigeneity, Education and Society*, 3: 2, 2014; J. Kēhaulani Kauanui, '"A Structure, Not an Event": Settler Colonialism and Enduring Indigeneity', *Lateral: Journal of the Cultural Studies Association*, 5: 1, 2016; Jodi A. Byrd, 'Still Waiting for the 'Post' to Arrive: Elizabeth Cook-Lynn and the Imponderables of American Indian Postcoloniality', *Wicazo Sa Review*, 31: 1, 2016, 75–89; Manu Vimalassery, Juliana Hu Pegues, and Alyosha Goldstein, 'Introduction: On Colonial Unknowing', *Theory and Event*, 19: 4, 2016; Cynthia G. Franklin, Njoroge Njoroge, Suzanna Reiss, 'Tracing the Settler's Tools: A Forum on Patrick

while a necessary condition for a decolonial passage, should be accompanied by a parallel moment of settler decolonial resurgence. If the aim is to decolonize the whole of society, Wolfe would have agreed, a critique of what settlers do and what they think they are doing when they do the things they do – a critique of their logic and its operation – is still necessary. Each settler nationalist historiography asserts discontinuity between present and past in order to express a local variety of exceptionalism. But the past was not past for Patrick Wolfe, and settler colonialism remains a global and transnational phenomenon. Two decades after he gave us *Settler Colonialism and the Transformation of Anthropology*, and after many recognitions and apologies in some settler societies, it still is. We see settler colonial studies as a continuing contribution towards this collective effort.

Wolfe's Life and Legacy', *American Quarterly*, 69: 2, 2017, 235–90. See also Shino Konishi, 'First Nations Scholars, Settler Colonial Studies, and Indigenous History', *Australian Historical Studies*, 50: 3, 2019, 285–304.

Introduction

Patrick Wolfe's Legacy and Method

Lorenzo Veracini

Patrick Wolfe's *Settler Colonialism and the Transformation of Anthropology* appeared in 1999, the result of his investigation into settler colonialism in the ongoing subjection of Indigenous peoples in the settler societies. While the contemporary settler polities, as Wolfe later argued, have been 'impervious to regime change', *Settler Colonialism* was an Australian-produced response to the consolidation and global spread of postcolonial studies as discourse and method (quite interestingly, postcolonial studies had also originally been an Australian intellectual export).[1] This call became very influential and inspired the consolidation in subsequent years of settler colonial studies as a distinct scholarly field. This introductory chapter reflects on Patrick Wolfe's legacy and method.

Patrick Wolfe was an unusual scholar. Always somewhat at the margins of Australian academia and yet holding at different times fellowships at Harvard and Stanford, he was able to contribute seminally to a variety of fields: anthropology, genocide studies, the historiography of

---

1 See Dipesh Chakrabarty, 'Subaltern Studies and Postcolonial Historiography', *Nepantia*, 1: 1, 2000, 9–32.

race, Indigenous studies, and the study of colonialism and imperialism. He was educated in excellent English public schools and was successful in the United States. The 'cringe', the notion that cultural and other standards are set elsewhere – mainly in Britain or in the US – still fundamentally shapes many aspects of Australian cultural life. But Wolfe remained marginal. In his case, the cringe did not apply.

He was my teacher, even if never in a formal capacity, but we had significant differences in approach. These differences have been neglected in criticism of settler colonial studies as a scholarly endeavour. We have been lumped together – and it was a great privilege. I'll get to some of these critiques in a minute, but first allow me to focus on our differences. To put it simply, in my thinking settler colonialism was like a waltz: a three-step dance involving settlers, Indigenous peoples and exogenous others; for Wolfe, it was like a salsa involving Indigenous and non-Indigenous peoples. Two is not three, and even though it sounds like a diatribe that medieval theology scholars may engage in, it was not a small difference.[2] He regarded all non-Indigenous peoples as 'settlers' and I do not. And there was another fundamental point of dissension: for Wolfe, settler colonialism was one type of colonialism; for me, they were antithetical modes of domination. One is not two, the medieval scholasticists again. Our focus was also dissimilar: my interest is settlers and what they do and what they think they are doing. For him, the focus was indigeneity under attack. He had promised that he would respond.[3] I will not enjoy that even greater privilege.

---

2   Wolfe noted: 'The "Natives"' irreducible externality to the settler social contract ... prompts me to register an appreciative disagreement with Veracini, who has aptly pointed out – my disagreement being with his inference rather than with the point itself – that settlers bring their sovereignty with them. This enables Veracini to distinguish between settlers and immigrants, the latter being those who do not bring a sovereignty with them. On its own terms, this distinction seems questionable (where, for instance, does it leave White settlers of Irish descent?)'. In a note he then added: 'My disagreement is not with Veracini's observation that, while settlers found political orders, immigrants encounter those orders already founded. It is with the implication that this distinction within sovereignty discourse detaches immigrants from the settler project of Native replacement, an implication that ultimately (or so it seems to me) hinges on voluntarism'. Patrick Wolfe, 'Recuperating Binarism: A Heretical Introduction', *Settler Colonial Studies*, 3: 3–4, 2013, 257–79, at 258, 276, note 11.

3   Concluding one of his interventions he had said: 'I am saving my

Wolfe typically proceeded against fashionable scholarly trends. Dialectics and binaries had ceased to be familiar methodological approaches in the social sciences decades before, but they still worked for him. And they worked for those who read his work, and they were many. Similarly, area specialisation was not his call. Reframing stubborn problems actually required him to think outside established disciplinary boundaries. As a result, as well as being interdisciplinary, his work was eminently and inherently comparative. He was thus able to contribute to educating a generation of younger scholars working in a remarkable variety of national settings: Australia, Hawaii, North America, Brazil, and Palestine.

Dialectics

This was, in my opinion, the first step in his dialectical method: anything could be better understood by looking at what it is not. He believed that the rigorous analysis of a specific topic could shed light on another; that one could understand, for example, the racialization of African Americans in the US by looking at the dispossession of Indigenous peoples; and that one could understand the current dehumanization of Indigenous Australians by looking at the ways in which a nascent scholarly discipline had at once proclaimed their humanity and reflected on their alleged failure to reproduce.

Related scholarly fields have generally refrained from crafting a response – although there are now exceptions to this non-engagement. Jared Sexton, for example, has offered a critical response to the consolidation of Indigenous and settler colonial studies.[4] Sexton is concerned with the ways that settler colonial studies and native studies neglect slavery as a problem as much as they neglect 'abolition' in their approaches to decolonization.[5] For Native studies, Sexton argues, 'anti-racism without

---

disagreement with Lorenzo over his next line – "This is why settler colonialism is not colonialism" – for another time. This article is long enough as it is'. See Patrick Wolfe, 'Purchase by Other Means: The Palestine Nakba and Zionism's Conquest of Economics', *Settler Colonial Studies*, 2: 1, 2012, 163, note 7.

4 See, for example, Jared Sexton, 'The *Vel* of Slavery: Tracking the Figure of the Unsovereign', *Critical Sociology*, 2014, 1–15.

5 Ibid., 2.

Indigenous leadership is a wager for Black junior partnership in the settler colonial state'.[6] He dismisses this link: there are ways out of settler colonialism other than being Indigenous or an 'ally'.[7] 'Abolition' (understood flexibly in this context and in an expanded way) will liberate all because abolition is not about Indigenous sovereignty as opposed to the settler one, but against sovereignty per se. Indigenous and settler peoples may be the 'peoples of sovereignty', Sexton argues, but it is genocide that unites radically different experiences. Genocide is, for him, inherent to slavery: enslavement is, after all, the prohibition for the enslaved to reproduce '*as* people'.[8] In the context of this analysis, slavery is thereby prior to Indigenous dispossession; it is an *Ur* dispossession, the mother of all dispossessions. Sexton concludes: 'Slavery is not a loss that the [Indigenous] self experiences – of language, lineage, land, or labor – but rather the loss of any self that could experience such loss'.[9] Wolfe was keenly aware of the strategic uses his scholarship could be made to work for, and his 2016 book on the 'elementary structures of race' constituted a response (even if the volume had been almost two decades in the making).[10] Sexton's conclusion and Wolfe's reconstruction of the evolution of racial categories were compatible. The racialization of Indigenous collectives was the complementary counterpoint to the racialization of Black people – they were distinct and yet depended on each other, and they should be considered jointly.

I once told Patrick that his work on racializations (note the plural) was recuperating a line of inquiry that was last seen with Colette Guillaumin's work in the early 1970s. He took it as a compliment and added a mention of her 1972 essay to his notes.[11] Guillaumin had seminally distinguished between 'hetero-referential racialisation' (that is, 'they are black and therefore we are white'; we are therefore defined as *not them*) and 'auto-referential racialisation' (that is, 'we are human and therefore they are not'), even though she had emphasized, as Patrick would, that

---

6 Ibid., 5.

7 See ibid., 7.

8 Ibid., 9 (emphasis in original).

9 Ibid.

10 Patrick Wolfe, *Traces of History: Elementary Structures of Race*, London: Verso, 2016.

11 Patrick Wolfe, 'Settler Colonialism and the Elimination of the Native', *Journal of Genocide Research*, 8: 4, 2006, 387–409, at 404, note 2.

different ways of constructing racialized alterities are always interwoven and very rarely operate in their 'pure' form.[12]

Comparisons in a register of difference and the theoretical implications of this work were central to Patrick's approach. He was suspicious of postcolonial discourse and its assertion of a putative discontinuity with the colonial past. He had been involved in the intellectual milieu that had developed the concept in the 1980s. The Institute of Postcolonial Studies in Melbourne was then an important referent and actively promoted subaltern studies. Patrick had begun his PhD with Greg Dening – a most respected figure of the 'Melbourne school' of ethnographic history (the 'anthropologic turn' of the 1960s was another Australian intellectual export – other contributors to the 'school' were Donna Merwick, Rhys Isaacs, and Inga Clendinnen) – but had continued under Dipesh Chakrabarty's guidance. Melbourne provided a very special intellectual environment and, in many ways, still does. With all due respect for Sydney's empiricism, this was (in Australia) where the thinking was done. But he had moved away from postcolonialism's embrace of 'hybridity'. Many argued about whether there should be a hyphen separating 'post' and 'colonialism'. In a settler colonial society, he had seen no 'post'. His rejection paralleled Peter Gran's and preceded Haim Hazan's.[13] Patrick's recuperation of 'binaries' preceded Kieran Healy's parallel and much more recent rejection of 'nuance'.[14] In 'Fuck Nuance' Healy concludes that

---

12 See Collette Guillaumin, 'Caractères spécifiques de l'idéologie raciste', *Cahiers Internationaux de Sociologie*, LIII, 1972, 247–74. As a rule of thumb, a colonial world would prefer the first type while a settler-colonial world would opt for the second. Auto-referential racialization (that is, what Leon Poliakov described as 'Arianization') fits in with settler colonialism's logic of elimination. On the contrary, hetero-referential racialization (that is, what Gayatri Spivak describes as 'Othering') works better within the colonial necessities of exploitation. Could this distinction be condensed in the opposition between an imperial form of whiteness and a republican form of whiteness? See Leon Poliakov, *The Aryan Myth*, New York: Basic Books, 1974; Gayatri Chakravorty Spivak, 'The Rani of Sirmur: An Essay in Reading the Archives', *History and Theory*, 24: 3, 1985, 247–72, especially 252–7.

13 See, for example, Peter Gran, 'Subaltern Studies, Racism, and Class Struggle: Examples from India and the United States', 2004. Available at: internationalgramscisociety.org; Haim Hazan, *Against Hybridity: Social Impasses in a Globalizing World*, Cambridge: Polity Press, 2015.

14 Kieran Healy, 'Fuck Nuance', *Sociological Theory*, 35: 2, 2017, 118–27.

'demanding more nuance typically obstructs the development of theory that is intellectually interesting, empirically generative, or practically successful'. He notes that academic 'connoisseurs'

> call for the contemplation of complexity almost for its own sake, or remind everyone that things are subtler than they seem. The attractive thing about this move is that it is literally always available to the person who wants to make it. Theory is founded on abstraction, abstraction means throwing away detail for the sake of a bit of generality, and so things in the world are always 'more complicated than that' – for any value of 'that'.[15]

Patrick was never constrained by nuance. He would have approved.

Largely following Patrick's lead, settler colonial studies consolidated into an autonomous comparative scholarly subfield. The scholarly journal of the same name and the emerging literatures that the settler colonial studies blog (that is, me) has monitored since 2010 are a testament to this strengthening.[16] Possibly an indication of its relative success, settler colonial studies as interpretative framework has more recently been the object of sustained critique. This criticism was not coordinated and emerged from quite different scholarly settings. It should be taken seriously.

I'd like to focus on two examples. In a brief note published in the October 2015 issue of *Perspectives on History*, the professional magazine of the American Historical Association, Nancy Shoemaker reminded historians that settler colonialism is only one among many types of colonialism (she identified twelve types). What prompted her reassertion, Shoemaker noted, was that 'settler colonial theory has taken over my field, Native American studies', and that 'settler colonial theory is now dogma'.[17] While the content of this reaction is incontrovertible, there are many colonialisms (and yet no one had suggested that this was not the

---

15   Ibid., 123.
16   See the *Settler Colonial Studies* journal, and 'Settler colonial studies blog' (settlercolonialstudies.blog). As of early 2019, the blog has posted on more than 1,700 scholarly works dedicated to various aspects of settler colonialism.
17   Nancy Shoemaker, 'A Typology of Colonialism', *Perspectives on American History*, 2015.

case), the context where this is stated is telling: settler colonial studies is forcing a redefinition of established disciplinary boundaries.

Similarly, but from an entirely different angle, Kēhaulani Kauanui, who has worked closely with Patrick, also distinguished in a recent piece between what Patrick actually said and the way his work is used. Settler colonial studies and its rapid consolidation can obliterate Indigenous presences, she noted before concluding: 'Settler Colonial Studies does not, should not, and cannot replace Indigenous Studies.'[18] Using an explicitly Wolfean turn of phrase, later Kauanui added: to 'exclusively focus on the settler colonial without any meaningful engagement with the Indigenous – as has been the case in how Wolfe's work has been cited – can (re)produce another form of "elimination of the native"'.[19]

If Shoemaker was concerned with the ways in which 'settler colonial theory' compromised the position of Native American studies within the historical discipline (but note: this theory cannot be characterized as 'settler colonial', as it remains programmatically critical of the mode of domination that it explores), Kauanui was concerned with the ways in which the reception of Patrick's work and its routine embrace was compromising the position of 'Indigenous studies' within American studies. This concern is now widespread. Kauanui referred to a paper by Alyosha Goldstein presented at a panel during the 2015 annual meeting of the American Studies Association tellingly entitled 'The Settler Colonialism Analytic: A Critical Reappraisal'. Goldstein criticized the ways in which Patrick's project had been reduced to the 'structure, not the event' quip. Kauanui also cited Robert Warrior's unease: 'I had a growing anxiety, however ... that the rise of Settler Colonial Studies has become – not everywhere by any means, but in some circles – an answer to the chronic need for more attention to and awareness of Native and Indigenous studies', an attention and awareness that, Warrior felt, should be fulfilled by native and Indigenous studies themselves.[20] While Kauanui took care in not blaming Patrick for the citational excesses of his followers, I feel

---

18 J. Kēhaulani Kauanui, '"A Structure, Not an Event": Settler Colonialism and Enduring Indigeneity', *Lateral, Journal of the Cultural Studies Association*, 5: 1, 2016.
19 Ibid.
20 Ibid.

that this apprehension may be unjustified. Unlike the settlers it studies, settler colonial studies does not aim to displace other approaches. Indeed, it is necessarily premised on them. It depends on Indigenous scholarship in the same way in which the study of 'masculinities' depended on the prior achievements of women's studies and the study of 'whiteness' depended on the prior accomplishments of Black studies. Deferral, a determination to not 'ventriloquize' does not, should not, and cannot be seen as elimination ('ventriloquizing' was Patrick's term; he was of the opinion that only Indigenous scholars should participate in Native studies).[21]

On the other hand, Shoemaker's search for primacy, with imperial and colonial histories holding on to subordinate fields, is perhaps as unwarranted as Sexton's search for priority.[22] In its diversity, settler colonial studies never suggested that colonialism did not shape the world we live in, and settler and Indigenous peoples are the 'peoples of sovereignty' only in the sense that one's sovereignty is asserted as the other is denied. The two dispossessions should profitably be thought of as simultaneous. They may ultimately be co-dependent. One could by the same logic respond that white and Black folks are the peoples of embodied property, whereby one's ability to own bodies is asserted precisely because someone else's is denied. Catherine Kellogg's recent reading of Judith Butler and Catherine Malabou's exchange regarding Hegel's *Phenomenology of Spirit* compellingly suggests that dispossession is necessarily and dialectically structured into two valences.[23] Beyond direct citations, Patrick would have recognized his seminal input.

Criticism aside, Patrick's work is truly reshaping scholarly boundaries, especially in the US. The role of Patrick's work in redefining American studies as a discipline was discussed at a well-attended roundtable session held at the 2016 meeting of the American Studies Association, a

---

21 Patrick Wolfe, *Settler Colonialism and the Transformation of Anthropology*, London: Cassell, 1999, 4.

22 See Iyko Day, 'Being or Nothingness: Indigeneity, Antiblackness, and Settler Colonial Critique', *Critical Ethnic Studies*, 1: 2, 2015, 102–21. Day's solution to the incompatibility of Indigenous and Afropessimist claims is to put 'colonial land and enslaved labor at the center of a dialectical analysis' (113). This is Patrick Wolfe's solution.

23 Catherine Kellogg, '"You be my body for me": Dispossession in two valences', *Philosophy and Social Criticism*, 2016.

meeting dedicated to the theme of 'home'. The rationale for the roundtable was telling:

> A central contention of *Traces of History* [Patrick's then recently published book] is that racialization 'represents a response to the crisis occasioned when colonisers are threatened with the requirement to share social space with the colonized'.[24] The implication of this argument – that race and space are inextricable, and that racialization results from colonizers being confronted with the threat of having to share social space with the colonized – leads to the proposition that race distinguishes those who belong in the national home from those who are deemed out of place in it … On this roundtable, scholars consider contributions *Traces of History* makes, including the challenges it poses and the possibilities it opens to American studies and its approaches to home. Panelists approach the discussion of Wolfe's book as experts in one or more of the racial discourses and histories it takes up, and from different disciplinary homes. As they do so, they explore how and why the study of sites of settler colonialism have and have not found a home in American Studies. Of particular interest will be how the book provokes a rethinking of erasure narratives that have characterized historical writing in what became the US. They also consider ways a comparative approach – their own, in dialogue with the one Wolfe takes in *Traces of History* – can enable new and necessary understandings of the articulations among racisms as they take place in disparate sites that are linked through circuits of imperialism. Interrogating how *Traces of History* is and is not at home in American Studies, in other words, offers an opportunity to take up larger questions about the future of American studies.[25]

I believe that we should collectively pursue this reappraisal beyond American studies. The participants to that roundtable thought the same and engaged in robustly critical debate.[26]

---

24   Wolfe, *Traces of History*, 14.
25   A record of this ASA Program Committee roundtable is available on YouTube: '#2016ASA - Racializing the National Home: Patrick Wolfe's "Traces of History"', 24 November 2016.
26   Ibid.

Disciplines

Patrick once mentioned to me that he was 'still a Marxist'. I wasn't surprised, even if I had grown up with very, very different Marxists. I'd like to suggest he was a Marxist especially because of his scholarship and methodology. The referent here was perhaps the young Marx: someone digesting the best that Hegelian traditions could offer and discovering that things are not things in and of themselves but through relationships. In a sense, he was a Marxian. Dialectical materialism was his method, and he wrote a book about settler colonialism by looking at anthropology (and vice versa), and another about the racial formation that follows the emancipation of slaves by looking at its opposite: Indigenous assimilation. The second step in his dialectical method was to interpret reality through the play of binaries and oppositions. The first step was propaedeutic and led into the second. It was a decolonizing dialectics.[27]

A parenthesis on what I mean here for 'dialectics' is perhaps warranted. Let me refer to another teacher of mine, Carlo Ginzburg. He once noted that the 'human species tends to represent reality in terms of opposites. The flow of perceptions, in other words, is scanned on the basis of markedly opposing categories: light and dark, hot and cold – high and low'. He referred to Heraclitus's motto, 'that reality is a War of opposites – a motto that Hegel retranslated in terms of their dialectical conception' to emphasise how dialectics is essential not to construe reality but to perceive it.[28] Dialectics in this context is needed not to express the way things 'actually' are, but to make them understandable. Likewise, the reason we may think dialectically is not metaphysical; we think dialectically because of perception, because of aesthetics. Dialectics is thus crucial for heuristics. It is here that I would like to base my claim that Patrick was a great teacher. Dialectics allowed him to make his students/readers/correspondents understand what settlers, bureaucrats, anthropologists, and various racists understood – his ability to explain how people came to think was exceptional. Dialectics allowed him to explain how it was that racism, for example, was primarily about space, that racial

---

27 For a recent and convincing argument similarly advocating dialectics as a decolonizing approach, see George Ciccariello-Maher, *Decolonizing Dialectics*, Durham: Duke University Press, 2017.

28 Carlo Ginzburg, 'L'alto e il basso', in Carlo Ginzburg, *Miti emblemi spie: Morfologia e storia*, Torino Einaudi, 1986, 109 (my translation).

distinction was premised on spatial indistinction. In this sense, Patrick's dialectics operated similarly to Edward Said's contrapuntal method and to Ginzburg's morphologies. The contrapuntal method was designed to unleash the heuristic potential inherent in relating apparently disconnected ideas, discursive tropes, and structures of references, while Ginzburg's morphology was an attempt to focus on recursive patterns characterizing seemingly unrelated phenomena.[29]

But there's more. Not only is Patrick's work contributing to reshaping scholarly boundaries, it may be useful in rethinking the very notion of 'boundaries', their utility, and the metaphors that underpin them. In academic settings knowledge is typically organized in spatial ways. No wonder that academics can be 'territorial', and that they work in specific 'fields'. Academics, however, typically relate to their fields not as hunter-gatherers accessing a commons but as proprietorial settlers exercising their rights of pre-emption as sanctioned by a particular title (Dr, Prof., and so forth) that is associated with a radical right of discovery. It is a recognizably Lockean right: 'I said this first', 'I first mixed my intellectual labour with this idea', 'I broke new ground, and demand recognition in the form of citations'. Some exceptionally good academics are referred to as 'pioneers'. (Incidentally: I personally decided earlier on that metaphorical fields were preferable to actually existing fields and became an academic rather than remaining where I grew up.)

Settler colonialism and its structures of reference may be more hegemonic than we may normally assume (they have been 'impervious to regime change', he noted).[30] This mode of domination organizes the 'metaphors we live by', and it is in this context that Patrick's work should be located (if I may be allowed to use yet another spatial metaphor).[31] Gramsci, and his lesson about hegemony, was never far from Patrick's thinking, and there is a reason why his latest book was called *Traces of History*.[32] His starting point was always hegemony and the ways it normalizes domination. Against the normalizing effects of settler colonial hegemony, the task was to recover the traces of its history. It was a

---

29   Edward W. Said, *Orientalism*, New York: Knopf Doubleday Publishing Group, 2014 [1978]; Ginzburg, *Miti emblemi spie*.

30   Wolfe, 'Settler Colonialism and the Elimination of the Native', 402.

31   George Lakoff, Mark Johnson, *Metaphors We Live By*, Chicago: University of Chicago Press, 2003 [1980].

32   Wolfe, *Traces of History*.

very political task but not a narrowly political one. Patrick knew about wars of position. There are scholars that imagine their interlocutors in a Machiavellian way, and there are scholars that imagine them in a Socratic way. They are either informing the prince or their students (there are many other possible approaches, of course). Patrick always had a Socratic approach, he was never Machiavellian; that is also why he was at times criticized for not proposing explicitly *political* solutions.[33]

Let me focus again on his books and his dialectics (even though it was in the shorter essay that he was, in my opinion, at his best). *Settler Colonialism and the Transformation of Anthropology* was ostensibly a history of Australian anthropology. He once told me that the reference to 'settler colonialism' in the title was only added at the very end and at the request of the publisher. As far as he was concerned, when he wrote it, settler colonialism as a mode of domination was not the main focus. And yet, to explain the evolution of this academic field, Patrick defined settler colonialism as a distinct mode of domination. No one had theorized it before and in a systematic way. It was his ability to understand settler colonialism that enabled him to frame the provenance and evolution of anthropology, and it was his knowledge of the ways in which anthropologists were embedded in a particular mode of domination that enabled him to conceptualize settler colonialism. Similarly, *Traces of History* utilizes his analysis of racism under settler colonialism in order to explain racism elsewhere (and vice versa). That such an explanation actually provides a compelling typology of racial formation is an added bonus.

In his last book, Patrick was able to outline the *process of formation* that leads to *formation as structure* (there are traces of history in our terms' etymologies too). Racial formation depends on its formation: he identifies three types and reconstructs the specific historical circumstances they develop through: the inassimilable race that follows the emancipation of slaves in the US and of Jews in Europe; the assimilable race that follows the settler colonial conquest of Indigenous peoples in Australia and the US; and the repressed race, the literal 'deracination', that follows the transition out of slavery in Brazil and the religious conversion of secular Zionism that enabled the importation of 'Oriental' Jews to Israel/Palestine after 1948. Denial is necessary when a settler

---

33 See Tim Rowse, 'Indigenous heterogeneity', *Australian Historical Studies*, 45: 3, 2014, 297–310.

colonial project aims at the fragmentation of the non-Indigenous non-settler collective (that is, when the settler project is unable to express a demographic supermajority).

They are all vicious racisms. The assimilation of Western Jews that followed the Napoleonic reforms could be perceived as almost complete by the end of the nineteenth century.[34] It was a genuine revolution arising out of another. Emancipation is revolution: emancipation reconstructs the fundamental structures of society; the reactionary response was 'anti-Semitism' (anti-Semitism – the word says it, there is 'anti' in it – is reactionary by definition). What is remarkable – proof that a line of inquiry that begins with settler colonialism as a mode of domination and proceeds to the analysis of racial formation is indeed productive – is that this reaction resulted in a settler colonial project. Zionism was, as Walter Laqueur noted and Patrick cites, 'the product of Europe, not of the ghetto'.[35] And, I would add, the product of Europe's revolution. The global 'settler revolution' emerged out of another, a point recently made by James Belich, and already made long ago by Louis Hartz.[36] The reverse is also true. Revolution defined itself against reaction and against settler colonialism; and Patrick also refers to Shaul Stampfer and his remark that for the Bund and for liberal religious Jews 'a denial of migration' was indeed crucial to their 'self-definition'.[37] Colonialism, but we are talking here about colonization, had been recurrently proposed by colonial advocates such as Friedrich Fabri (the 'father of the German colonial movement') as a 'solution' to all of Germany's problems: national, political, economic, demographic, and so on. It was an external solution. But German colonialism was fundamentally frustrated.[38] There were only internal solutions left. The Final Solution was final in both senses of the term: it followed previous ones.

---

34 Ibid., 97.
35 Cited in ibid., 107.
36 See James Belich, *Replenishing the Earth: The Settler Revolution and the Rise of the Anglo-World, 1783–1939*, Oxford: Oxford University Press, 2009; Louis Hartz, 'A Theory of the Development of the New Societies', in Louis Hartz (ed.), *The Founding of New Societies: Studies in the History of the United States, Latin America, South Africa, Canada, and Australia*, San Diego: Harvest/HBJ, 1964, 3–48.
37 Wolfe, *Traces of History*, 110, note 61.
38 See ibid., 98.

Patrick's ability to tease out the dialectical tensions pitting emancipation and assimilation is what I believe is his most relevant legacy. They are antithetical 'solutions', and yet they do not dissolve. Thinking about 'solutions' is in itself somewhat self-defeating (current debates surrounding the future of Israel/Palestine come to mind: we may be suspicious of all solutions that are presented as full and final). Wolfe concludes his book with a genuine call for further exploration and indeed for further struggle: 'emancipation and assimilation are not merely distinct. They are strategic alternatives. Emancipation is a way not to assimilate: where assimilation denies the existence of difference, emancipation preserves liability for it'.[39] Assimilation is a type of genocide that follows frontier genocides. The genocidal impulse follows emancipation, which follows genocidal collective social death. We should look at these formations' formation. We should recover the traces of history.

The definition of settler colonialism – the structure – and the typology of racial formation – the logic – are heuristically compelling and were not even the main point. Or were they?

Conclusion

He was my teacher, but he was also my friend. Patrick taught me how to make sure a fire shelter is okay. I mentioned how removed he was from Australian academia. But he wasn't removed from the community he lived in. The Coranderrk Aboriginal community were his neighbours and mentors. He was a victim of the 2009 Victorian bushfires. In succeeding months, we visited often and my eldest daughter was the first one to dance on top of the cement water tank he had built in front of what would become his new house. New building regulations demanded that a wider clearing be opened before rebuilding. So, we worked to clear the land. I worked at settler colonialism with him as well as on it. I say all this not to claim privileged access in interpreting his work, but because I would like to emphasize how Patrick's scholarship was especially grounded. He was unconcerned with departmental squabbles, metrics, rankings, measurable impacts, workload models and ERA eligible outputs (the latter is an Australian government-led exercise aiming to measure scholarly

---

39 See ibid.

quality – something that I am sure has a corresponding equivalent in other parts of the world). He took my daughters to rustle water from loggers. Referring again to Gramsci, I would like to think of him as what once would have been called an 'organic intellectual'. This still is a compliment; these days if you want to sell anything wholesome it must be 'organic'. He was organic. He was staunchly organic to his community if not his class in a way that was indeed revolutionary. This included an ongoing recognition of the importance of emotions (for him the scholarly, the political and the emotional were always intimately intertwined and part of a single whole, which when I think of it, is as good a definition of integrity as there can be). After losing his house, in a letter that was widely syndicated in the national Australian press, Patrick had noted:

> My house was on 4.8 hectares of bush outside Healesville, above Chum Creek. It went up in flames on Saturday. There's nothing left but some unusable steel framing and a cracked concrete slab. Friends, neighbours, family, colleagues, strangers have all been wonderful. Alongside the sadness and the not knowing what's going to happen, their humanity has been truly uplifting.
>
> I wasn't impressed to see the Prime Minister cuddling a crying man on camera. If he'd come across me while I was crying, I would have resisted his embrace, especially if the media had been present.
>
> I don't need a public show of empathy from the Prime Minister. I need him to do something meaningful about climate change so that fewer of us will have to lose our houses, our animals and each other.[40]

His scholarship was adopted globally but it was irreducibly Australian. It was conceived in relation to Australian developments.

Whether it is cited too often or not, Patrick's work is famous principally for two statements: one was about the 'structure', the other about the 'logic' of settler colonialism.[41] But attention to the specific context in which these statements were developed is necessary. That 'settler invasion is a structure, not an event', should be contextualized in the 1990s: the 'Age of Mabo' – the period that followed the belated legally

---

40   Patrick Wolfe, 'Cuddles not required', *Sydney Morning Herald*, 10 February 2009.

41   Wolfe, *Settler Colonialism and the Transformation of Anthropology*, 163; Wolfe, 'Settler Colonialism and the Elimination of the Native', 387.

sanctioned recognition of native title's existence in Australian jurisprudence.[42] Similarly, his contention that settler colonialism is driven by a 'logic of elimination' should be contextualized in the 2000s: the age of forced 'normalization' (the age that would see the Northern Territory 'intervention', the armed invasion of Aboriginal communities in 2007, a military intervention that required that the government unilaterally suspend the Racial Discrimination Act, and ATSIC's executive dissolution, ATSIC being an elected Commonwealth statutory authority representing Aboriginal and Torres Strait Islander peoples).[43] The former was a warning against what Elizabeth Povinelli would call the 'cunning of recognition'; the latter a warning against a type of normalization that resembled forced assimilation.[44] Crime fiction novelist Catherine Aird said that if 'you can't be a good example, then you'll just have to be a horrible warning'.[45] Patrick focused on crimes that were not fictional and issued two exemplary warnings instead.

He was somewhat removed from academia but never out of touch with the world that surrounded him. And yet, the 'structure' and the 'logic' are somewhat incompatible: one identifies permanence, the other supersession. Some have recognized a focus shift between these approaches, but I'd like to emphasize methodological continuity.[46] Writing in 1990s Australia when, following Mabo and the Native Title Act, many felt a new beginning was possible, he warned against settler appropriations of Indigenous struggles. Writing in the mid-2000s, he insisted on the need to prioritize resistance. There is no contradiction here and the two stances are merely two sides of the same coin. The times had changed.

---

42   See Bain Attwood (ed.), *In the Age of Mabo*, Sydney: Allen & Unwin, 1996.

43   A note is needed here: he referred to the 'logic of elimination' *precisely* because he knew the difference between elimination and its logic. Referring to the former therefore implies a denial of the latter. In settler colonial studies, the observation of settler colonialism does not proclaim the elimination of Indigenous unsurrendered sovereignty. This is crucial and should not be controversial.

44   Elizabeth Povinelli, *The Cunning of Recognition*, Durham: Duke University Press, 2002.

45   Quoted in Grenville Kleiser, *Dictionary of Proverbs*, New Delhi: APH Publishing, 2005, 95.

46   Marcelo Svirsky, 'Resistance is a Structure not an Event', *Settler Colonial Studies*, 2016.

He was planning to work on territorialization and I was able to read an early draft of his next project. I suspect that he would have relied on his analysis of the ways in which settlers organize their relationship with the land to understand the ways in which other collectives do the same. Understanding settler colonialism as a mode of domination was in his scholarship always an accessory for something else, a means to some other end, one way of understanding a relationship. The British had supposedly set up an empire without really wanting to (I am referring to nineteenth-century British settler apologist and historian John Robert Seeley, who famously noted: 'we seem, as it were, to have conquered half the world in a *fit of absence of mind*'[47]). Like them, this committed anti-imperialist scholar kick-started a scholarly field in a fit of absent-mindedness. Or did he?

---

47   John Robert Seeley, *The Expansion of England*, Chicago: University of Chicago Press, 1981 [1883], 12.

Part 1

Assimilations

1

Colonization, Land Registries, and the Torrens Act in French Algeria, 1863–1903

Sung Eun Choi

Throughout all of his writings, Patrick Wolfe was concerned with the duality of nineteenth-century settler-colonial systems in which racial regimes were imposed upon the colonized always in tandem with the dispossession of native lands. Ultimately replacing the native on their soil – the logic constitutive of all European settler societies – was grounded in the ideology of private property and its attendant idea of *terra nullius*. In Australia, as Wolfe explained, native entitlement to land was never historically recognized and the path to removal of natives was achieved via assimilation policies that aimed to erase their presence altogether. This chapter draws attention to yet another settler-colonial context, that of French Algeria where, unlike in Australia, the colonized Muslim population was left intact in large numbers and where native entitlement legislation became integral to European settler domination. In mid-1860s French Algeria, as European French settlers sought to expand control over what remained of Muslim holdings – and beyond what was willingly recognized by the Metropole – they began advocating for a law with foreign origins to advance their case for expanded settler claims to land. What came to be known generally as the Torrens Act had been applied first in South Australia in 1858 and subsequently adopted in the United States and its dominions. The choice of the Torrens Act was context specific, as it was just one of multiple methods being applied globally for registering land ownership. The Act, however, was mainly being touted in settler colonies above other kinds of land registration methods, leaving clear implications for the study of settler colonialism. This chapter examines how and why a particular land registration law was promoted actively by the European settlers in Algeria just as Metropolitan officials sought to affirm the French status of Muslims in Algeria. It addresses the historical variability of settler land policy by examining a colony where *terra nullius* was not always the prevailing logic, where settlers aggressively fought against Metropolitan constraints, and where civil status was an important means for achieving racial differentiation as well as restricting native entitlement to land.

For Patrick Wolfe, land and labour were 'elementary structures' that determined the racial ordering of settler societies and their successor states. In the settler-colonial context, native occupants on the land had little chance of long-term survival in the face of European colonization while those enslaved in service of the colony were provided with the basic conditions of sustenance. The colour-coded vocabulary that emerged in reference to each of these groups became an enduring ledger for racial violence. For Wolfe, in Australia, where Indigenous peoples were decimated or in the Americas where foreign labour was imported and native populations removed, the material conditions of expulsion, segregation, enslavement, and genocide all resulted in variant structures of racial differentiation that were relayed by complex colour codifications.[1]

In this chapter, I revisit the case of French Algeria in the late nineteenth to early twentieth century to offer a comparative perspective on settler colonialism.[2] Unlike in North America or Australia, where native peoples were all but exterminated in the process of colonization, the long and bloody period of French colonial conquest in Algeria that began in 1830 never realized the ambition of eradicating the 3 million Arabs and

---

[1] Patrick Wolfe, 'Land, Labour, and Difference: Elementary Structures of Race', *American Historical Review*, 106: 3, 2001, 866–905; Patrick Wolfe, *Traces of History*, Verso: London, 2016, 'Introduction'.

[2] Wolfe was not as concerned with settler societies that gained independence from colonial powers, Algeria being a case in point. See Sung Choi, 'French Algeria, 1830–1962', in Edward Cavanagh, Lorenzo Veracini (eds), *The Routledge Handbook of the History of Settler Colonialism*, London: Routledge, 2017.

Berbers who inhabited the lands north of the Sahara. Throughout the entire colonial period, Europeans accounted for about 7 per cent up to 10 per cent of the entire population.[3] The doctrine of *terra nullius* was untenable in such a context. Nor was such a claim promoted by a France eager to renew colonial expansion under the guise of a virtuous empire shorn of its Atlantic slave plantation economies. In 1851, three years after Algeria was constitutionally annexed as French territory, Napoleon III reaffirmed Algeria's identity as a *royaume arabe* ('Arab kingdom'), a notion promoted primarily by the French military in Algeria, with its own set of codes and practices. French jurisdiction would supersede the defunct power of the Turks, and the *royaume arabe* would soon surrender to distinct laws that would facilitate civilian colonization while mediating racial, political, and socio-economic difference. The most infamous of these would be the 1874 'Native Code' or *Code de l'Indigénat*, which lasted until 1946 and excluded Muslim subjects from the regime of French rights.

Insofar as land expropriation was concerned, the conquering army could not effectively take immediate and full control of the vast stretches of territories placed under French control. Nor could the imperial administration of Napoleon III exercise seamless control over Muslim customs and practices that continued to govern everyday local land rights and usage. French Algeria was to remain, therefore, a juridical quandary even after its constitutional annexation in 1848. The history of French Algeria was defined by the assimilation of lands and the refusal to grant Muslim subjects full rights. In other words, assimilation was desirable only where land, and not people, were concerned. While Islamic laws were invoked as a separate legal realm and a convenient instrument to deny Muslims French citizenship and rights, the Islamic regime of rights concerning land was undermined at every turn. To fully appreciate how this was achieved, it is important to survey the series of laws through which lands were expropriated in Algeria.

In 1863 during the Second Empire, the imperial *Sénatus-consulte*, or Senate Laws, were passed by Napoleon III to confiscate lands by way

---

3 Choi, 'French Algeria'. As Jennifer Sessions has explained, North Africans had a long history of interaction with Europeans and had become immune to the pathogens that would ravage the Indigenous peoples of North America. Jennifer Sessions, *By Sword and Plow: France and the Conquest of Algeria*, Ithaca: Cornell University Press, 2011, 181.

of sequestration, a method of seizing lands in exchange for debt payments. Imperial France recognized the Arab councils of notables, or *djêmmas,* along with jurists or *cadis* in affairs concerning land transactions between Muslim Algerians, however.[4] The recognition of local authority fomented battles between settler representatives and the French military, which oversaw administrative affairs in Algeria until the fall of Napoleon in the Franco-Prussian War of 1870. Since the passage of the Senate Laws in 1863, the civilian administration in Algeria proposed multiple laws to expand colonial settlements, prompting decades of juridical and material contest between settlers on the one side who agitated in favour of further colonization, and the existing regime of customary practices recognized by the Metropole on the other. In face of the juridical and practical schemes of colonization in Algeria, Muslim communities struggled to remain on the land either by evasion of French laws or through armed resistance, neither of which could successfully thwart settler attempts to persist with amendments to the Senate Laws and their push for maximum dispossession.

It is important to trace the history of land acquisition and colonization achieved through a series of laws and legal debates in the latter three decades of the nineteenth century, a period which some historians have associated with the attenuation of land expropriation and a demographic rebound in Algeria of the Arab and Berber populations.[5] Given the demographic imbalance in French Algeria, we can see how settlers tackled and surmounted their demographic inferiority while continuing to encroach upon Indigenous rights and properties over the long nineteenth century. Because historians have focused more intently on the brutality of sequestration as enacted by the 1863 Senate Law, the decades that followed have been perceived as relatively relaxed in terms of colonial brutality. The destructive legal measures put in place at this time to achieve further colonization have therefore eluded critical analysis even though land expropriation occurred with ever more ferocity in the decades after 1863.

The first half of the 1860s was indeed decisive for French Algeria, as hundreds of thousands of Muslim inhabitants were displaced and

---

4 The *Sénatus-consulte* of 1863 was spearheaded by Minister of War Maréchal Randon, and was the most important expression of the dual jurisdiction in Algeria.

5 Sessions, *By Sword and Plow,* 181.

forced into debt and submission to French laws.⁶ But the policy of grouping communities into new territorial units and assigning titles as set in motion by the Senate Law of 1863 remained, for the most part, incomplete. Not until the civilian administration took over from military governance in 1870 and issued a new title system, did the pernicious policies of the 1860s take full effect. The extensive growth of a real estate market in the 1880s and 1890s in Algeria also allowed colonists to shore up arguments about turning the page on a violent past, obscuring what could arguably be considered a much more pervasive dissolution of Arab and Berber societal structures. These decades are replete with cases of what historian Didier Guignard has referred to as *l'abus colonial* or 'colonial abuses', whereby an entrenched settler network of political bosses, elected officials, and bureaucratic agents diffused throughout the communes forced Algerians to routinely forfeit rights to property.⁷ The land laws of the 1880s and 1890s, although accomplished with arguably minimal bloodshed and force, continued to undermine the Senate Law's formal recognition of Indigenous practices on communal lands by introducing as many measures as necessary to assimilate these properties and extend the full reach of real estate transactions throughout Algeria.

Central to land expropriation in Algeria during the last three decades of the nineteenth century was the title registry system, which sealed the ultimate titleholder's rights while nullifying all previous claims connected to the property. Officials in the governor general's office debated the possibility of introducing a modern title registry system in the 1880s after nearly two decades of wrangling over the restrictions that were placed on certain tribal properties by the imperial Senate Law. The Torrens Act, first introduced in Australia in 1858, appealed to settlers and investors in Algeria precisely because it guaranteed the proprietor exclusive rights

---

6   Historian Patricia Lorcin has skilfully analysed land sequestration and the *cantonnement* or confinement of entire tribes after displacing them from seized territories. Patricia M.E. Lorcin, *Imperial Identities: Prejudice, Stereotyping, and Race in Colonial Algeria*, Lincoln: University of Nebraska Press, 2014. For critical studies of the 1830s to 1840s, see Sessions, *By Sword and Plow*.

7   Didier Guignard, *L'abus de pouvoir dans l'Algérie colonial (1880–1914)*, Paris: Presses universitaires de Paris Ouest, 2010. Guignard's work is a must-read, and cites multiple ways in which Europeans misled or simply reneged on promises to Muslim clients, bypassed legal procedures, and abused elections in order to transfer properties and monies to interested parties.

as title holder. By using a public registration system, the Torrens Act secured the title holder's rights and barred competing claims once the title was registered. If introduced in French Algeria, it would, settlers hoped, help invalidate Arab or Berber claims and grievances and would dissolve the intervention of local courts recognized by the Senate Law. The final version of the modern registry system in Algeria was modelled on the Torrens Act and would allow colonists swift access to Arab and Berber properties while overriding tribal rights in the process.

Historians of property law have noted the settler-colonial origins of the Torrens Act and its contribution to the commoditization of land, first in Australia and later in the imperial centre in England.[8] As Brenna Bhandar has noted, the Torrens system introduced new abstractions with regard to property ownership, which in turn gave credence to such myths as 'security' and 'mortgaging power' in land transactions. In the Australian context, the fictitious identification of land as commodity became intertwined with ongoing *racial* abstractions expressed through such typologies as 'Savage' and 'Whites' whereby qualities of whiteness and property ownership would define material and racial difference.[9] Such works on the Torrens Act have established Australia as the model for scholarly inquiry.[10] But what of those settler colonies that could not simply ignore the presence of native populations on the land or the validity of the latter's written laws? How were the rights of the colonized effaced if not through the doctrine of *terra nullius*?

This chapter leans on Patrick Wolfe's historical analysis, situating the French land laws of the 1880s and 1890s in Algeria in the broader context of civilian juridical power during the time of the French Third Republic (1870–1940). It reassesses the importance of the laws that appeared subsequent to the 1863 Senate Law to identify the legal strategies by which settlers overcame bureaucratic obstructions to colonization.[11] Historians of law in colonial societies have often pointed to the 'analytic constraints'

---

8   Brenna Bhandar, 'Title by Registration: Instituting Modern Property Law and Creating Racial Value in the Settler Colony', *Journal of Law and Society*, 42: 2, 2015, 253–82.

9   Ibid., 255.

10 See also Ranajit Guha, *A Rule of Property for Bengal: An Essay on the Idea of Permanent Settlement*, Durham: Duke University Press, 1981 [1963].

11 Patrick Wolfe, *Settler Colonialism and the Transformation of Anthropology: The Politics and Poetics of an Ethnographic Event*, London: Cassell, 1999, 44.

of settler colonial studies including the overly 'monolithic view of the expressions of law, legality, and sovereignty'.[12] Renisa Mawani and others have taken issue with Wolfe's 'logic of elimination', which, she claims has 'afforded far too much power to the colonial state', thereby overlooking the 'shifting, heterogeneous, and deeply contested asymmetries of colonial and legal power'.[13] The dynamic engagement of Indigenous jurisprudence and legal practices, as Mawani argues, become abstractly 'colonial' in settler-colonial analyses.[14] That is, the native–settler binary cannot account for contingent shifts in imperial or colonial objectives.

I would argue, however, that while civilian officials in Algeria were confronted with challenges as they attempted to overturn past imperial restrictions placed on colonization, the kinds of strategies settlers then devised to overrule local customary practices helped to reinforce a settler–Indigenous structure. Contingencies and their impact were invariably tied to the binary structural conditions of settler colonialism. Patrick Wolfe's work encourages us to go beyond the appreciation of site-specific contingencies, anxieties, and ambiguities in power relationships as evidence of complex dynamics of power, to investigate the conditions that gave the settler–Indigenous binary its particular expression in different settler societies. In short, structural investigations must accompany studies of contingencies while analyses of contingencies must bear in mind the structural limitations of their impact. In the case of French Algeria, the question is how settlers retained power in the face of a resilient Muslim population, and overcame the anxieties that beset early efforts to expand colonization.

Inspired by Wolfe's analyses of the modes by which racial difference was expressed across settler societies, I draw attention to the legal procedures that not only subjugated Algerian family life, inheritance practices, and land conveyance practices under a French framework, but also relegated Muslim communal practices concerning landed property to an ineffectual role in face of the rise of landed capital. In Algeria, racial difference became encoded in the legal taxonomy concerning land usage, rights, and proprietorship, which cast Muslim codes as unscrupulous and impotent in the face of economic development. In brief, French

---

12   See Renisa Mawani, 'Law, Settler Colonialism and "the Forgotten Space" of Maritime Worlds', *Annual Review of Law and Social Sciences*, 12, 2016, 113–17.
13   Ibid., 114.
14   Ibid.

land registries in Algeria imposed a new order on Algerian communities, which resulted not only in colossal material losses, but also in the recasting of tribal ties to the land in proprietary terms, leaving little or no room to retrace a patrimonial lineage.

The History of the Modern Land Registry System

Various land registry systems existed in Europe since feudal times. In England, it was customary in the centuries leading up to the Victorian era for estate holders to use privately held bills, and then deeds or deed titles, to document the lineage of the land as a private inheritance whose origins could be traced back to the grantor of the estate: the Crown.[15] Where primogeniture had once prevailed in England, the chain of deeds and accompanying documents would have remained intact with relative stability. Land agents worked in the service of maintaining the estate, surveying the boundaries of the property, dealing with tenants, and accounting the income in order to ensure the real value of the estate. During this period, land and its upkeep were private affairs, and estates were considered the material foundation of the deedholder's social prestige and status. But, as land became commoditized and aristocratic estates more frequently divided in the latter half of the nineteenth century, deeds and lands were dispersed, sometimes in multiple directions that made it difficult to maintain track of the entire chain of deeds or titles.

As common law required that all such deeds and documents should be submitted for any transaction involving land, speculators and investors making their way into the real estate market were often the strongest advocates of reform with respect to land registries. Investors in real estate called for a system of registration that could certify each property's discrete identity and provide legal protection for the prospective investor from third party claimants with possible claims to the property. Such a registry system should also provide assurances against undisclosed liens and other residual debts on the land freeing the parcel from any obstacles as might obstruct the transfer. To meet this end, Britain passed the 1871 Land Transfer Act, which allowed prospective investors to register titles

---

15 W.N. Harrison, 'Transformation of Torrens's System into the Torrens System', *The University of Queensland Law Journal*, 4: 2, 1962, 125.

to the land if they should want such protections. After multiple modifications, the subsequent Land Transfer Act of 1897, which was modelled on the key elements of the Torrens Act – most notably its public registration of titles and guarantees of proprietorship – was passed.[16]

The introduction of the Torrens system in the imperial metropolitan centres remained largely voluntary, however, and older practices died hard. In reality, despite the active lobbying by land investors, the modernization of land registries in Europe was achieved only after a long and contentious process as it confronted strong opposition from the landowning class and their staunch defence of custom and conventions with respect to land holdings. To fully convert land into uninhibited capital, there had to be a radical shift away from the perception of land as an inalienable extension of social prestige. The final step in modernizing land registries came about with the dual practice of making public the records pertaining to proprietorship, which gave, for the first time, primacy to the ultimate registration of the title, and thereby deposed claims to the land derived from past ties to the property. The most recent rendition of this step towards modernizing land registries can be found in the World Bank's statement in 2005, which emphasized the importance of assuring investors that 'the land has no more encumbrances than those publicised'.[17]

The modernization of land registries was attended by a certain liberal conception of political progress. Real estate enthusiasts in nineteenth-century Europe saw the commoditization of land as part and parcel of building democracy; only a true liberation of land from the clutches of the few would allow for the free flow through the markets of the object most profoundly associated with a feudal past. As some would also argue, such were the developments representative of civilized societies. As Sarah Keenan has pointed out, however, the openness and fluidity ascribed to the modern land registry and mortgage system were largely fictitious with all the fantastical characteristics as might be found in the literary

---

16 William Niblack, *An Analysis of the Torrens System of Conveying Land with References to the Torrens Statutes of Australasia, England, Ireland, Canada and the United States*, Chicago: Callaghan and Co, 1912, 3.

17 World Bank and International Finance Corporation, *Doing Business in 2005: Removing Obstacles to Growth*, Oxford: Oxford University Press, 2005, 40, cited in Luis J. Arrieta-Sevilla, 'A Comparative Approach to the Torrens Title System', *Australian Property Law Journal*, 20, 2012, 207.

imaginings of time travel.[18] The modern registry system, with its simplified formalities, admittedly eased the circulation of land, but in the end, created a system with a different set of exclusionary conditions of means and access to capital.[19] The Torrens Act, as Keenan notes, had tremendous impact as communal lands and their material conditions were converted into free-floating real estate parcels. In the settler colonial context, where the history being effaced from Indigenous lands mirrored the brutality of colonial expansion, land registries were a discreet but powerful extension of military conquest and dispossession. If the use of force came up against limitations in removing colonized peoples from the land, as was the case in Algeria, title registries made it all but impossible for native claimants to retrieve or contest their losses.

Land ownership and the rise of liberalism

Before a discussion of the Torrens Act in the colonial context, it will be useful to take a brief detour to examine how the modernization of land ownership laws became entwined with the rise of liberalism and imperialism. Until the early 1800s, estate transactions in Europe were affairs concerning a small cohort of the land-owning class. In 1871, when the first version of the Land Transfer Act was passed in Britain, there were all of 200,000 landed proprietors in England.[20] It was not until the wide-ranging dissolution of aristocratic estates in the latter half of the nineteenth century that the need for a simpler system of land transaction could be achieved.[21] In the French case, decades after the 1789 revolution had committed to doing away with the landed class, the 1804 Napoleonic Code adhered to the principle of 'conservation' or preservation when it came to laws concerning land. Landed property was regarded as an element of social stability and the premier form of familial heritage. Laws

---

18 Sarah Keenan, 'From Historical Chains to Derivative Futures: Title Registries as Time Machines', *Social and Cultural Geography*, 2018, 3.

19 Ibid., 3, 6–7.

20 Niblack, *An Analysis of the Torrens System*, 3.

21 Various forms of title systems were in place across Europe in the 1860s, by which time some form of title system was being used in: Australia (1825), France (1855), England (1862), Spain (1861), and Italy (1865). Although 'title-dependent', these laws still required the documentation and submission of all previous titles and records of ownership. Arrieta-Sevilla, 'A Comparative Approach to the Torrens Title System', 207.

regarding land were first and foremost about preserving one's *patrimoine*, not about its conversion into property.[22]

France, too, saw growing interest in real estate investments by the 1880s, however, and enthused investors turned their energies to invigorating the market and finding ways to bind land to finance capital. The main venue for such investments was the mortgage market where landed property was now the measure of credit. The real estate market in Europe functioned on the premise that each property had distinctive qualities in terms of dimension, fertility, location, buildings, and other such components that made each parcel a worthy purchase and investment. In the era of liberal democratization, the easing of regulations with regard to acquiring landed property and securing relevant rights was considered essential to the levelling of social and political opportunities. This notion, when transposed into the settler colonial context, would fuse with prejudices against the disorderly, unwritten rules of 'primitive' societies.

The expansion of the real estate market in nineteenth-century Britain and France coincided with the expansion of their respective settler-colonial empires. In the French case, imperial conquest, land expropriation, or colonization, or both, took hold in North Africa, and large areas across West and sub-Saharan Africa. Europeans who arrived in the North African colonies with the specific goal of acquiring land brought with them ideas about the democratization of property ownership along with a deep-seated prejudice against all customs that impeded the conveyance and transaction of land. In a 1900 doctoral thesis on the successful adoption of the Torrens Act in the French protectorate of Tunisia in 1885, one law student, René Viollette, opened with a praise of civilized countries where land was no longer the source of power restricted to the feudal lord or a patriarch, as the 'land [was] now democratized'.[23]

From the perspective of the settler, the bearers of tradition and custom were not the nobility or wealthy landowners as it was in Europe but the native occupants on the land. In the French settler colonies, drawing

---

22   *Projet de loi sur le régime de la propriété foncière en Algérie préparé par la commission instituée par M. Tirman, Gouverneur-Général de l'Algérie*. Gouvernement Général de l'Algérie, 1886. Archives nationales d'outre-mer (ANOM) Bib AOM 6856.

23   René Viollette, *L'Act Torrens: Son application en Australie et Tunisie*, Paris: Jouve et Boyer, 1900, 5.

up a clear description of landed properties faced distinct challenges, not least because the perimeter of properties was often demarcated by rivers, treelines, forests, and other such natural barriers. Records pertaining to lands consisted of inheritance rights, names of beneficiaries, communal histories, and such elements that were not legible or admissible under French land tenure laws. For Muslim communities in Algeria, for example, it was the genealogical tree that identified family lines and inheritance rights and claims, which were often maintained by the local tribal councils or *djêmmas*. This discrepancy in the conception of rights to landed properties meant that European colonists entering into monetary exchange with Muslim landowners were often ensnared in the complicated task of substantiating the transaction and securing claims on the land in the local courts.

Dealings with native populations were not the only challenge to the facile expansion of colonization in the empire. The Crown in the British case, or the metropolitan government in the French case, also lay claim to inalienable rights over lands that had been conquered and confiscated in the name of empire. It was evident to European settlers that in order to acquire landed property, a more advantageous system would be imperative by which land could be identified, acquired, and alienated. Enter the Torrens Act: the registry system devised by Sir Robert Torrens who had begun his career as a Customs House official in South Australia and who later became representative of Adelaide in the House of Assembly in 1857, mainly for his contribution to devising the registry system. Torrens would finally become the first premier of South Australia.[24]

Originally, Torrens was inspired by the system of ship registrations already in practice in Australia.[25] Upon the sale of a ship, the seller would cancel the certificate of ownership and the buyer would then record a

---

24 Eugene C. Massie, 'The Torrens System of Land Registration and Transfer', *The Virginia Law Review*, 6: 4, 1900, 215; Greg Taylor, *The Law of the Land: the Advent of the Torrens System in Canada*, Toronto: University of Toronto Press, 2008. Ironically Australia – Victoria and now New South Wales – has taken steps to privatize public title registries. As Karen Strojek writes, such sales of registries have generated concerns about 'transparency, security of title and loss of government revenue'. See 'Torrens, Our Land-title Pioneer Might Have Approved of Privatised Registries'. Available at theconversation.com.

25 For literature on the importance of the sea as a critical colonial space, see Mawani, 'Law, Settler Colonialism, and the "Forgotten Space" of Maritime Worlds'.

new certificate in its place. The cancellation of the previous certificate was the critical step in assuring the subsequent buyer that the property had been securely transferred.[26] After some modification, the Act was adopted in North American and some Latin American countries at the turn of the century. By the eve of the First World War, fourteen states in the United States had recognized the law, and the Act was passed in Hawaii and the Philippines shortly thereafter.[27] The Torrens system would go on to survive in variegated ways in the United States well into the early 1990s.

In the Australian colonies, the Torrens Act came into operation first in July 1858, and was then amended to pass as the Real Property Act. In 1860, further modifications were made in quick succession to free the proprietor from any 'encumbrances, liens, estates, or interests' as might be put forth by other claimants.[28] The Torrens Act appealed to settlers whose primary obligation when entering into a land transaction was first to produce a title, and second, to file it under a public registry at which point their full possession and rights to conveyance would be inaugurated. In addition, all subsequent 'retrospective investigation' of the property was also prohibited.[29] This registration system protected the ultimate titleholder with rights that superseded all others, including those that at one point might have been granted by the Crown as 'paramount' rights. With the Torrens Act, it was not the Crown but the registration of a title that became henceforth the grantor of rights. The Australian colonies' implementation of the Torrens Act had in fact assimilated Crown grants into a modern land registry, gaining it a reputation for having democratized common law instruments.[30]

---

26   Most explicit was article 33: 'Every certificate of title or entry in the register book shall be conclusive, and vest the estate and interests in the land therein mentioned in such manner and to such effect as shall be expressed in such certificate or entry'. Cited in W.N. Harrison, 'The Transformation of Torrens's System into the Torrens System', 126.

27   D.H. Van Doren, 'The Torrens System of Land Title Registration', *Columbia Law Review*, 17: 4, 1917, 354.

28   Article 41 of the 1860 Real Property Act in Australia, cited in Harrison, 'Transformation of Torrens's System into the Torrens System', 127.

29   Ibid., 129.

30   John Baalman, 'Approach to the Torrens System', *Sydney Law Review*, 2: 1, 1956, 89. Baalman was a known critic of Harrison's interpretation of the Torrens system.

According to Luis Arrieta-Sevilla, the immediate embrace of the Torrens Act in Australia was possible primarily because lands recently freed by the Crown had become, in practice, 'virgin' properties on which fresh laws could be enforced to set precedents. The regime of rights and the material foundation for such rights were, in effect, born together. Australia's situation drew stark contrast with that in England where private ownership of land and the long-standing sanctity of deeds prevented the introduction of the Torrens system.[31] In France, too, when the Act was first debated in the 1880s, advocates of the Act were met with opposition from those who upheld the immutability of the Napoleonic Code. Subsequently, multiple legislative battles were waged against perpetuities and existing modes of conveyance before revisions to land registries were put through in the legislative chamber. As much as convenience was key to the Torrens Act, I would argue that factors more complex than convenience made the Torrens system more amenable to the settler colonies than in metropolitan centres, namely the availability of uncolonized lands and the power exercised by Europeans over colonized communities. The following section analyses the land registry system as it arrived in Algeria in the 1870s and the debates that ensued to put the system into practice.

The Evolution of Land Laws and the Torrens Act Debate in French Algeria

French Algeria at the time of annexation consisted of an enormous stretch of territory, comprising the Tell region, which encompassed the land mass south of the Mediterranean shoreline and north of the Sahara, from the Moroccan to Tunisian borders. In total, the Tell measured 14 million hectares (each hectare being equivalent to 10,000 square metres or almost 2.5 acres) and was home to approximately 1.5 million Arabs and some 700,000 Kabyles.[32] From the invasion of Algeria in 1830

---

31   Arrieta-Sevilla, 'A Comparative Approach to the Torrens Title System', 216.

32   Accounts of Algeria's demographic divide between European and Muslim populations vary widely between historians. Jennifer Sessions cites 483,000 Europeans, though in imperial documents, the census notes 200,000 European cultivators. 'Rapport de M. le comte de Casablanca, chargé de l'examen

onward, the French state claimed inalienable rights to all public domain, or *beyliks*, previously under the control of the former Ottoman authorities, or *beys*. These domains made up nearly one-third of the Tell region, and included forests, rangelands, and arable lands. To these state domains were later added the *habous*, or lands reserved for religious functions and additional 'dependencies' co-opted by France throughout the nineteenth century.

With the 1851 coup of the Eighteenth Brumaire, Louis-Napoléon Bonaparte, president of the Second Republic, crowned himself emperor of a new Second Empire, and proclaimed inalienable rights to all state domains in Algeria as well as in the imperial metropole. Algeria was proclaimed a *royaume arabe* and Napoléon III proclaimed his commitment to the safeguard of all lands that were now under imperial French control, including those that had been occupied 'since time immemorial' by sedentary tribal communities. As stated in the Senate Law of 1863, 'we did not come to oppress or defraud but to civilize'.[33] 'Civilized France' now superseded the 'Turkish despotism' that had deprived the peasants of land and their living.[34]

By imperial accounts, 'a mere half' of the total arable lands in the Tell, or approximately 450,000 hectares, were being cultivated by some 200,000 European colonists, the rest by Arab and Berber sedentary or semi-sedentary communities whose numbers remain unknown. Out of the entire 1.5 million Arabs and 700,000 Kabyles, a large majority lived in nomadic or semi-nomadic pastoral communities, with some regularly traversing the Sahara and the Tell region. Apart from the public domains were the 'communal lands', much of it being rangelands occupied by Algerian pastoral communities, amounting to approximately 15 per cent of the Tell region. Lastly, there were 'private' properties also occupied by

---

du projet de sénatus-consulte relative à la constitution de la propriété en Algérie dans les territoires occupés par les Arabes; Séance du Sénat du 8 avril 1863', *Constitution de la propriété en Algérie* (Gouverneur-général de l'Algérie, 1863), 19. ANOM Bib AOM 6852.

33   'Sénatus-consulte relative à la constitution de la propriété en Algérie dans les territoires occupés par les arabes', Art. 6, in *Statistique et documents relatifs au Sénatus-consulte sur la propriété arabe*, Paris: Imprimerie impériale, 1863, 8.

34   Land farmed by 'industrious' colonists would supplant the plantations that had crumbled under the Atlantic revolutions. See Sessions, *By Sword and Plow*.

Arab and Berber communities, which made up more than one-third of the Tell. These were divided into two primary types: the *melk* – private lands belonging to families and considered indivisible – and the *arch* – also indivisible and inalienable lands belonging to *douars*, or larger tribal units administered by tribal elites. These 'private' properties remained closed off to European colonization even after they were placed under French constitutional jurisdiction after 1848. As a result, they would become the most hotly contested tracts of land in the later decades of the nineteenth century.[35]

The contest over land would remain twofold in French Algeria throughout the colonial period. On the one hand, settlers or European private individuals – in possession of approximately 6.5 per cent of the arable lands by 1860 – sought to expand their personal investments in lands still under Arab or Berber ownership, including *melk* and *arch* properties. The French imperial state, on the other hand, sought to maintain control over all public domains and Muslim properties that might be given over to colonization. The stated goal of the empire was to absorb more arable lands being farmed by Arabs in order to distribute them as plots or further agricultural development.[36] Over time, European private investors with the help of settler officials would persist with attempts to reduce state controls over restricted territories while achieving more freedom as to where they might invest or acquire property. These efforts would bear fruit as the nineteenth century drew to a close.

The two *Sénatus-consultes* laws of 1863 and 1865, which maintained Algeria as a *royaume arabe*, were in fact the result of significant pressure placed on the empire to alleviate the frustration of colonists and investors seeking landed properties, especially those in Muslim hands. The influx of immigrants from Europe's Mediterranean coastal regions to Algeria throughout the 1850s and 1860s and the pleas of commissioners and special envoys dispatched to Algeria during the Second Empire to expand civilian settlements forced the empire to consider releasing

---

35 The descriptions of these types of land holdings appear in multiple texts related to Algeria. See, for example, Maurice Wahl, *L'Algérie. Deuxième édition, revue et augmentée,* Paris: Félix Alcan, 1889, 310.

36 Gouverneur-Général, *Constitution de la propriété en Algérie,* 19; see also Émile Larcher and Georges Rectenwald, *Traité élémentaire de législation algérienne,* Paris: Librairie Arthur Rousseau, 1923, 386–7; also cited in Guignard, *L'abus colonial,* 172.

more land to colonization.[37] In the letter, the 1863 Senate Law declared all erstwhile 'indivisible' lands administered by local custom as falling under French jurisdiction. This juridical assimilation allowed imperial and military officials, still in control in Algeria, to begin the work of dividing these lands into parcels that could be distributed to tribal family units or *douars*. These *douars* would be considered property holders with the right to make decisions about conveyance, and each *douar* was to be assigned discrete titles. Within each *douar*, individual members were to be held accountable as proprietors, and were to be assigned titles to this effect, though this was never fully achieved.[38] The 1863 Senate Law took the 376 tribes occupying 6,970,000 hectares in the Tell, and subdivided them into 676 *douars*, each with a claim to a unit of land.[39]

This policy was intended to facilitate the conveyance of land and pave the way for further acquisition of Muslim properties by the state as well as by private investors. With regard to the goal of creating landed properties out of private holdings, the Senate Law was an expression of state interest in expanding public domain. The law, spearheaded by an imperial officer, invoked the notion of 'public utility' to define colonization not only in terms of 'favour[ing] individual initiatives and facilitat[ing] exploitation', but also in terms of 'companies and their expropriation of land for public utility'.[40] For the imperial state, the extension of public domain was necessary for modern irrigation systems and engineering projects, which would presumably generate agricultural and financial wealth. Imperial law viewed private initiatives as incapable of generating mechanized agricultural industry essential to aggrandizing capital investments, as the law also noted. If colonization required the release of public lands and conveyance of Indigenous properties, then public initiatives also required the acquisition of more land in the Tell. As noted in the Senate Law: 'how could development be at all possible if most of the territory is discredited and not available for sale or lease?'[41]

The 1863 Senate Law introduced a double set of interests. At the same time as the law restructured tribal societies and prepared the grounds for land development and land conveyance, it continued to allow transactions

---

37 Among the experts called on to visit Algeria was Alexis de Tocqueville.
38 *Statistique et documents relatifs au Sénatus-consulte*, 304.
39 Wahl, *L'Algérie*, 311.
40 *Statistique et documents relatifs au Sénatus-consulte*, 14.
41 Ibid., 8.

between Muslim landowners to be administered by the local jurists or *cadis*. The enormous stretch of land subject to the Senate Law made it all but impossible to carry out the enterprise of assigning titles to all *douars* all at once, and local notables were still able to exercise their authority in matters concerning land conveyance, including in instances involving European claimants. Civilian investors were aggravated, however, by the slow process by which military officials assigned proper titles, and expressed their frustration with the perceived delinquency of the *cadis* who appeared to evade Senate Law regulations.[42] Over the ensuing decades, aspiring investors kept their sights fixed on the 11.9 million-plus hectares in the Tell and sought to access public domains as well as private *melk* and *arch* lands, which meant that the problem of imperial control over Algerian soil via the Senate Law would preoccupy settlers in the coming decade.

France's defeat in the Franco-Prussian War in 1870, which culminated in the loss of Alsace-Lorraine to Germany, resulted in the newly inaugurated French Third Republic's offer to aid citizens fleeing the German takeover by granting them land in Algeria. With the end of the Second Empire, Algeria was no longer under the control of the imperial army, and with the arrival of new Alsatian settlers from the metropole, colonists gained more confidence in asserting their case with civilian officials. Land-hungry investors in Algeria saw an opportunity to lobby for a more effective and simplified land registration system, which would facilitate the conveyance of properties belonging to Muslim titleholders. In making their case, settler officials appealed to juridical rationality, and contested the contradictory practice of validating Muslim customary practices in *French* Algeria. As one colonist argued, Muslim legal practices were chaotic and obstructive: 'the absence of land agents, registers, maps, or archives or any other authentic documents from the Ottoman period made it impossible to establish a base codification of the French government's administrative authority in Algeria'.[43] It was time to rationalize land laws in Algeria and demote the Senate Law.

---

42   Wahl, *L'Algérie*, 311.

43   *Statistique et documents relatifs au Sénatus-consulte*, 19. There is strong evidence to suggest that during the conquest, much of the Ottoman papers were burned. See Alexis de Tocqueville, 'Second Letter on Algeria, (1827)', in Alexis de Tocqueville, *Writings on Empire and Slavery*, Jennifer Pitts (ed.), Baltimore: Johns Hopkins University Press, 2001, 15.

The only resolution in the minds of land-hungry Europeans would be a total and uncompromising division of all Muslim properties, the complete eradication of local custom, and the implementation of a less arduous system with regard to land transactions. Colonists cited fundamental flaws in a double jurisdiction in Algeria. The Muslim landowner, they argued, had no real French status, and therefore should not receive the patronage of the state:

> Thus we find here by fate, a system, which has placed all of the population in Algeria divided into two separate legal systems ... But the situation has ... maintained properties in an insecure state impeding the development of transactions and credit ... While the Muslim is protected under French jurisdiction for troubles encountered during transactions ... the European finds himself in face of the unknown and can only seek *ad hoc* redress.[44]

In the years that followed the promulgation of the Senate Law, settlers called for nothing short of a 'complete mobilization' of the land and its corollary: the unwavering disintegration of Algerian society as the Arab and Berber populations knew it. Free colonization and 'public wealth' could only be achieved to its fullest if all conditions necessary for making land the principal instrument of that wealth, were optimized.[45] The practical tenets of the Senate Law were as radical as they were brutal, but none of the consequences of displacement and *cantonnement* (or confinement) really made an impression with investors consumed in removing all barriers to dividing up lands and distributing them to *douars* with corresponding titles. Algeria was 'languishing' under such barriers and constraints.[46] Forceful arguments were made to remove all customary practices with regard to land transactions and do away with perpetuities, land buybacks, and the use of oral testimonies during mediations. As far as the colonists were concerned, the time to give French laws absolute pre-eminence was long overdue. Investors called upon civilian authorities in Algeria: elected officials, mayors, heads of communes, tax agents,

---

44 *Nécessité d'une Réforme dans le Régime de la Propriété musulmane en Algérie*, Alger, 1868, 5. ANOM Bib AOM B/6854.

45 *Régime de la propriété foncière en Algérie*, Gouvernement Général de l'Algérie, 1886, 6. ANOM Bib AOM B/6856.

46 Ibid., 6.

and court officials to broker their interest with legislators in Algeria and in Paris.

The efforts of investor lobbyists in Algeria resulted in the so-called Warnier Law in 1873, two years into the Third Republic. As stated by a European official representing the interest of colonists in the legislative debates leading up to the law, the new law should bring the following results:

> First, to make the native *indigène* a property holder and the true cultivator of his land. In submitting all properties to the regime of French laws, we should prepare for a complete mobilization of the soil and the transformation of Arab society itself. We should render possible real estate transactions, negotiations of purchases by Europeans, and the full extension of a free colonization [*colonisation libre*].[47]

As one colonist maintained, to 'mobilize property was to obey natural law in the *new* agrarian economies; in this, there was no conflict with the preservation of patrimony'. The first article of the 1873 Warnier Law stated that 'the establishment of immobile property in Algeria, its conservation, and the contractual transfer of buildings and property rights, whoever the proprietor, shall be governed by French laws'.[48] With the Warnier Law, the policy of title registrations begun under the Senate Law was enforced on all lands without any exception, including the *arch* lands previously considered the indivisible domain of tribal communities. To impose the law, an army of investigator-commissioners was sent out to survey all collective and privately held properties in the Tell in order to assign new titles and numbers to each property.[49] Such titles as assigned in accordance with the 1873 law were to supersede all previous documents pertaining to rights on the property. The Warnier Law thus introduced elements that would resonate with the Torrens Act:

> All rights previously accorded 'Muslim or kabyle' landowners, such as easement – the use of someone else's property for specific purposes –

---

47   Wahl, *L'Algérie*, 312.
48   'Loi du 26 juillet 1873', *Loi 2252-Loi relative à l'établissement et à la conservation de la Propriété en Algérie,* ANOM Bib AOM B/6853, 135.
49   Wahl, *L'Algérie*, 311.

and other rights related to land as practiced by custom were henceforth abolished. In addition, the registration of new titles would inaugurate new rights to the exclusion of all previous rights connected to the said property.[50]

By some accounts, the 1873 law marked a resounding victory for colonists as it left no lands beyond the reaches of French laws. But the Warnier Law was still lacking in the eyes of resident Europeans, as it required documentation of the civil status and identity of all parties involved in transactions, whether European or Muslim in addition to monetary fees. Prospective investors complained about the difficulty of distinguishing between names of Muslim titleholders who, according to custom, were often found to share similar or even identical names with extended family members.[51] Some investors found themselves in Muslim courts in order to settle the identity of past titleholders. Consequently, the European settlers called for measures that could implement more effective ways to verify the civil status and family surnames of titleholders.

Starting in the 1880s, a coterie of legal experts and settler representatives in Algeria began calling for the adoption of a land registry system analogous to the 1858 Torrens Act to amend the gaps in the Warnier Law. In the process, some called for a revamping of the taxonomy of landed property in Algeria and a complete restructuring of laws that governed practices of conveyance. The expansion of the real estate market was not the only matter at stake; the ability to impose land taxes on Muslim titleholders also took on urgency. As noted by one tax official, G. Cahn, first and foremost, there should be no such category as communal property in Algeria. In fact, Warnier himself had attempted to redefine 'communal' properties by insisting that these were properties owned by a group of individuals who occupied the land but who had no familial ties to one another, as opposed to private properties, which were under the ownership of a family of multiple individuals who held a single title together

---

50   'Loi du 26 juillet, 1873', 136.
51   The French established standardized names for Arab subjects in Algeria at the same time land laws were being amended. As explained by Susan Slyomovics, 'the law of 23 March 1882 imposed French ID cards and patronymic surnames on all Algerian households'. Susan Slyomovics, *The Performance of Human Rights in Morocco*, Philadelphia: University of Pennsylvania Press, 2005, 103.

as a family.[52] 'It is twelve years since the *Sénatus-consulte* and General Chanzy have officially confirmed that the third and most serious operation of the 1863 law – the dividing of all collective lands – remained unfinished, with seven hundred and twenty three tribes still claiming some form of customary rights in Algeria.'[53]

Advocates for a new land registry system in Algeria highlighted the precedent set in 1885 in the French protectorate of Tunisia where the importation of the Torrens Act had allegedly achieved great success in fulfilling democratic principles and simplifying land registries.[54] Jurists and law professors in Algeria actively contributed editorials and statements in the European papers to call for similar measures. For instance, in the 1886 March issues of the *Akhbar* – a journal dedicated to legal matters – one professor of law, Alfred Dain, explained the advantages already seen in Australia and similar advances it would bring to Algeria.[55] The Torrens Act had the advantage of offering retroactive protection for the investor from all competing claims that might invoke imprescriptible rights on the property.

Europeans advocating for a new registry system also made their case on grounds that only a homogeneous and legally consistent registry system would resolve any problems related to contradicting claims on land rights in Algeria. When Indigenous property changed hands and became the property of the European investor, it should become 'French property' and subject solely to French laws. Muslim practices should have no bearing on the rights of Europeans once the latter registered their titles.[56] Dain argued that as the situation stood, 'only natives benefited' from legal disputes that concerned tribal lands. The Warnier Law had taken the radical step towards partitioning and registering all lands belonging to Arab and Berber communities, but it did not hold the 'indigenous' party accountable for any charges incurred during

---

52 Maurice Pouyanne, *La propriété foncière en Algérie*, Alger: Adolphe Jourdan, 1900, 409.
53 G. Cahn, *Algérie: De la constitution de la propriété indigène,* Paris: Challamel Ainé, 1880, 9. At this juncture, Cahn argued, private initiatives should be allowed to mediate land transaction.
54 René Viollette, 'L'Act Torrens: Son application en Australie et Tunisie', 99.
55 Alfred Dain, 'L'Act Torrens et la purge spéciale de la loi du 26 juillet 1873', in *AKHBAR, Journal de l'Algérie*, 4 March 1886, in ANOM Fonds 91 1N/7.
56 Ibid.

the transaction. It was still up to the 'European to carry the charges of administrative titles and notarization fees, all the while deprived of real guarantees of full and uninhibited proprietorship'.[57]

The argument for modifying land laws was therefore couched as an important means to invalidate not only Muslim customary practices related to land rights, but also Muslim laws as a whole. Not only were Muslim laws confusing, argued settlers, they were not really laws; they were derived from the Qur'an, a religious text.[58] The Qur'an, as Viollette argued, could not possibly be used as a legal code since Allah was considered the sole proprietor of all lands. Men were mere caretakers entrusted with God's property. The Qur'an also gave to multiple interpretations as seen in the four conflicting schools of legal thought that existed across the Muslim world, Viollette protested.[59] Even if Muslim proprietors could obtain *outikas*, or notarized claims to a parcel, multiple *outikas* were sometimes registered in connection to a single piece of property, raising suspicions of fraud. Such documents as titles were 'illusory'.[60] In his thesis, Viollette explained that in civilized societies, land performed a social function as commodity procuring financial gain for the proprietor.[61] Such conceptions unfortunately did not carry over in Muslim laws, he argued.

Drawing from the Tunisian situation, the French in Algeria opposed all recognition of customary practices. In a series of articles in *Le Petit Colon* in the summer of 1884, Dain emerged again to argue for the 'Algerianization of the Torrens Act'. Citing an actual legal case, the author explained that 'a well-meaning European' had tried to create an estate out of 800 hectares near Affreville, on land registered to a community of 400 to 500 Muslim occupants of a *douar*. In acquiring this land, the said European was burdened with over 22,500 francs to complete the transaction. The case appeared in the Blida court where the colonist had offered to pay the price of 850 francs to be shared equally among the 400 to 500 residents who were to be displaced into a neighbouring *douar*. 'To the blind defenders of Arab rights', Dain had this to say: 'the expropriation, which placed this land in European hands did at least permit the

---

57 Ibid.
58 Viollette, 'L'Act Torrens', 114.
59 Ibid., 116.
60 Ibid., 116.
61 Ibid., 6.

'indigenes' to get a fair price for their land even if the mass displacement was morally questionable'.[62] Such statements underlined the juridical rather than moral or political qualities of the case, arguing for a law that could provide protection for the buyer while sparing her any exorbitant fees stemming from the acquisition. What might befall the Muslim landholder was not considered pertinent to the legal issue at hand.

The French in Algeria also made the case for capital investments, which were allegedly hindered for fear that anyone willing to take out a mortgage on land or invest in property risked the chance of running into contending claims by family members of former Muslim occupants.[63] High interest rates on mortgage repayments and the general pattern of underestimation with respect to the value of the property were all factors that delayed meaningful colonization. When metropolitan officials expressed reluctance with regard to passing an Act in Algeria before it was considered in Paris, one jurist, Yves Guyot, in siding with the French in Algeria alluded to Algeria's distinctive situation: Algeria could not be treated in the same light as France. In Algeria, so much more land was available but placed under restrictions and occupied by Muslim inhabitants. Only 1 million hectares, which amounted to less than 1 per cent of all land in the Tell, sat in European hands. The Torrens Act, which recognized titles as bearing the identity of a specific parcel and protected the person acquiring the land by conferring sole rights of possession and conveyance, would finally complete the step of severing the archaic familial and personal ties that colonized populations had with their land.

Amendments were indeed made to the Warnier Law in ways that would further advance the de-structuration of colonized communities and their property regimes. In 1883, commissioners from the governor general's office acted as land surveyors and were given absolute authority to enter Muslim communities to carry out the work of dividing parcels and registering titles for all properties, including those unresolved by the 1863 and 1873 laws.[64] The ultimate goal of the mission was to eradicate all

---

62 'La propriété en Algérie', *Le Petit Colon algérien.* 27 Août 1884, ANOM Fonds 91 1N/7.

63 Dain, 'L'Act Torrens et la purge spéciale de la loi du 26 juillet 1873'.

64 Gouverneur-Général Tirman, *Instruction sur le mode de reconnaissance des biens indivis entre familles indigènes et sur le partage de ces biens, en exécution de l'article 3 de la loi du 28 avril 1887*, Alger: Giralt, 1887, 2. ANOM Bib AOM B/6860.

private properties considered 'indivisible' including *melk* and *arch* properties. Commissioners could carry out all operations at their discretion with full immunity. They would only have to follow the rule of identifying the 'core members' of the family occupying the land. Only these core members of the family would be regarded as having proprietary rights.[65] According to the instructions laid out by the governor general's office, these commissioners were to carry out their duties not just as land surveyors but also as investigators of family relations. All customary interpretations of consanguinity as practised in Arab or Berber communities would be disregarded and overruled via the new titles. Any claim by extended family members judged to be defunct, or any claims made by persons perceived by the commissioner to be outside the immediate bounds of the family, including relatives, would be removed from the list of beneficiaries.[66] As indicated by the governor general's office, the commissioners operated not by the letter of existing regulations, but by decisions made on the ground with the ultimate goal of dissolving all properties that were once considered indivisible by the Senate Law.

The Chamber of Deputies in Paris also weighed in, suggesting that if the situation required it, the very parameters of what constituted an Arab or Berber family unit could be adjusted to ensure the transfer of land.[67] What emerged out of these debates at the governor general's office were ethnographic observations that would inform legislation and colonial governance: 'If one looks deeper into [the state of] "indigenous lands", one recognizes that a typical home or *foyer* never has more than a small family unit in it whose members share only the most intimate ties: a husband, a wife, children, and somewhat rarely sisters, under-aged nephews, an old mother and frail father'.[68] The observation trailed into an ambiguous point: 'there was no obvious difference between families in rural France and the peasants in Algeria, outside of bigamy and polygamy, which were exceptions [in Algeria]'.[69] Such observations implied that communal lands or properties belonging to large family units, including *arch* properties, had no real social distinctions as to warrant inalienable status or indivisibility. All lands in French Algeria therefore

---

65 Tirman, *Instruction sur le mode de reconnaissance des biens indivis*, 1.
66 Ibid., 2.
67 Ibid., 3.
68 Ibid., 3.
69 Ibid., 3.

shared the same qualities of being *alienable* properties. But to perceive this fact was one thing; it was quite another to enter these alienable properties into financial transaction with full legal backing.

In 1888, while commissioners were actively engaging in their duties, a conference was held in the city of Oran on the possible benefits of the Torrens Act to Algeria precisely to ensure the legal validity of transactions involving communal and indivisible properties. The French Association for the Advancement of the Sciences hosted the conference and the debate was led by a Paris municipal deputy and legal expert, Léon Donnat. Having advocated for the American Homestead Act as a possible model for Algeria in the past, Donnat was now one of a growing pool of politicians and legislators interested in implementing the Torrens Act in Algeria. Under the Torrens Act, he maintained, landowners could register their property by simply sending in a title with the description of the parcel to an office of registration whereby a notice would be posted in a local newspaper. If no one made a counterclaim on the plot within six months, the parcel would be registered pending fees and other payments bearing the name of the individual. Publicity was key, as the public bore witness to the title.[70]

The Act was considered much less laborious and economical than regulations set by French codes, and was regarded by its advocates as a beneficial policy in Algeria 'where the very survival and success of colonists depended on the swift and immediate access to newly cleared lands'.[71] The Torrens Act as it was applied in Australia, unlike other land registry systems, had allowed certified copies and photographs of original titles as evidence of registration. Once their titles were registered, the titleholder would be assured adjudication and receive reimbursements for fees pertaining to such processes. To receive such protection, however, titleholders were required to pay insurance. As those advocating the Act would argue, such insurance was precautionary as one had only to refer to the statistical accounts from New South Wales, which showed a zero-success rate for cases brought against titleholders since the inception of the law. 'Imagine how much more advantageous the Act would be if brought to Algeria', Donnat argued. 'Our current Civil

---

70 Léon Donnat, *Deux institutions à introduire en Algérie, Conférence faite à Oran*, Paris, Aux bureaux de la France commerciale, 1888, 5.
71 Ibid., 6.

Code has even granted family members of the native seller the [inalienable] right to buy back lands that were sold off. We can understand how dangerous it is for the colonist'.[72] Europeans were in fact victims of 'the scourge of the [Muslim] landowner' who often rented out land at prices crushing to cultivation and obstructive to colonization.

The debate surrounding the Torrens Act also highlighted the distinction that certain jurists hoped to make between metropole and colony. To officials who opposed the import of the Torrens Act in Algeria for reasons having to do with the prevention of juridical inconsistencies across metropole and colony, Donnat argued that colonization had already created such distinct circumstances in Algeria that freedoms such as those being pursued by colonists could not be the same ones sought in the metropole. Having detected the hesitation among legislators in the metropole to grant colonists more autonomy, Donnat insisted that allowing colonists the freedom to adopt their own land registry method would in fact strengthen, rather than weaken, the ties between colonists and metropolitan authorities.[73] Muslim occupants on the land had become inconvenient obstacles to the acquisition of property. In 1880, it was affirmed that landed property made up as much as 44 per cent of the total land surface in Algeria as opposed to only 13 per cent in the metropole. To capitalize on the available land in Algeria, it was only a matter of ensuring that Muslim occupants could no longer delay or prevent land transactions.

Although the Torrens Act was not applied in Algeria at this time, another law was issued in 1897 to further amend the Warnier Law and help smooth land transactions for European investors buying land from Muslim property holders. The Torrens Act was never far from the minds of jurists who promoted such amendments. The 1897 law introduced features that were again similar to those of the Torrens Act: publicity and the suppression of unverified liens, related debts, and claims that might have negative repercussions for the prospective titleholder. All prospective investors would receive the visit of an administrator-agent who would examine the property, survey and demarcate its exact perimeter, and render public the intent and title of the applicant along with all descriptions pertaining to the property. The notice would then be posted

---

72 Ibid., 9.
73 Ibid., 10.

in the *Journal officiel de l'Algérie*. All decisions regarding the property would be posted in the marketplaces, town halls, and other public places if necessary, in French and Arabic. Declarations related to accepting the rights to the property would be recorded in formal minutes.[74] The mayoral office and 'indigenous' parties would receive the information in French and Arabic respectively. Any objections to the assessor's report and minutes would have to be lifted before the title was finally issued.

Following upon such measures as were instituted to help safeguard the property rights and titles of European investors, some proposed adopting the actual Torrens Act to officially reinforce these measures. In October 1901, a commission was convened in Algiers for the study of 'Reforms Relevant to Landed Property' under the auspices of the 'Direction of Indigenous Affairs', a subdivision of the Office of *Indigène* Property, which answered to the governor general's office. The goal of the commission was to deliberate proposed revisions to Algeria's property laws, weigh the benefits and weaknesses of the Torrens Act, and debate possible resolutions to ongoing challenges faced by Europeans with regard to land transactions. But this was not simply about the technicalities of the land or title registry system. If we follow the evolution of the debates surrounding land registries since 1863, the implications for a long-term de-structuration and destruction of Algerian society become apparent.

Although the newly revised law passed in 1897 did offer similar conditions of security as the Torrens Act for the prospective investor-titleholder, only the particular features of the latter would be, for the governor general, 'the most perfect instrument in the acquisition of indigenous lands as it provided all the desired guarantees Europeans desired'.[75] The import of the Act would bring success where past laws had failed: 'consolidating properties [in European hands] and mobilizing [Indigenous] lands to help develop credit'.[76] Once and for all, the Act

---

74 'Loi du 16 février 1897', in *Service de la propriété indigène: Instruction sur les enquêtes partielles à effectuer en exécution de la loi du 16 février 1897 sur la propriété foncière en Algérie*, Gouverneur-Général de l'Algérie, 1898, 108. ANOM Bib AOM B/6862.

75 *Commission d'Étude: Réformes à apporter dans le Régime de la Propriété Foncière en Algérie* (Européenne et indigène), 8 octobre 1901, Gouvernement Général de l'Algérie, Direction des Affaires Indigènes: Service de la Propriété Indigène, 1901, 19. ANOM AOM Bib /6863.

76 Ibid., 8.

would help purge the histories of Muslim properties and all of the legacies and bequests that were associated with the land, which long predated the French registry system but remained in practice still. Not all officials trusted such a simplified registry system as the Torrens Act in Algeria where local customs created additional steps involving Muslim titleholders to finalize a transfer, but for enthusiasts, it promised the ultimate goal of fuelling the financial credit system in Algeria by encouraging landowners to mortgage their property. Misgivings, if there were any, had mainly to do with the complications such reforms would entail in Algeria. As one official noted, Europeans in Algeria 'lacked the same freedoms enjoyed by Australians' who were unburdened by the recognition of native title.

The main question, as officials saw it, was what to do with the intractable presence of Muslim landowners who 'failed to comply' with French regulations but whose lands were coveted by investors? When titles were reassigned to the villages or *douars* starting in 1873, Muslim proprietors were required to report and transcribe all of their mortgage debts. As one official remarked, however, even where French laws were applied, there was constant wrangling over the accuracy of mortgage debts and confusion because of the discrepancies that resulted from divergences in legal practices.[77] French officials cited the lack of rigour in 'indigenous' habits as outdated impediments that stifled the Warnier Law.[78] Commission members agreed that the most obvious question was how to contend with the most obstinate element in Muslim local practices: the codes managing inheritances, beneficiaries, and mortmain – lands held by religious orders.

Officials in the commission were divided as to whether it was truly feasible to abolish Muslim practices completely and successfully, and to subjugate all land management under French laws. Memories of the fearsome uprisings in the Kabyle in 1871 and 1872 against French rule and colonial taxation on grain, were still very much on the minds of colonist officials. Some feared opposition from Kabyle representatives who sat on the Financial Delegation, which oversaw budgets. The governor general, however, continued to maintain that France should completely do away with all categories of rights pertaining to tribal collective ownership

---

77 Ibid., 17.
78 Ibid., 17.

including *arch* lands: 'juridical scruples should be set aside' where the future of the colonists was at stake.[79] To investigate the situation of places where the Torrens Act was already in effect, a subcommission was sent to Tunisia. Upon its return, members reconvened to reaffirm their confidence in the Torrens Act foremost because it allowed European titleholders more security with regard to land transaction and therefore more confidence in mortgaging landed properties.[80]

The commission members in Algeria analysed the utility of the Torrens Act for colonists and debated the possible methods by which it could be implemented in the Algerian context. It became apparent that the presence of indivisible properties still under Arab and Berber ownership, including *arch* lands, remained intractable impediments to the full and unobstructed transfer of lands to Europeans in Algeria. To successfully implement the Torrens Act in Algeria, all 'indigenous' properties would have to be registered. The notion of a universal and comprehensive mandatory registry across all of Algeria raised critical questions, not only about its feasibility, but also about the rights and benefits that would be accorded to Muslim titleholders who entered the registry. So far, much of the effort to register properties held under communal titles was done piecemeal, by administrators on the ground. The Torrens Act would streamline such processes.

The debates surrounding the future of the Torrens Act in Algeria brought to light a profound dilemma that would continually resurface for European settlers and investors in Algeria. If the Torrens Act seemed to offer opportunity to assimilate more of the communal properties hitherto deemed out of reach or too thorny for interested investors because of the complex inheritance and usage rights dictated under Muslim code, then the risks associated with bringing Muslim titleholders and communal lands into the Torrens registry were also becoming apparent. Some of the concerns had to do with the feasibility of a mandatory registry and the challenges of enforcing full compliance among Muslim titleholders whose properties would be bound by the terms of the Torrens Act. Officials were especially apprehensive as the Act would in effect bar any future claims brought forth by family members and descendants and prohibit appeals to custom and Islamic inheritance laws.[81]

---

79 Ibid., 8.
80 Ibid., 30.
81 Ibid., 61.

There was more to the problem of introducing the Torrens Act across all populations, however, should the Act take full effect – in Algeria. The Torrens Act would fall under French jurisdiction and the Civil Code, which governed French citizens. How would the *indigènes* who held property titles on communal lands, but were not full French citizens, be made answerable to the Torrens Act, a French law? If the 1863 Senate Law, and later the Warnier Law, accorded nominal French status to the colonized while recognizing Muslim codes and practices, the Torrens Act would go one step further and force Muslim titleholders to relinquish any and all legal ties to Islamic law including all future inheritance claims. The fundamental question remained: how could the French assimilate Arab and Berber lands under French law without assimilating their claimants as French citizens?

Ultimately, officials decided on a procedure that would allow for a system of land registration that would force any titleholder entering into transaction to register their titles for posterity, and thereby relinquish any rights associated with inheritance. Those who wished to enter into transaction would therefore be compelled to submit their rights over the land exclusively to French laws and a public registry. After sale or registration, tribunals would adjudicate any subsequent claims Muslim titleholders or other family members might wish to raise. Such courts would provide French officials the opportunity to make provisional decisions with regard to Indigenous rights. Here, any deviation from French laws could be adjudicated as needed. Muslim subjects were left with a difficult choice: to submit their property to French laws and cede all familial rights to the land, or be forced to live off lands that could only provide minimum sustenance. For communities wanting to capitalize on land sales, there was little option but to relinquish their ties to existing customs and practices that had once allowed Muslim inhabitants in Algeria familial grounding and security of inheritances.

Conclusion

Decades after the brutal conquest of Algeria, the French in Algeria relentlessly pursued a legal mechanism to abrogate as many customary practices as possible and undermine Indigenous governance over communal and collective lands. In the end, Muslim codes were not so much made subordinate to French laws as they were made ineffectual. The notion of having ties to tribal lands became something of a legal encumbrance rather than a meaningful foundation to maintaining social ties for Arab and Berber peoples living in the Tell. With the extension of a real estate market and with mounting legislation that enabled greater acquisition of land for European investors, Muslim titleholders were forced to compromise the future of their family's rights to land inheritances if ever they entered into land transactions. The pressure to do so only intensified throughout the late nineteenth to early twentieth centuries.

When probing the in-depth discussions that attended the importation of the modern title registry system into Algeria, it is easy to consider laws as having a less deleterious effect on colonized societies than military force. But such legal strategies and policy decisions were the direct extension of brute policies that included *regroupement* – forced rounding up of populations – and *cantonnement* or confinement, among other forms of forced displacement. These laws continued the work of violently uprooting colonized communities, and did so in the name of energizing capital investments and rationalizing the legal infrastructure of the settler society. In addition to declaring exemption from taxes otherwise shouldered by Algerians, settlers continually devised legal channels to sever the historical ties that once bound Indigenous societies to the lands they inhabited. They did so not only by applying new regulations, but also by redefining the very notions of personhood, family, and property.

The land registry system that was finally adopted in Algeria shared many points in common with the Torrens Act that had first emerged in Australia. Its aim was to achieve what the 1863 Senate Law of sequestration and *cantonnement* could not: to make French regulations a *sine qua non* for retaining any rights and ties to all land. Ultimately, almost all lands in Algeria became subject to laws that simply rejected the very idea of Indigenous rights. The assimilation of lands resulted in the complete dismissal of existing local customs, practices, and land laws. In the meantime, settlers were successful in overturning imperial restrictions and the Senate Law. While 'turning the page', colonists sought to destroy whatever regime of rights remained for the Muslim inhabitants, leaving later generations incontrovertibly disconnected from their patrimonial legacy. If there were limits to how much settlers could achieve with land registries in Algeria, this could hardly have comforted Muslim communities increasingly pressured not only to give up lands but also those customary practices that expressed their connection to that land.

French officials in Algeria continued to apply measures that allowed for investors to enter into transactions with reluctant Muslim titleholders after 1863 with more security than was possible before. Although the registration of Muslim communal properties remained incomplete by the turn of the twentieth century, the extensive use of public title registries disinherited a large number of Muslim titleholders whose lands were being acquired by Europeans. Titles once entered into registries signalled the forfeiture by Muslim titleholders of further appeals to local courts. The very idea that there were too many limits and constraints to Algeria's land assimilation was a settler colonial one. For the Muslim inhabitant, these constraints proved to be the outer limits of an ever-shrinking regime of rights and claims to land in French Algeria. Although the notion of *terra nullius* could not help carry through the near complete removal of the population in Algeria as it had in North America and Australia, settlers certainly devised policies with the concept of *terra nullius* in mind.[82] Land expropriation by Europeans was far-reaching in Algeria and worked wholly against native Muslim interests, advancing as far as possible the severing of ties between the colonized and their lands. Constraints towards this aim were contingencies that were determined by the binary that shaped European and Muslim relations throughout the history of French Algeria – a binary structure, which would remain entrenched throughout the entire settler-colonial period until independence.

---

82   For a fuller account of how *terra nullius* was conceived by the French in Algeria, see Sessions, *By Sword and Plow*.

2

'False Friends?' On Algeria, the Algerian Jewish Question, and Settler Colonial Studies

Susan Slyomovics

Where does French Algeria fit in the field of settler colonial studies? I begin by asking a hypothetical, counterfactual question: during the 132 years of French colonization between 1830 and 1962, if France had granted citizenship to Muslim Algerians, would such an action have made the natives free?

This question of what freedom means to the native applies also to Algerian Jews, who were throughout the Maghreb categorized in French colonial terminology as natives of the Israelite and Mosaic faith. In contrast to Algerian Muslims, the benefits of citizenship became the political and legislative solution applied uniquely to Algerian Jews transforming them into that compound phrase *français d'Algérie de religion juive* that seems to subdivide the French of Algeria by religion but resonated in the local idiom with a racial distinction. As a minority component of the nineteenth-century native population of Algeria, Algerian Jews represented a rare instance of mass naturalizations of a colonized population enacted into law by a European imperial power through the Crémieux Decree of 24 October 1870. What made the Crémieux Decree so politically potent was that, coincidentally or not, it was passed the same year that the three Algerian *départements* – namely the regional divisions of Algiers, Oran, and Constantine – became an integral part of metropolitan France garnering French citizenship, the right to vote in French elections, and representation in France's governing bodies. These rights, bestowed on the European settler population regardless of origins across the Mediterranean from Italy, Spain, Malta, and Corsica, encompassed native Algerian Jews.

This chapter focuses on the time period when Algerian Jewry were forcibly returned to indigeneity between 1940–3 after Germany defeated France in May 1940. Second World War Vichy-era fascism expanded from France to its overseas North African colonies against those racially classed by colonial bureaucracy as *indigènes* or 'natives', a term perennially applied to the Algerian Muslim and, due to Vichy laws between 1940–3, to the Algerian Jew. More specifically, I investigate the case of Algerian-Jewish soldiers under Vichy Algeria who not only lost their citizenship and became 'native' but were also imprisoned as Jews in forced labour camps. This historical moment foregrounds the precariousness of citizenship for the category of 'natives' as embodied by the disenfranchised racialized minority of Jews, who were a minority within the archipelago of French colonial prison camps. I then trace the ways in which Vichy's innovation, which was to include Jews in the colonial racialization of religious communities, continues to reverberate postwar and globally.

Where does Algeria fit in the field of settler colonial studies and, consequently, in our understanding of the Indigenous community of Algerian Jews? As a minority component of the nineteenth-century native population of Algeria, Algerian Jews, who came under the varied legal regimes of French Algeria after the 1830 conquest, represented a rare instance of mass naturalizations of a colonized population by a European imperial power. An exceptional process of political emancipation was enacted into law through the Crémieux Decree of 24 October 1870, named after Adolphe Crémieux (1796–1880), a French Jewish statesman notable for his successful political work on behalf of abolishing slavery in the French colonies. Yet there is no escape from reproducing the very colonial terminology surrounding the Algerian Jew transformed from native, or more precisely the colonizer's subcategory of *indigène israélite*, to French citizen. My subtitle deliberately echoes Karl Marx's 1844 essay 'On the Jewish Question' since French citizenship for France's Jews maps somewhat onto Algerian Jews. This is because even prior to the establishment of the Third Republic (1870–1940), which encompassed the first period of Algerian Jewry's enfranchisement, Marx noted presciently that France, labelled as a constitutional state, offered 'incompleteness':

> Who is to emancipate? Who is to be emancipated? Criticism had to investigate a third point. It had to inquire: *What kind of emancipation* is in question? What conditions follow from the very nature of the emancipation that is demanded? Only the criticism of *political emancipation* itself would have been the conclusive criticism of the Jewish question and its real merging in the *'general question of time'* … In France, a *constitutional* state, the Jewish question is a question of constitutionalism, the question of the *incompleteness of political emancipation*. Since the *semblance* of a state religion is retained here, although in a meaningless and self-contradictory formula, that of a *religion of the majority*, the relation of the Jew to the state retains the *semblance* of a religious, theological opposition.[1]

Marx's reflections on French Jewry are pertinent to Algeria especially in relation to the striking contrasts afforded by a secular republican France engaging with Jews as a 'semblance of a religion', while simultaneously implacably antagonistic to Islam embodied in its Algerian Muslim subjects who remained almost always the native.

An historically specific configuration emerged consisting of the French secular and republican metropole – France's North African empire of Algerian provinces settled by Europeans, and the Algerian Muslim native subject – that frames the people of this chapter: namely the twice-enfranchised Algerian-Jewish citizen (in 1870 and 1943) and once disenfranchised Algerian-Jewish native subject of 1940. In Algeria, the native Jew became a French citizen, returned briefly to native status, reverted to French citizen albeit a liminal and imperfect European settler in the colony, and finally was reconfigured to *Pied-Noir* in the metropole. To unpack such complex intertwined relationships from the perspective of settler colonial studies, I pose the counterfactual question: If France had extended citizenship to all its Algerian native subjects, would such an action have made those Muslim natives 'free'?[2]

---

1 Karl Marx, 'On *The Jewish Question*', 1844, available at: Marxists.org (emphasis in original).

2 Alina Sajed raised this same question minus my quotes around 'free' in

Terminological *Faux Amis*

To begin answering such a hypothetical and cruelly untrue historical conjecture – and even before unpacking the various ways in which the Jewish and Muslim natives as *indigènes* were seen, known, described, and transformed for French Algeria – some preliminary reflections are in order about definitional overlaps: What is a settler colony and who are and were the settlers of French Algeria? These are meta-discursive avenues that set boundaries and ask questions about which knowledge practices rely on and continuously reformulate the field of settler colonial studies. Therefore, I focus on critical terms deployed in French and Francophone studies about Algeria because they appear to confound the certainties of Anglophone researchers faced with scores of linguistic 'false friends'. Words and phrases are recurring *faux amis* lurking at the intersections between the French and English languages; they deceptively resemble each other in sound and spelling but nonetheless differ in meaning, nuance, and origin.[3] When moving from French to English, at least the French term *colonization* is safely the English 'colonization'. However, the English 'colonist' may translate as *colon* and less commonly *coloniste*, both available to stand in for the English word 'colonist', although older dictionary definitions for the latter include: 'during early colonisations in North Africa, a supporter of maintaining and developing these colonies'. A third word, *colonisateur,* means both 'colonizer' and again 'colonist'.[4] More ambiguously, 'settler colonialism', produces a durable categorical misalignment when the French translation for 'settler colonies' resurrects *colonies de peuplement* or literally 'colonies of settlement', a venerable nineteenth-century phrase that emerged to distinguish

---

Alina Sajed, 'Fanon, Camus and the Colour Line: Colonial Difference and the Rise of Decolonial Horizons', *Cambridge Review of International Affairs*, 26: 1, 2013, 15.

3 For French approaches to specific social science 'nomadic' terms (but not settler colonialism), see Olivier Christin, *Dictionnaire des concepts nomades en Sciences Humaines*, Paris: Éditions Mérailié, 2004. See also Sophie Dulucq, Jean-François Klein, and Benjamin Stora, *Les mots de la colonisation*, Toulouse: Presses universitaires du Mirail, 2008, 29–32.

4 On the term 'colonialism' as applied to Algeria by France's historians, see Guy Pervillé, 'Qu'est-ce que la colonisation?' *Revue d'histoire moderne et contemporaine*, 22, 1975, 321–68.

between colonies of exploitation as opposed to colonies of settlement. Colonies are for exploitation, but if they are empty, one needs to people them first, but what if people are already there? The 'peopling' or *peuplement* part of the phrase once carried opposed meanings to refer not only to the obvious condition of settlers coming to settle but also to designate whether the target territory for settlement was *peuplement* in the sense of 'already peopled' by a native population and not uninhabited lands capable of exploitation. *Peuplement* meant not just empire's active populating occasioned by the arrival of European settlers from elsewhere. The word acknowledged the existence of densely populated or 'peopled' territories that dynamically shaped configurations of settler–native relations so much so that according to Sophie Linon-Chipon, policies envisioned by Louis XIV for Madagascar and Napoleon III for Algeria were intended to lead to the formation of a united single people from an Indigenous population conjoined to the incoming settlers.[5] In other words, there are no French phrases to match the English 'settler' and 'settler colonialism' without becoming enmeshed in discourses at odds with these concepts.

Although colonialism was the prevailing term from 1830 onward for Algeria, France was also an empire. The Second Empire, 1852–70, ruled by Emperor Napoleon III famously attributed to Algeria in 1860 the status of 'Arab kingdom' (*royaume arabe*) with himself as its leader. In 1865, a mere ten days after he returned from his official state visit to Algeria, Napoleon III published his approach, which articulates classic definitions of colonialism but not settler colonialism:

> No one can possibly have the idea to exterminate the three million natives [*indigènes*] who are in Algeria, nor pushing them back into the desert, following the example of North Americans in regards to the Indians; we have therefore to live with the Arabs and mould them to our laws, get them used to our domination, and convince them of our superiority, not only through our weapons, but also by our institutions … Pacification of the Arabs is therefore the indispensable basis of colonisation, and seeking the means to achieve this, is to favour European interests.[6]

---

5 Sophie Linon-Chipon, *Gallia orientalis: Voyages aux Indes orientales, 1529–1722*, Paris: Presses de l'université de Paris-Sorbonne, 2003, 691.

6 'Il ne peut entrer dans l'idée de personne d'exterminer les trois millions d'indigènes qui sont en Algérie, ni de les refouler dans le désert, suivant l'exemple

The emperor's letter foregrounds the false friends that lurk between languages on academic topics related to French colonialism but even more so do the taxonomic categorizations that serve to construct, elide, oversimplify, and finally enumerate the various components of Algerian society as if they were different species. Drawn from the archive of French colonial terminology, vocabularies of colonialism and empire continue to influence critical engagements across transnational academic communities. They are symptomatic of difficulties that animate how the colonizers ordered, named, renamed, and reconfigured peoples, tribes, groups, and individuals with whom they came into contact under conditions of imperial conquest. Terms used during the colonial era bleed into the textual remains of colonialism's afterlives especially in case studies of countries such as Algeria, where the brutal political ruptures of 1962 established an independent Algeria.

To understand comparatively the case of Algeria, an impressive array of major thinkers has grappled with the varieties of colonial contact as an object of knowledge; in what follows, the terms they produced to structure the racialization of Algeria's inhabitants and its associated order-making efforts and knowledge production emerging from the shadow of empire assist in the determination of categories such as settler colonialism or colonialism. As one example, anthropologist Udo Krautwurst enumerated the following concepts and dyads in 2003: settler colonies/colonies of intervention and exploitation; settler colonial mode of production/capitalist mode 'proper'; settler colony/administrative colony; trading colonies/colonies of settlement; white settler colonies as a hybrid between temperate colonies of immigration and settlement/tropical colonies of exploitation and administration; settlement colonialism/exploitation colonialism; settler societies/colonial societies; peasant political economy/settler political economy; settler/non-settler colonies; emigrant metropolitans/migrant metropolitans; emigrationist colonial

---

des Américains du Nord à l'égard des Indiens; il faut donc vivre avec les Arabes, les façonner à nos lois, les habituer à notre domination, et les convaincre de notre supériorité, non seulement par nos armes, mais aussi par nos institutions ... La pacification des Arabes est donc la base indispensable de la colonisation, et chercher les moyens de l'obtenir, c'est favoriser les intérêts européens'. Napoléon III, *Lettre sur la politique de la France en Algérie adressée par l'empereur au maréchal de Mac Mahon duc de Magenta, gouverneur général de l'Algérie*, Paris: Imprimerie impériale, 1865, 10.

ideologies/economic colonial ideologies; settler states/colonial states; and dependent colony/settler colony.[7] Krautwurst's solution to confusions of terminological and categorizing excesses is, in his own words, to conclude boldly and in italics that '*all colonialism is settler colonialism*'.[8] Such attendant terminological binds are bound up in the search for an escape from the knotty Bourdieusian 'struggle of classification' (*lutte de classement*) that has led scholars who think about French colonial Algeria in several directions.[9]

One path followed by historian Guy Pervillé is to focus on definitions emerging from the strategies and outcomes that French colonization adopted to deal with large native populations in conquered territories. He considers three:

> [Colonization] can involve [the native] in its work by sharing its techniques and letting them a share of space that they can develop and use. This combination can lead to assimilation. It can exclude them by blocking them or confining them to waste land, where the ploughshare breaks. This exclusion provokes war and often genocide. It can also use them as labour. This exploitation makes integration into subordination, which does not allow the merger of two populations.[10]

---

7 See Udo Krautwurst, 'What is Settler Colonialism? An Anthropological Meditation of Frantz Fanon's "Concerning Violence"', *History and Anthropology*, 14: 1, 2003: 59–60.

8 Ibid., 58. For a succinct summary of the intellectual lineage or *silsila* of settler colonial studies, see Gabriel Piterberg, *The Returns of Zionism: Myths, Politics and Scholarship in Israel*, London: Verso, 2008, 54–61.

9 Pierre Bourdieu, 'L'identité et la représentation [Éléments pour une réflexion critique sur l'idée de région]', *Actes de la recherche en sciences sociales*, 35, 1980, 63–72. See also Pierre Bourdieu, 'Classement, déclassement, reclassement', *Actes de la recherche en sciences sociales*, 24, 1978, 2–22.

10 La colonisation 'peut les associer à son œuvre en leur communiquant ses techniques et en leur laissant la part d'espace qu'ils peuvent mettre en valeur en les utilisant. Cette association peut conduire à une assimilation. Elle peut les exclure en les refoulant ou en les cantonnant sur des terres de rebut, où le soc de la charrue se briserait. Cette exclusion provoque la guerre et souvent le génocide. Elle peut aussi les exploiter comme main-d'œuvre. Cette exploitation réalise une intégration dans la subordination, qui ne permet pas la fusion des deux populations'. Pervillé, 'Qu'est-ce que la colonisation?', 350.

Patrick Wolfe's interventions in these discussions are pertinent and influential. The consequences of Perville's last two strategies are collapsed by Wolfe when he writes that 'the question of genocide is never far from discussions of settler colonialism. Land is life – or, at least, land is necessary for life'.[11] Here, Wolfe returns to his fundamental articulation of settler-colonial domination that is not with the colonized but directly with the land. In this way, by judging the state of settler colonialism through outcomes and strategies, which in turn helps distinguish a colony from a settler colony, Wolfe relegates French Algeria to the category of 'so-called settler colonies'.[12] This is because theorists, among them Patrick Wolfe, are influenced by D.K. Fieldhouse's earlier 1966 taxonomies which looked to dominant tendencies to typify his four categories. Fieldhouse enumerates occupation colonies, mixed settlement, plantation, and pure settlement to emerge with his definition of Algeria as a 'mixed colony'.[13]

For Wolfe, productive analyses of settler colonies reside ideally in the mode of 'pure settlement' colony. Examples of pure settlement, cited by Gabriel Piterberg, are to be found in the early Virginia and New England colonies, or much later in the Israeli kibbutz in which the salient feature is the rejection of native labour thereby rendering the native superfluous:

> But the fundamental point about a white-settler colony – New England, Virginia, Australia, New Zealand, Argentina – is that it is predicated on white labour, on complete closure vis-à-vis the natives, on gradual territorial expansion, under the bayonets of a metropole colonial power for as long as necessary; and on the creation of a self-sufficient economy that can attract more settler immigration.[14]

---

11 Patrick Wolfe, 'Settler Colonialism and the Elimination of the Native', *Journal of Genocide Research*, 8: 4, 2006, 387.

12 Wolfe, 'Land, Labor, and Difference: Elementary Structures of Race', *American Historical Review*, 106: 3, 2001, 868.

13 D.K. Fieldhouse, *The Colonial Empires: A Comparative Survey from the Eighteenth Century*, London: Macmillan Press, 1966, 250. See also George M. Frederickson, *The Arrogance of Race: Historical Perspectives on Slavery, Racism, and Social Inequality*, Middletown, CT: Wesleyan University Press, 1988, 216-35.

14 Gabriel Piterberg, 'Settlers and Their States: A Reply to Zeev Sternhell', *New Left Review*, 62, 2010, 117.

What do categories and taxonomies classify, why the struggle for classification, and, above all, why should we care about them? To characterize French Algeria and reckon with its importance to the field of settler colonialism at the very least ensures further refinements in the study of modes of settler domination. Despite Algeria's perennial 'unstable status' as a settler colony, yet another category introduced by Gershon Shafir is influenced by French Algeria.[15] A settler colony may be one of two kinds according to Shafir: the 'ethnic plantation' of early Zionist settlement which relied on land and cheap labour from the native followed chronologically by Fieldhouse's model of the 'pure settlement colony'. In pre-1948 Palestine, the move from 'ethnic plantation' to 'settler colony' was occasioned by

> frustration with the inability of the ethnic plantation colony to provide sufficient employment for Jewish workers, i.e., from opposition to the particular form of their predecessors' colonization ... the dominant Zionist method, was but another type of European overseas colonization – the 'pure settlement colony' also found in Australia, Northern US, and elsewhere. Its threefold aim was control of land, employment that ensured a European standard of living, and massive immigration ... This form of pure settlement rested on two exclusivist pillars ... The aims were the removal of land and labor from the market, respectively, thus closing them off to Palestinian Arabs.[16]

So, for Shafir, Algeria most resembles an ethnic plantation. In contrast, historian David Prochaska weighs in by categorizing French Algeria as a settler colony. His conclusions are based on the creation of a settler society whose demographics, class, and race taxonomies place the native at the bottom rungs and in the minority in spaces where the settler–native nexus mattered most, which were the economic powerhouses of the city:

---

15 Fiona Barclay, Charlotte Ann Chopin, and Martin Evans, 'Introduction: Settler Colonialism and French Algeria', *Settler Colonial Studies*, 2017.

16 Gershon Shafir, 'Zionism and Colonialism: A Comparative Approach', in Michael N. Barnett (ed.), *Israel in Comparative Perspective: Challenging the Conventional Wisdom*, Albany, NY: State University of New York Press, 1996, 235.

A settler colonial society in which the European colonizers outnumber the Algerian colonized two to one. A French colony in which the Italians, Spanish, and Maltese are as numerous as the French, and form colonies within the colony. A French colonial society created largely by naturalizing Jews and Europeans. A colonial society stratified along lines of race and class, and typified by residential segregation, vertical occupational stratification, functional occupational specialization, plus unequal pay for equal work. It all fits together.[17]

If the rural agricultural kibbutz is the pre-eminent ethnic plantation for Palestine, then Prochaska's focus on cities takes us to where the native is largely absent. Surrounded and cordoned off in the Casbah of Algiers or in the second city of Oran and its *villes nègres* (literally 'Negro towns'), these were spaces allocated to the native in urban centres. Urban segregation highlights the intersections of colonial authority, the deliberate underdevelopment of racialized native quarters, and the concomitant economic development of vibrant European *villes nouvelles* or 'new cities' inhabited by settlers (or *colons* in Fanon's original French text). Colonial Algerian urban centres were 'compartmentalized' in Fanon's words and built upon constricting pre-existing precolonial urban formations of the *medina* and *mellah*, the walled city and Jewish minority quarters respectively:

> The settlers' town is strongly built all made of stone and steel [*La ville du colon est une ville en dur, toute de pierre et de fer.*] It is a brightly lit town; the streets are covered with asphalt, and the garbage cans swallow all the leaving, unseen, unknown and hardly though about ... The town belonging to the colonized people, or at least the native town, the Negro village, the medina, the reservation, is a place of ill fame, peopled by men of ill repute ... It is a world without spaciousness, men live there on top of each other, and their huts are built one on top of the other. The native town is a hungry town, starved of bread, of meat, of shoes, of coal, of light. The native town is a crouching village, a town wallowing in mire. It is a town of niggers and dirty Arabs.[18]

---

17 David Prochaska, *Making Algeria French: Colonialism in Bône, 1870–1930*, New York: Cambridge University Press, 1990, 178.
18 Frantz Fanon, *The Wretched of the Earth*, New York: Grove, 1968, 39.

However we come to define the formation in French Algeria – in which the presence or absence of native labour is one determinant – it is the case, following Gabriel Piterberg, that on-the-ground realities in colonized Algeria are unthinkable without exploitable native labour. Therefore, he concludes that the fault line between colonizer and native becomes more porous and more difficult to maintain.[19] To pay attention to the ways in which Algeria has much to say about settler colonial studies as an ethnic plantation dependent on native labour in the ways Gershon Shafir outlines for Israel/Palestine, I look at how French colonialism not only created the category of the *indigène* or native in the first place, but also, having created the category, how it incessantly destabilized, indeed played havoc with, nativeness. Following on from my explorations of classification's porosity leads me to the next step. How do the topics, concerns, definitional boundaries, and questions on which knowledge practices both rely and continuously reformulate overlap, and how is the *indigène* known and categorized in French Algeria? Classifications by and about settler colonialism come to tell us what the settlers think when they do what they do. As Lorenzo Veracini emphasizes, settler colonialism projects look forward to focus on the future of a society which is their society to come.[20] The history of settler ideas about settlement and Indigenous peoples matters, since they could not imagine their place in the future Algeria without a vocabulary that is both generic and specific to French Algeria.

The Crémieux Decree and a French Jewish Consistory Modelled for Algerian Jews

In the beginning is the French word *indigène,* translated as 'indigene' and 'native' in English. The word remains widespread in popular French speech, still bearing the weighty histories of France's overseas empire

---

19 On differences between the ethnic plantation colony and the pure settlement colony shaping the consciousness of those who experience those material realities (including in their literary imagination), see Gabriel Piterberg, 'The Literature of Settler Societies: Albert Camus, S. Yizhar, and Amos Oz', *Settler Colonial Studies*, 2: 1, 2011, 1–52. Albert Memmi questions the colonizer–colonized binary, especially in relation to his own community of Tunisian Jews positioned as 'historically ambiguous'. Albert Memmi, *Pillar of Salt*, Boston: Beacon, 1992, 282.

20 Lorenzo Veracini, 'Settler Collective, Founding Violence and Disavowal: The Settler Colonial Situation', *Journal of Intercultural Studies*, 29: 4, 2008, 363–79.

and its variegated populations. *Indigène* also speaks pejoratively to and about non-French subjects who are not full citizens far more so than its less common English cognate.[21] Specific examples of French-constructed indigeneity after France's conquest of Algeria in 1830 produced concepts of the 'Arab' and the 'Berber' as France's oldest stereotypes for Algerian natives.[22] Endlessly repeated and circulated with variations throughout much of the vast French ethnological literature about Algeria, these categories were hierarchically arranged which, among other attributes, systematically pitted the 'good Kabyle' farmer of the mountains against the 'bad Arab' nomads of the lowlands. Colonial anthropologists abstracted physiological characteristics to create racial types, which were then given visual attestation through the drawings, photographs, and captions provided by photographers and ethnographers.[23] While French anthropology, medicine, travel writing, and military reports produced a plethora of records and descriptions of the physical attributes about what they perceived to be Algeria's two principally different races, these attributes of good Berber and bad Arab, Patricia Lorcin argues, were never scientifically measurable but rather opinionated descriptors masking as science that were 'measured according to philosophical, sociological and moral indexes'.[24] It is noteworthy that while the nativeness of Muslim

---

21 Laure Blévis, 'L'invention de l'"indigène", Français non citoyen', in Jean-Pierre Peyroulou (ed.), *L'Histoire de l'Algerie à la periode colonial*, Paris: La Découverte: 2014, 212–18.

22 Nicolas Bancel and Pascal Blanchard, 'To Civilize: The Invention of the Native (1918–1940)', in Pascal Blanchard, Sandrine Lemaire, Nicolas Bancel, and Dominic Thomas (eds), *Colonial Culture in France since the Revolution*, Bloomington: Indiana University Press, 2014, 173. See also Pascal Blanchard and Nicolas Bancel, *De l'indigène à l'immigré*, Paris: Gallimard, 1998.

23 Susan Slyomovics, 'Visual Ethnography, Stereotypes, and Photographing Algeria', in Ian Richard Netton (ed.), *Orientalism Revisited: Art, Land, and Voyage*, London: Routledge, 2102, 128–50.

24 Indigenous peoples become labelled good or bad in various contexts – for example, according to Israeli settlers, the terms Druze, Christian Arab, or Muslim Arab divide and categorize Palestinians as good allies for the first category ranging to bad enemy indigenes for the last one. Similarly, for North American native tribes (which are often reversed as mirror images depending on whether they are named by French or English settlers). On images specific to Algeria's natives, the Berbers and Arabs, see Patricia Lorcin, *Imperial Identities: Stereotyping, Prejudice and Race in Colonial Algeria*, London: I.B. Tauris, 1995, and Patricia Lorcin, 'Imperialism, Colonial Identity, and Race in Algeria,

Algerians is fixed, the settlers, drawn from a population arising from the northern shores of the Mediterranean, labelled themselves *Algériens*.[25]

In contrast, my approach to French Algeria, which remains within the framework of Shafir's concept of the ethnic plantation in Algeria and its potential to provide nuanced re-examinations of settler colonial studies, returns to colonial anthropological knowledge production in order to repeat my previous hypothetical, counterfactual question posed at the beginning of this chapter. So, what would freedom really mean for the native of French Algeria? In the post–Second World War period, when political pressures for citizenship and rights for the native reached an apogee, notable advocates such as Albert Camus and Germaine Tillion proposed their preferred solution, which was to turn the Muslim native into French citizen through 'assimilation'. On the other side of the French political divide regarding the place of colonized peoples were Frantz Fanon and Pierre Bourdieu, each in their own words maintaining that colonialism in regards to the native population was not reformable. Frantz Fanon famously described conflictual dyads pitting native and colonizer. The 'colonial world is a Manichean world':

> In its bare reality, decolonization reeks of red-hot cannonballs and bloody knives. For the last can be the first only after a murderous and decisive confrontation between the two antagonists ... There is no conciliation possible ... This compartmentalized world, this world divided in two, is inhabited by different species.[26]

My counterfactual historical query about what freedom would really mean for the native of French Algeria, as it happens, is relevant even though French citizenship was never bestowed on the majority of

---

1830–1870: The Role of the French Medical Corps', *Isis*, 90: 4, 1999, 655. Distinctions between good Berbers/Kabyles and bad Arabs were already in place in Alexis de Tocqueville, *Travail sur l'Algérie* (1841). Available at classiques.uqac.ca/classiques.

25 Julia Clancy-Smith, 'Islam, Gender and Identities in the Making of French Algeria, 1830–1962', in Julia Clancy-Smith and Frances Gouda (eds), *Domesticating the Empire: Languages of Gender, Race, and Family Life in French and Dutch Colonialism, 1830–1962*, Charlottesville: University Press of Virginia, 1998, 154.

26 Fanon, *Wretched of the Earth*, 41.

Muslim Algerians – excepting some 7,000 before the end of the Algerian War of Independence from a population of 9 million natives. The question of what freedom means to the native applied powerfully to Algerian Jews, hitherto *indigènes* of a different religion categorized in French colonial terminology throughout the Maghreb as natives of the Israelite and Mosaic faith, confessional descriptors rather than the racial and nationalist valences ascribed to 'Muslim'. The dialectic of emancipation for Algerian Jews and assimilation for Algerian Muslims is one outlined by Patrick Wolfe. Pertinent to my question is his emphasis that freedom is stubbornly contextual, as in the Algerian-Jewish case when the context is constantly shifting and subject to the struggle inherent to the politics of classification.[27]

Historian Joshua Schreier exemplifies Wolfe's position because he views the Crémieux Decree as intentionally emancipating Algerian Jews from Islam precisely in order to exclude Muslims.[28] French citizenship would be emancipatory for the native Algerian Jew. Indeed, Schreier locates one of the earliest uses of the French colonial phrase *mission civilisatrice* ('mission to civilize') to the year 1847 when uttered by a certain Amran Senanes, an Algerian Jew, as yet still a native in the terminology of the 1840s. Identifying vociferously with the French Jewish rabbinical mission to civilize Algerian Jewry, Senanes lamented that the Jewish 'consistory' system in France set up to oversee French Jewish communal and religious affairs was unworkable in his own backward, Jewish Algeria. To establish first a French consistorial model for Algerian Jews preceded, perhaps even set forth, pathways to the eventual civilizing mission inextricably intertwined with mastery of the French language for the entire Jewish community; it also entailed centralization, a seemingly neutral reorganizing, yet one that would model new top–down hierarchies to ordain and hire a Jewish religious bureaucracy of rabbis, ritual slaughterers, and deacons, as well as to raise tax revenues from kosher butchers, merchants, and alcohol vendors who would become invested with a metropolitan authority no longer anchored in local Algerian-Jewish practices. A 'mission to civilize' for Algerian Jews meant reorganizing the community and included 'securing control and extending surveillance to

---

27 On the dialectic of emancipation and assimilation, see Patrick Wolfe, *Traces of History*, London: Verso, 2016.

28 Joshua Schreier, *Arabs of the Jewish Faith*, Stanford, CA: Stanford University Press, 2010.

the hitherto personal spheres of life' by state-sanctioned and often secular officials in making doctrinal and communal decisions.²⁹

Nonetheless, Schreier describes clearly and sympathetically in his second chapter on 'Revolution, Republicanism and Religion: Responses to Civilizing in Oran, 1848', the multiple engagements of Algerian Jews whether with France, their own French co-religionists arriving in Algeria from France, or their fellow Oran Jews to produce a case study about the struggle for control over local synagogues. Schreier reads complex and ambiguous responses by the prominent Jewish community of Oran, one that is not entirely 'resistance' (my word not Schreier's) by Algerian Jews to similar claims to a civilizing mission by French Jews, and the ways in which even defining 'civilization' was clearly understood as part of contestations for political authority within the confines of Oran synagogues. Historically, from the 1847 official opening of the consistory of Oran, the position of grand rabbi would be held by a French, not an Algerian, Jew. The first holder, as Schreier recounts based on archival correspondence, was Lazare Cahen, an Alsatian-educated Jew chosen because of his duties as a chaplain to Jews in prison. Schreier conjectures that since the Oran Jewish community was understood as heavily invested and represented in criminal activities (the men constituting some 25 per cent of the inmates of the civil prison and the women engaged in prostitution), the most useful skills were held by those who ministered to Jewish incarcerated criminals in the metropole. Moreover, the one extensive social interaction between a rabbi and a Jewish criminal that did not taint the rabbi was the role of prison chaplain. In striking ways, French colonial discourse about the criminality of their Algerian non-Jewish Muslim-majority population resembled attitudes by French rulers about Algerian Jews. Yet the differences between native Jews and Muslims in Algeria were that eventually Jews became redeemable and civilizable in French terms in the 1840s. This was partly owing to the consistorial system

---

29   Joshua Schreier, 'Napoléon's Long Shadow: Morality, Civilization, and Jews in France and Algeria, 1808–1870', *French Historical Studies*, 30: 1, 2007: 77–103. See also Sung Eun Choi, *Decolonization and the French of Algeria: Bringing the Settler Colony Home*, New York, NY: Palgrave Macmillan, 2016, and Valérie Assan, *Les Consistoires israélites d'Algérie au XIXe siècle*, Paris: Armand Colin, 2012. Comparative population figures for Algerian Jews and Muslims are in Laure Blévis, 'En marge du décret Crémieux: Les Juifs naturalisés français en Algérie, 1865–1919', *Archives Juives*, 45: 2, 2012, 47–67.

devised and imposed for Algerian Jews which carried out this role for over two decades in the period of 1847 to 1870 before Algerian Jews were enfranchised as French citizens.

According to such a reading, the 1870 Crémieux Decree was uniquely successful when viewed as an example of a European power making claims to afford comprehensive protection for the entirety of the Jewish community and then doing so through the extension of French citizenship to natives inhabiting a French overseas colony. In contrast to Algerian Muslims, the benefits of citizenship became the political and legislative solution applied uniquely to Algerian Jews transforming them into that compound phrase *français d'Algérie de religion juive* that seems to subdivide the French of Algeria by religion but resonated in the local idiom with racial distinctions. What made the Crémieux Decree so politically potent was that, coincidentally or not, it was passed the same year that the three Algerian *départements,* namely the regional divisions of Algiers, Oran, and Constantine, became an integral part of metropolitan France, garnering French citizenship, the right to vote in French elections, and representation in France's governing bodies. These rights, bestowed on the European settler population regardless of origins across the Mediterranean from Italy, Spain, Malta, or Corsica, enfolded native Algerian Jews.

The exception among Algerian Jewry, which numbered some 35,000 people in 1870, was the several thousand Algerian Mzabi Jews residing in what became the southern military territories only fully conquered by France in 1882, twelve years after the Crémieux Decree. There, Jews as well as Muslims came under direct military oversight and both groups were categorized as *indigènes*. French military authorities viewed the southern Algerian territories differently from the three northern provinces conquered fifty years previously. According to Sarah Abrevaya Stein, Saharan Jews became an exogenous category, one created by the military as opposed to the settler authorities. Stein notes that the purpose of this military-induced and therefore legal sub-classification of Indigenous Mzabi Jews was not to isolate southern Algerian Jewry from their northern Algerian co-religionists, the latter already enfranchised in 1870 before the conquest of the south in 1882. Rather, the military's main purpose was to avoid jeopardizing the precarious protectorate framework imposed on the region's Ibadite leadership, which called both for Jews remaining Indigenous and prohibiting European settlement. The

Algerian south was where indigenes, certainly Muslims but especially Jews, stayed Indigenous.[30] This was adjudged to be best implemented if, and only if, the Saharan south excluded Algerian Jews from French citizenship and excluded European settlers from establishing colonies. A zealously guarded preserve of the military, this vast region was the object of centuries of French imaginary constructions coupled with savage colonial violence directed at the varied populations of Mzabi Jews, Ibadis, Tuaregs, and more.[31] The scholarly literature on colonialism in French Algeria is concerned exclusively with the three littoral provinces of Oran, Algiers, and Constantine, all three of which were integrated into the French polity and where the majority of enfranchised Algerian Jews resided, even though this coastal region represented a mere tenth of Algerian territory. Nonetheless, when comparing settler colonies, Algeria (coastal and Saharan), along with South Africa, Southern Rhodesia, and Kenya, are usually lumped together in sharing the African experience of not-quite-genuine settler colonialism.

Pierre Bourdieu on Algerian Jewry

Given the pervasive pseudo-scientific divisions and descriptions of the Algerian 'native' along racial and ethnic lines, where did the Algerian Jew fit in ethnographically? As late as 1958, the fourth year of the brutal eight-year Algerian War of Independence, eminent social scientist Pierre Bourdieu published *Sociologie de l'Algérie* in the popularizing French university press series *Que sais-je?* ('What do I know?'). Although constrained by both the press' 128-page limit, and more so because he produced the manuscript during the very first years of an Algerian sojourn regulated by his French military service in Algeria in the middle of a war, Bourdieu in hindsight concluded in 2004 that the purpose of this first slim book was above all else to enlighten a French audience:

---

30 Sarah Abrevaya Stein, *Saharan Jews and the Fate of French Algeria*, Chicago: University of Chicago Press, 2014.
31 See Benjamin Brower, *A Desert Named Peace: The Violence of France's Empire in the Algerian Sahara, 1844–1902*, New York: Columbia University Press, 2009.

Being seconded to the military staff of the French administration (*Gouvernement général*) in Algiers, where I was subjected to the obligations and schedules of a second-class private assigned to clerical duties (drafting correspondence, contributing to reports, etc.), I was able to embark on writing a short book (for the *Que Sais-je? series*) in which I would try to tell the French, and especially people on the Left, what was really going on in a country about which they often knew next to nothing – once again, in order to be of some use, and perhaps also to stave off the bad conscience of the helpless witness of an abominable war.[32]

This was Bourdieu's first book. It was about Algeria and it became a bestseller. Even as he wrote, he was already moving from his academic training in philosophy to on-the-ground reports that drew on ethnology and sociology. Five chapters in the first 1958 edition were written according to prevailing mid-twentieth-century ethnographic conventions that described in broad strokes each element of the native population in French colonial Algeria. His approach returns to the colonial archive with its institutionally approved descriptions, typologies, and surveys of peoples according to their characteristics, manners, and customs. Only towards the end, in his sixth chapter 'Disintegration and Distress', the last in the original 1958 French volume, does he set aside retrograde ethnographic approaches and append a seventh chapter entitled 'The Revolution within the Revolution' (which only appeared in French two years later in the 1961 edition but simultaneously with the English translation). These publication histories demonstrate Bourdieu's evolution in thinking about Algeria. His ensuing publications and especially the next 1961 edition of *Sociologie de l'Algérie* are ruptures with this debut 1958 volume marred by stereotypical descriptions of the Algerian natives.[33] At best, his first book underscores Bourdieu in the mode of his 'struggle of classification' in which he produces an excess of categories about Algerian society.

Weberian 'ideal types' were transformed into archetypes and stereotypes powerfully frozen for the French reading public and sustained in

---

32 Pierre Bourdieu, 'Algerian Landing', *Ethnography*, 5: 4, 2004, 419.
33 On Bourdieu's evolving sociology of Algeria it is worth comparing the French 1958 and 1961 editions to tease out the changing role of a scholar engaged in political debates. See André Nouschi, 'Autour de *Sociologie de l'Algérie*', *Awal*, 27–28, 2003, 29–36.

the popular imagination by visual representations. Each country of colonized French North Africa, according to anthropologist Malek Chebel, typified a different visual stereotype usually geographical or architectural. For French audiences, Algerian stereotypes in particular centred around racial, even erotic, distinctions about a colonized society because the ultimate outcome of the *colonie de peuplement* is its peoples:

> In Morocco, it is above all the architecture of cities (gardens, gates, fountains, markets, *medersas*) that intrigue and hold the attention of colonial painters and illustrators. In Tunisia, the landscape and artisanat were priorities. In Algeria it was the society: 'scenes and types' rained down, *moukères* (Arab women), demi-mondaines, professions (barbers), Tuareg chiefs (*amenokals*), dancers (*nailiyate*) were at the same time occasions that permit discerning the Other in the immeasurable challenge of the image. These tendencies were obviously not neutral: they reflected the contradictions of the moment, often the will [wish or desire (*volonté*)] to find some paradigms in an ocean of uncertainties.[34]

Bourdieu follows similar rigid paradigms seeking stable classificatory units amid Chebel's 'ocean of uncertainties' and fixes sociological categories that divide, subdivide, and further subcategorize the components of what he terms an 'original Algerian society'; he conjures familiar divisions by setting up individual chapters and headings for the Kabyle, the Shawia, Mozabites, and other Arabic-speaking peoples of Algeria such as the Kouloughlis.[35] His fifth chapter joins together these sundered subcategorizations of native peoples through an evocation of culture subsumed

---

34 Malek Chebel, 'L'image de l'autochtone maghrébine', in Nicolas Bancel, Pascal Blanchard, and Laurent Gervereau (eds), Images et colonies: Iconographie et propagande coloniale sur l'Afrique française de 1880 à 1962, Paris: UNESCO, 1993: 272, and Malek Chebel, '"L'Arabe" dans l'imaginaire occidentale', in Pascal Blanchard (ed.), *L'autre et nous: 'scènes et types'*, Paris: Association Connaissance de l'histoire de l'Afrique contemporaine, 1995, 39–44. For anthropology's histories and photography about Algeria into 'scene and types' (*scènes et types*), see Susan Slyomovics, 'Visual Ethnography, Stereotypes, and Photographing Algeria', in Ian Richard Netton (ed.), *Orientalism Revisited: Art, Land, and Voyage*, London: Routledge, 2012, 128–50.

35 From the English translation of Pierre Bourdieu, *Sociologie de l'Algérie*, in *The Algerians*, Boston: Beacon, 1961 [1958], 111.

under his umbrella rubric of 'Common Cultural Heritage'.[36] Only there is to be found a brief mention of Algeria's native Jewish population in that quintessential textual aside, a footnote, which further subdivides into two varieties what appeared to Bourdieu as two more subcategories of Algerian Jewry. Both kinds of Jewish types draw on fifteenth-century distinctions about origins to describe the telling category of 'autochthons who are very similar in manners and civilization to the other natives of Algeria':

> The Israelites, about 150,000 in number, are divided according to origin into two groups, the 'Spaniards', driven from Spain in 1492, and the autochthons, who are very similar in manners and civilization to the other natives of Algeria. While conserving a number of their traditions, they are for the most part engaged in the Moslem business sector and follow the European mode of life. They are particularly numerous in the cities.[37]

Bourdieu's footnote barely gestures towards the complexity of the post-1870 Crémieux Decree era, which dramatically reconfigured the population of European colonists: Algeria's Jews had moved categories legally and juridically from native to French citizen. After the 1830 conquest and prior to the 1870 enfranchisement, Algerian Jewry were frequently perceived by the European colonisers as obvious intermediaries between themselves and the other great masses of natives, the Arab, and Berber. Jews were structurally the native colonized but also liminally the go-betweens who did not fully belong to but interpreted the variety of cultures that existed in the region to the colonizer.[38] Algerian

---

36 These first five chapters of Bourdieu's *Sociologie d'Algérie*, a book purporting to explain Algerian society to the French public, perhaps merited the caustic review in the prestigious *Annales* journal by noted historian of Algeria Marcel Émerit, who underscored glaring gaps surrounding the topic of colonization in Bourdieu's book. Marcel Émerit, 'Pierre Bourdieu *Sociologie de l'Algérie*, Collection "Que sais-je?" [compte rendu]', *Annales: Economies, sociétés, civilisations*, 15: 2, 1960, 402–4.

37 Bourdieu, *Sociologie de l'Algérie*, 93.

38 Geneviève Dermenjian, 'Les juifs d'Algérie dans le regard des militaires et des juifs de France à l'époque de la conquête (1830–1855)', *Revue Historique*, 284, 2, 1990, 333–9.

Jews retained a shared native culture mediated through economic interchanges between Jew and Muslim, according to Bourdieu, who modelled culture metaphorically onto linguistic contacts found in the Greek *koinè*:

> In the dialogue that brings the different groups of Algeria face to face, there is being worked out in original form of civilization, a cultural *koinè*. As a final example, it may be noted that the way of life peculiar to the Israelites indicates that they were very closely related to the other Algerian 'cultures'; a few characteristics will suffice: intensity of community feeling, patriarchal structure of the family, whose head is revered as much as any overlord, simultaneous or successive polygamy, a cult of saints resembling the cult of marabouts, superstitions and magic beliefs, Arab language, etc. Thus no group escapes this intense cultural interpenetration.[39]

For Bourdieu, cultural interpenetration trumped French citizenship to determine his alignment of Algeria's Jews with native Muslims. He tempered this with his observations that 'while conserving a number of their traditions, they are for the most part engaged in the Moslem business sector and follow the European mode of life. They are particularly numerous in the cities'. Bourdieu's summary about Algerian Jewry emphasized their conservative traditions, noted their investment more in the Muslim than European commercial sector, and saw them demographically and geographically as a community of urban dwellers. As townspeople, Jews readily conformed to Prochaska's views when he situated the pinnacle of the Algerian settler colony in the cities. Prochaska therefore overlaps with Shafir's descriptions of ethnic plantations despite the fact that Shafir's formation described agricultural Zionist colonies. Instead, ethnic plantations were to be found in the cities of Algeria with their transformational urbanized settler demographics.

Bourdieu's blanket characterizations are similar to those found throughout the vast colonial-era literature on Algerian Jews. Indeed, as we have argued elsewhere, this distinctive history and understanding of Algerian Jews, similar to concepts about the 'Arab' and 'Berber', also owed its historiographical beginnings to French colonialism:

---

39 Bourdieu, *Sociologie de l'Algérie*, 93.

Even as the French conquest of Algeria was underway, military and colonial officials, as well as Franco and Franco-Jewish reformers sympathetic with the colonial mission, began to produce literature about Algeria's Jews. The resulting ethnographies, travelogues, Orientalist musings, official reports and surveys, works of medical literature, and military and colonial reports have provided scholars with vivid (if usually problematic) depictions of the pre- and early-colonial Jews of Algeria: all told, they offer a complex – and inevitably partial – picture of Algerian Jewish life, and also of the way in which Jews figured in the French *mission civilisatrice*.[40]

Jews were made integral to France's civilizing mission in Algeria, underpinned by metropolitan French Jews' efforts to assure uplift to their co-religionists by an attachment to France.[41] As Lisa Leff notes, in France Jews did not become less Jewish as they became more French once granted equal citizenship in 1791.[42] Extending her insight to Algeria, I conclude that Jews did not become less Jewish as they became more French but instead became less or even non-Arabophone and non-Berberophone and hence less Algerian. My approaches to a native subgroup, namely Algerian Jews, who were effectively and synecdochically sliced off from the majority Algerian Muslim indigenes, were tested during the Second World War. This rare case of native enfranchisement in the colony and

---

40   Susan Slyomovics and Sarah Abrevaya Stein, 'Jews and French Colonialism in Algeria: An Introduction', *Journal of North African Studies*, 17: 5, 2012, 749–55.

41   Among works on French Jews and their civilizing mission towards Algeria's Jews are Schreier, *Arabs of the Jewish Faith*; Pierre Birnbaum, 'French Jews and the "Regeneration" of Algerian Jewry', in Ezra Mendelsohn (ed.), *Jews and the State: Dangerous Alliances and the Perils of Privilege*, Oxford: Oxford University Press, 2003, 88–103; Richard Ayoun, 'Les efforts d'assimilation intellectuelle et l'émancipation législative des Juifs d'Algérie', in Centre Georges Pompidou (ed.), *Cultures juives méditerranéennes et orientales*, Paris: Syros, 1982, 171–88; and Nathan Godley, '"Almost Finished Frenchmen": The Jews of Algeria and the Question of French National Identity, 1830–1902', PhD diss, University of Iowa, 2006.

42   See Lisa Moses Leff, *Sacred Bonds of Solidarity: The Rise of Jewish Internationalism in Nineteenth-Century France*, Stanford, CA: Stanford University Press, 2006, 2, which contrasts with French Jewish assimilation proposed in Arthur Hertzberg, *The French Enlightenment and the Jews*, New York: Columbia University Press, 1968.

the ways in which, unlike Arab and Berber subjects after 1870, Algerian Jews were 'at once coloniser and colonised',[43] is doubly unusual because they reverted forcibly, albeit temporarily, to the previous century before French citizenship was granted. For Algerian Jews, rights, citizenship, and enfranchisement were revoked during the Vichy years.

The Algerian Jewry's Return to Indigeneity (1940–3)

After the German defeat of France in May 1940, conquered France was divided between the Nazi-occupied zone and the so-called unoccupied zone to the south headquartered at Vichy. Second World War Vichy-era fascism expanded from France to its overseas North African colonies against those racially classed by colonial bureaucracy as *indigènes* or 'natives', a term perennially applied to the Algerian Muslim and, due to Vichy laws between 1940–3, to the Algerian Jew. Anti-Jewish laws were enacted beginning with the Jewish Statute of 3 October 1940 defining a Jew as a person with three grandparents 'of the Jewish race' or with two Jewish grandparents if the spouse were Jewish. As Jews were singled out and foreign Jews targeted for special abuse in France, juridical strategies unique to Algeria came to undermine the legal foundations of the Algerian-Jewish community. The law of 7 October 1940 abrogated the Crémieux Decree, which had granted French citizenship to Algerian Jews since 1870. Once stripped collectively of their status as French citizens, approximately 110,000 Algerian Jews (according to the census of 1931) were subjected to discrimination in every sphere.

Inspired by Nazi Germany's racial classifications of the Jew, Vichy policies from France were extended to settler Algeria's concepts of race.[44] What was the longstanding legal application to the Indigenous Muslim colonial subject was administered to Algerian Jews with additional constraints. Relegating the Jew to the Muslim category of 'native' served to stabilize and strengthen those who inhabited that very category of indigene by claiming to render both equal in the sense that they were equally

---

43   Schreier, *Arabs of the Jewish Faith*, 10.
44   See Samuel Kalman, *French Colonial Fascism: The Extreme Right in Algeria, 1919–1939*, New York: Palgrave MacMillan, 2013, who insists on the specificity and extremism of 'colonial fascism' unique to the European settler society in Algeria.

without the rights of citizenship, while holding out to the mass of Muslim natives the possibility of a controlled naturalization process of becoming French. French Algeria's forms of anti-Semitism had traditionally opposed granting Algerian Jews French citizenship because once a group such as the Jews were emancipated and enfranchised, others, such as the Arabs, could conceivably also be emancipated. When the Crémieux Decree was abolished and Jews were returned to the category of natives, some of the settler fears were realized: the two groups' identity resulted in the prospect of undifferentiated decolonization. The Crémieux Decree had made a settler society by adding native Jews to the category, while its abolition remade a colonial society by unmaking a people and diminishing the colony of *peuplement*. Moreover, the abolition of the Crémieux Decree also reversed the settler project back to a colonial one, if one follows Lorenzo Veracini's distinction between colonialism, which is characterized by a focus on production (that is, articulating with networks of international trade) and contrasted with settler colonialism, which focuses on reproduction and peopling.[45]

Wartime intensified Muslim–Jewish 'triangular relations' mediated through France:

> Jews and Muslims related to one another through their respective relationships to the French state and society and to definitions of French national and imperial belonging. Thus, competing understandings and institutional manifestations of 'Frenchness' inflected how Jews and Muslims saw one another and framed every interaction. To a significant extent the reverse was also true: Jews and Muslims often appraised their relationship to France through their relations with one another.[46]

Their respective relationships to France and to each other were marked by additional factors unique to the Algerian context under Vichy. New laws eliminated any possibility for Algerian Jews to request French citizenship even in ways made contingently possible to the Algerian Muslim native since 1919, notably through service in the French armed forces. During the First World War, some 14,000 Algerian Jews mobilized to

---

45   Lorenzo Veracini, email correspondence, 21 October 2016.
46   Ethan Katz, *The Burdens of Brotherhood: Jews and Muslims from North African to France*, Cambridge: Harvard University Press, 2015, 5.

fight for France alongside 125,000 Algerian Muslims and 92,000 Europeans of Algeria. Jews of France and Algeria answered a second time the call to arms to defend France during the so-called phony war that lasted from September 1939 to April 1940. Soldiering in the French military formed the primary counterweight to racist stereotypes in the metropolitan imagination about both the cowardly, cunning Jew and the passive, untrustworthy Arab. Fighting and dying for France in two world wars symbolically elevated the colonized Muslim native to temporary fraternity with his colonizers, if not to equality. Natives conscripted for military service were viewed positively reinforcing earlier conquest-era stereotypes of the ferocious Muslim Algerian warrior and aligning these stereotypes with demands for their obligatory service since 1912. As Pascal Blanchard and Nicolas Bancel have concluded, 'Only the 'backup native troops' [*supplétif indigène*], auxiliaries to the military conquest of Africa and therefore a symbol of the acceptance of the colonial act, escaped this negative stereotype'.[47] Notwithstanding positive aspects in the French public's views of the native soldiers, the 'savage' North African cavalier of old evoked subliminal aspects of the armed Arab fighter stubbornly attached to Islam. This image inspired settler fears. Only during war were rights for the empire's subjects even raised and only on behalf of citizenship for decorated war heroes, and the possibility of equal pensions, little of which ever materialized. Once Jews were denied French citizenship in 1940, Vichy jurists swiftly revoked the possibility of regaining citizenship for Jews who served in the French military during the First World War (according to the law of 11 October, *Journal officiel* of 13 October 1940). Many Vichy functionaries in Algeria, often members of the European settler population, were notorious for virulent anti-Semitism of more than one variety: they were both anti-Jewish and anti-Muslim Algerian.

Algerian-Jewish Soldiers as Indigenous Native Labour

In addition to property spoliation and expulsions from education and the professions beginning in 1940, laws stripping Jews of French citizenship in Algeria combined with metropolitan strictures excluding Jews from

---

47 Pascal Blanchard and Nicolas Bancel, *De l'indigène à l'immigré*, Paris: Gallimard, 1998, 20.

the military and ordering foreign Jews into camps. A small number of Algerian Jews were subjected to confinement in camps. Under Vichy, Algerian-Jewish soldiers, conscripts, and volunteers were either dispatched to serve in Algerian Muslim units or transformed into forced labour through confinement in military camps that resembled prisons.[48] Jews, both Algerian and foreign, were a minority in the vast network of North African internment camps predominantly populated by a variety of other groups labelled by the Vichy regime 'dangerous individuals' and 'undesirable foreigners'. Nonetheless, the case of the disenfranchised, imprisoned Algerian-Jewish soldiers foregrounds the importance of citizenship for the disenfranchised, re-indigenized and racialized Jewish minority in the archipelago of French colonial prison camps. The double loss of citizenship and military service as citizen-soldiers was articulated by one imprisoned group. Hypermasculine Vichy military attitudes revived differences that naturalized the Jew, unlike Muslim Algerians serving as subjects of empire, as innately inferior according to hierarchies of nativeness that referenced combat aptitude. Algeria's Bedeau Camp was one camp reserved for Algerian-Jewish soldiers who issued the 'Manifeste des Juifs de Bedeau' in which Jewish citizenship is defined by praising their own historically valorous military service as French citizens. Addressed to General Henri Giraud during the Second World War, the manifesto is preserved in the archives of Centre de Documentation Juive Contemporaine in Paris:

> We Jews mobilised to Bedeau, declare the following:
> We hate Nazism, we hate it because it tortures a wounded France and because it specifically persecutes Jews.
> Two months ago a great hope was born in us, to take on again fighting with modern armies and contribute to the final crushing of the enemy of humanity.
> The realisation of this wish was denied us.
> That we were withdrawn from our respective units and all transformed

---

48 On Algerian-Jewish soldiers singled out for internment in all-Jewish forced labour camps during the Second World War era of Vichy Algeria, see my case study of Bedeau camp in Susan Slyomovics, '"Other Places of Confinement": Bedeau Internment Camp for Algerian Jewish Soldiers', in Aomar Boum and Sarah Abrevaya Stein (eds), *The Holocaust in North Africa*, Stanford, CA: Stanford University Press, 2019, 95–112.

into workers, contrary to using our skills, this fact has only one consequence for the public: to present us as suspect or unable to fight with weapons in hand.

We declare that no one has the right to doubt our fighting capacity: it would be an insult to the memory of our elders who rest by the thousands in the ground in France.

We express profound regret at seeing ourselves deliberately excluded from the current fighting for which we remain ardent champions…

In 1940, we fought as French. Since then we are excluded from the national community.

Let us all automatically be assigned to the units to which we were normally intended, that we be allowed to fight each according to our skills, but with dignity like other soldiers.

Let this be permitted, and all united we will answer: 'Present'.[49]

The Bedeau manifesto documents a direct appeal to the French Army, the institutional upholder of longstanding republican French ideals towards its minority Jewish population in France and Algeria, an entity

---

49 Centre de Documentation Juive Contemporaine (CDJC), CCCLXXXV-5, 'Manifeste des Juifs de Bedeau' (dated by Sidney Chouraqui to early January 1943): 'Nous juifs mobilisés à Bedeau, déclarons ce qui suit: Nous détestons le nazisme, nous le détestons parce qu'il torture la France meurtrie et parce qu'il persécute spécialement les juifs. Il y a deux mois est né en nous un espoir immense, celui de reprendre la lutte avec des armées modernes et de contribuer à l'écrasement définitif de l'ennemi de l'humanité. La réalisation de ce voeu nous a été refusé. Rassemblés pêle-mêle, fantassins, artilleurs, cavaliers, aviateurs, nous avons été transformés en pionniers […]. Qu'on nous ait retirés de nos unités respectives et qu'on nous ait tous transformés en travailleurs, au mépris de l'utilisation de nos compétences, ce fait ne peut avoir qu'une conséquence dans le public: nous présenter comme suspects ou incapables de combattre les armes à la main. Nous déclarons que personne n'a le droit de douter de notre valeur combattive: ce serait insulter à la mémoire de nos ainés qui reposaient encore par milliers en terre de France. Nous exprimons le profond regret de nous voir délibérément exclus de la lutte actuelle dont nous demeurons les champions ardents. […] En 1940, nous nous sommes battus comme Français. Depuis, on nous a exclus de la communauté nationale. […] Qu'on nous affecte tous automatiquement dans les unités auxquelles nous étions normalement destinés, qu'on nous permette de combattre chacun selon nos compétences, mais dans la dignité comme les autres soldats. Qu'on nous le permette, et tous unis nous répondrons "Présent"'.

that should supersede rather than succumb to the depredations of Vichy government in Algeria allied to Nazi rule. Lorenzo Veracini's 'triangular system of relationships', drawn from his *Settler Colonialism: A Theoretical Overview*, is present in the manifesto: 'settler coloniser, the Indigenous colonised and a variety of differently categorised subaltern exogenous alterities'. The metropolitan imperial state that originally meddled in the colony in 1870 to enfranchise Jews had failed Algerian Jewry because it is represented by the French military in Algeria sympathetic to fascist Vichy and unwilling to respond, mediate or reverse inequities as Algerian Jews expected:

> Indigenous and subaltern exogenous Others appeal to the European sovereign to articulate grievances emanating from settler abuse, the metropolitan agency interposes its sovereignty between settler and Indigenous or subaltern exogenous communities and settlers insist on their capacity to control Indigenous policy.[50]

On 20 October 1943, almost a year after the Allied landing in Algeria, Vichy's abrogation of the Crémieux Decree was itself revoked. Pressure from the Allied forces, De Gaulle's leadership of the Free French Army high command, and the force of world opinion helped to restore Algerian Jews to French nationality. Only after 1943, therefore, were Algerian-Jewish soldiers then dispersed among various fighting units in North Africa.

Decolonization and Rabbi Léon Askénasi

A second reason Algeria is peripheral to settler-colonial theory is by virtue of decolonization, which makes it incompatible with Patrick Wolfe's definition of settler colonialism as unfinished and ongoing. Algeria seems to offer closure for settler colonial studies because it appears as a self-contained, neatly bracketed history of colonization and decolonization. This is especially so since independence was marked by the dramatic exodus of most European settlers in the early 1960s beginning with the last years of the Algerian War of Independence and

---

50 Lorenzo Veracini, *Settler Colonialism: A Theoretical Overview*, London: Palgrave Macmillan, 2010, 16.

continuing throughout the decade. European settlers departed en masse in the twentieth century, reversing the routes across the Mediterranean of the nineteenth century. So too did Algerian Jews depart, lumped together with the departing Europeans to become the 'repatriated' (*rapatrié*) in legal terminology and *Pieds-Noirs* in popular usage. Neither of these two categories fit them; rather, the repatriated were constituted by their mass exodus, which attached them to the settler community once Algerian Jews arrived in the metropole. While Algeria after independence should refuse the constraints that such an arbitrary closure imposes about decolonization being equal to independence, it is important for my argument to consider the ways in which the case of Algerian Jews post-1962 escapes formal endings.

Vichy's innovation, which was to include Jews in the colonial racialization of religious communities, continued to reverberate postwar and globally. While the majority of Algerian Jews as French citizens settled in France after Algerian independence, there were those who immigrated to Israel. One of the internees in Bedeau Camp was Léon Askénasi, the Oran-born son of Algeria's last chief rabbi. A rabbi, educator, and towering scholarly figure of postwar French Judaism, he was posted to the French Foreign Legion as a military chaplain, which was the absurd alternative unit available to Algerian Jews unwilling or unable to join the native Algerian Muslim regiments. His choice of the Foreign Legion transformed him into a foreign Jew in his own country as opposed to a native Jew, either status entailing the loss of his prewar identity as a 'Frenchman of Algeria of the Jewish religion'. His sojourn in Bedeau camp from 1943 produced these nuanced reflections in 2001. His belief in an untenable future for his Algerian-Jewish compatriots in Algeria post–Second World War is confirmed as long as his Algerian-Jewish co-religionists hold fast to French identity as opposed to their origins:

> We were mobilised as foreigners and in particular in the Foreign Legion. The vast majority of Jews mustered in the Legion camp thought that this was the vicissitude of history and that the time would come when French citizenship would be returned to us. I was in Bedeau Camp between 1943 and 1944, then I was a soldier in the war in the Colonial Army, a regular corps in the French infantry. What I lived during this period certainly affected me in a subterranean way and the moment I encountered the Israeli reality, that was the way it was settled

naturally. Fundamentally, if I had to live in the diaspora, I would have been seen more as an Algerian Jew of French culture than as a French Jew of Algerian culture. Algeria became later an Arab country and I could not consider myself an Arab.

Even today, I cannot comprehend the way in which North African Jews consider themselves French. Independent of the anti-Jewish and anti-Israel character of Arab countries, it does not occur to them to consider themselves Arabs but as French. This attitude is a kind of racism. It can be explained by the fact that Jews consider the mark of French culture superior to the mark of Arab culture. Objectively this is nonsense because cultures cannot be measured by the same criteria. But there is evidence for a Jew who has lived in an Islamic country: the difference between Jew and Arab is not only according to religion, it is also national. This double difference does not exist in relation to the European. This explains the continuity of the diaspora in a European milieu. After the fact, it was a very enriching experience for me to know the milieu of the Foreign Legion, but we were not organised as Jews in order for us to develop a national conscience. We considered ourselves as a kind of minority of the diaspora type. Religious life in the camp was very intense and it was there perhaps that I began to understand the condition of exile, which I have completely rid myself of on becoming Israeli. I felt that I was not at home and consequently, that I had no rights to claim. I could only attempt, through a strategy of submission, to obtain favours.[51]

---

51   Léon Askénasi, *L'histoire de ma vie*, 2001. Available at: manitou.org.il. 'Nous avons donc été mobilisés en tant qu'étrangers et, en particulier, dans la Légion étrangère. L'immense majorité des Juifs rassemblés dans le camp de la Légion pensait qu'il s'agissait d'une péripétie de l'Histoire et que le temps viendrait ou` l'on nous rendrait la citoyenneté française. J'ai été au camp de Bedeau de 1943 à 1944, puis j'ai fait la guerre dans la Coloniale, un corps de métier de l'infanterie française. Ce que j'ai vécu au cours de cette période a certainement travaillé souterrainement et, au moment où j'ai rencontré la réalité israélienne, cela s'est dénoué tout naturellement. Au fond, si j'avais dû vivre en diaspora, je me serais davantage considéré comme un Juif algérien de culture française que comme un Juif français de culture algérienne. L'Algérie est devenue par la suite un pays arabe et je ne pouvais pas me considérer comme un Arabe. Encore aujourd'hui, je n'arrive pas à comprendre la manière dont les Juifs nord-africains en France se considèrent comme Français. Indépendamment du caractère anti-Juif ou anti-israélien des pays arabes, il ne leur vient pas à l'idée de se considérer

More than 90 per cent of Algerian Jews settled permanently in France after Algerian independence in 1962, while a minority of Algerian Jews, like Askénasi in the 1960s became part of the waves of North African immigration to Israel. Although his surname in Hebrew means 'German', Léon Askénasi was not an Ashkenazi Jew, since variations on the word were family names as common among Sephardic families as Eastern European ones. Jews from North Africa became part of the Zionist story both to dispossess the native Palestinian Arabs and to be subsumed under the category of 'Mizrahim', literally 'Jews from the East'. Patrick Wolfe structures their role in Israeli Jewish society as:

> a settler-colonial labour force that is racialized in contradistinction to their Ashkenazi superiors, Mizrahim are more like American slaves than Australian convicts, their subordination being phenotypically encoded across generations. On the other hand, like Australian convicts, they share the settlers' common denominator vis-à-vis the Natives, only in their case it is religious rather than phenotypical.[52]

First in colonial Algeria and then in the State of Israel, Algerian Jewry's religion could be said to raise them above the native Arab masses. But only in France, while maintaining Jewishness under the protective umbrella of French republican rights, did Algerian Jews attain full metropolitan

---

comme des Arabes mais comme des Français. Cette attitude relève du racisme. Elle s'explique par le fait que les Juifs considèrent que l'indice culturel français est supérieur à l'indice culturel arabe. Ce qui est objectivement un non-sens parce que ces cultures ne se mesurent pas aux mêmes critères. Mais il y a une évidence pour un Juif qui a vécu en pays d'Islam: la différence entre le Juif et l'Arabe n'est pas seulement d'ordre religieux, elle est aussi d'ordre national. Cette double différence n'existe pas par rapport a` l'Européen. C'est l'un des éléments qui explique la perpétuation de la diaspora en milieu européen. A posteriori, ce fut pour moi une expérience très enrichissante de connaître ce milieu de la Légion étrangère, mais nous n'étions pas organisés en tant que Juifs pour pouvoir développer en nous la conscience nationale. Nous nous considérions comme une espèce de minorité de type diasporique. La vie religieuse dans le camp était très intense et c'est là peut-être que j'ai commencé à comprendre la condition d'exil, dont je me suis complètement débarrassé en devenant Israélien. J'ai senti que je n'étais pas chez moi et que, par conséquent, je n'avais aucun droit à réclamer. Je ne pouvais qu'essayer, par une stratégie de soumission, d'obtenir des faveurs'.

52   Wolfe, *Traces of History*, 259.

equality and citizenship, not as Jews but as European settler-returnees. It is noteworthy that for Léon Askénazi, Jewish identity is immutable but not racialized. Coincidentally, he too summons the same phrase as Bourdieu's essay in *Qui suis-je?* ('Who Am I?'), while rejecting Bourdieu's ethnically inflected paradigms for Algerian society.

> For the Jews find there [that is, the Bible] not only meaning in their relationship with nations, but also information, the only true one beyond all sociology and psychoanalysis, about their inner being, the final definition of their specificity, the immediate answer to their 'What am I?' to their 'Who am I?' Reading the Bible, the Jew reads his own identity card. [The Jew] is defined by horizontal time, he reinserted in the vertical of an uninterrupted history – in relation to those Hebrews who, three thousand years ago, heard the Torah at the foot of Mount Sinai. There is no idea of racism in this. The Jew today can descend through the flesh, of Abraham, Isaac and Jacob; but he descends from those who, throughout the centuries, came to add themselves to the Hebrew readers of the Bible.[53]

Léon Askénasi's trajectories mirror some of the scholarly approaches to Algerian Jews which emphasize linguistic and religious allegiances first solidified in the colony post-Crémieux Decree, then intensified in France to the extent that the community of Algerian Jews emerged more French, non-Arabophone, and more Jewish.

Related approaches in Jewish studies, affirmed by Askénasi, attribute the inevitable exodus of Jews living in Muslim-majority countries to the rise of anti-colonialism, independence, and nationalist movements. This

---

[53] 'Car les Juifs n'y trouvent pas seulement le sens à leur rapport avec les nations, mais aussi une information, la seule vraie par delà toutes les sociologies et toutes les psychanalyses, sur leur être intime, la définition finale de leur spécificité, la réponse immédiate à leur Que suis-je?, à leur "Qui suis-je ?" Lisant la Bible, le Juif lit sa propre carte d'identité. Il se définit par rapport à l'horizontale du temps, il se réinsère dans la verticale d'une histoire ininterrompue - par rapport à ces Hébreux qui, il y a trois mille cinq cents ans, entendirent la Torah au pied du mont Sinaï. Nulle idée de racisme en cela. Le Juif d'aujourd'hui peut descendre par la chair, d'Abraham, d'Isaac et de Jacob ; mais plus souvent, il descend de ceux qui, au long des siècles, sont venus s'ajouter aux lecteurs hébreux de la Bible'. Léon Askénazi, *La parole et l'écrit: Textes réunis et présentés par Marcel Goldmann*, Paris: Albin Michel, 56.

body of scholarship assumes pervasive anti-Semitism in the lives of Jews under Islam and teleologically concludes with the inevitable progress towards Zionism.[54] North African Jews were less fortunate as putative 'returnees' to Zion. In Israel, religious practice for those who followed that path is patterned on the leadership of SHAS, the ultra-Orthodox political party whose acronym is formed from *Shomrei Sfarad* or 'Guardians of Sepharad', which may proclaim Sephardic origins but belie religious formations that are largely in the Ashkenazi religious schools or *yeshivot*. As a result, the practice and study of religious texts undergird the traditional religious aspect of religious Zionism: according to these views, Jews, regardless of origins, have more in common with each other than the varied societies in which they live. When moved to the eastern shores of the Mediterranean Sea, Algerian Jewry were and are inserted into another settler-colonial matrix, albeit this time and place through the establishment of the State of Israel, where they precariously reside between the dominating European Ashkenazi Jews and the subordinated native Palestinians.

Reparations for Algerian Jewry under Vichy in 2018

Despite their small numbers during the Second World War period, Algerian-Jewish detainees would figure in two different sets of reparation protocols – Germans ones, because they were imprisoned as Jews, and French ones, because they were *Pied-Noir* European settlers 'repatriated' to France. In terms of the major postwar German indemnification protocols for the crimes of National Socialism negotiated from the early 1950s, Algerian-Jewish internment under Vichy Algeria resurfaced in 2004. Germany, not France, offered indemnifications that acknowledged incarceration of Algerian Jews for racial reasons since in French Algeria religion was racialized.[55] Additional debates have flourished to

---

54   On the 'lachrymose' nature of Jewish studies scholarship which emphasizes anti-Semitism, Jewish victimhood, and dispersion for European Jewry, see Salo W. Baron, 'Ghetto and Emancipation: Shall We Revise the Traditional View?' *Menorah Journal*, 14, 1928, 515–26. Reprised for Jewish studies of the Middle East and North Africa, it is labelled 'neo-lachrymose' in Marc Cohen, 'The Neo-Lachrymose Conception of Jewish-Arab History', *Tikkun*, 6: 3, 1991, 50–5.

55   Susan Slyomovics, 'French Restitution, German Compensation: Algerian Jews and Vichy's Financial Legacy', *Journal of North African Studies*, 17: 5,

frame reparation histories of Algerian Jewry in Israel, France, and North Africa. In Israel, one debate calibrates lesser Sephardic suffering during the Second World War versus the Ashkenazi Jewish Holocaust. Another layer of debates surrounds the role of Arab regimes during the Holocaust (or whether there was even a Holocaust in the Arab world). Yet a third approach, one that draws on the large-scale North African immigration to Israel, exploits the notion of population exchanges: Palestinian expulsion and indemnification claims are set against the dislocation of Jews from Arab lands and their claims for financial indemnification.[56] To ask who merits reparation is perhaps another example of 'false friends' because determining the worthy beneficiary becomes mired in questions of categorization, comparison, and translations of terminology.

In contrast, a settler colonial studies approach views the life and fates of an individual to be determined according to his or her place in settler-colonial hierarchies that still resonate in France and Israel. This is exemplified by the latest 2018 German reparation decrees that have enlarged the 2004 group of financial reparations. Those targeted the imprisoned, disenfranchised Algerian Jews incarcerated in camps because they were Jews. The 2018 protocols go beyond to the fact of Jews as settlers in French Algeria. Germany offers a one-time symbolic payment of €2,556.46 to designate the enlarged category of the compensable to the surviving Algerian-Jewish community if they resided in Vichy Algeria between July 1940 and November 1942, respectively the dates of Vichy's anti-Jewish laws and the Allied landings in North Africa: 'This is a long overdue recognition for a large group of Jews in Algeria who suffered anti-Jewish measures by Nazi allies like the Vichy Regime', said Greg Schneider, Executive Vice President of the Claims Conference. 'The Vichy government subjected these people to restrictions on education, political life, participation in civil society and employment, abolishing French citizenship and singling them out only because they were Jews'.[57]

2012: 881–901, and Susan Slyomovics, *How to Accept German Reparations*, Philadelphia: University of Pennsylvania Press, 2014.

56 Ibid.

57 Conference on Jewish Material Claims against Germany, 'Claims Conference to Compensate Algerian Jews Recognized for First Time by the German Government', Claimscon.org.

Germany's reparations to Algerian Jews, no less than France's reparations to Algeria's settler French citizens 'repatriated' to France (which included Algerian Jews), are consistent. Both countries identify the settler colonizer to compensate for the end of colonialism. Reparations were never for the native. The 1870 Crémieux Decree was uniquely successful as an example of a European power making claims to afford comprehensive protection for the entirety of the Algerian-Jewish community and then doing so through the extension of French citizenship to natives inhabiting a French overseas colony. Did Algerian Jews in French Algeria ever fully inhabit the appellation of 'Jewish settler community' of Algeria, as Pal Ahluwalia maintains?[58] Even symbolic sums of money emerging from Germany's 2018 reparations serve to affirm that this was so. The Algerian Jew of French Algeria as a historical phenomenon seems over. Yet German indemnifications of 2018 resurrect the purposes and provisions of the Crémieux Decree to financially enfranchise this entire community. For those 25,000 Algerian Jews still alive in 2018, a majority of whom reside in France and not Israel nor Algeria, histories of French and German indemnification protocols entrench layers of false friends within the category of the settler.

---

58 Pal Ahluwalia, *Out of Africa: Post-Structuralism's Colonial Roots*, New York: Routledge, 2010, 11.

Part II

Preaccumulations

3
Mormonism, Primitive Accumulation, Preaccumulation

Lorenzo Veracini

This chapter approaches Mormon history in the context of a global study of settler colonialism as a mode of domination and its political traditions.[1] It engages, in particular, with the religion's prehistory and with Patrick Wolfe's notion of 'preaccumulation' in order to interpret the Mormon commitment to settlement beyond the normal operation of capitalist accumulation.[2] My reconstruction of Mormon settlement and engagement with Wolfe's intuition about a settler-colonial endowment interprets Mormonism as an example of what I have elsewhere defined as

---

1   I have relied extensively on Richard Lyman Bushman's biography of Joseph Smith. Bushman's ability and commitment to reconstruct Smith's world is extraordinary. See Richard Lyman Bushman, *Joseph Smith: Rough Stone Rolling; A Cultural Biography of Mormonism's Founder*, New York: Vintage Books, 2007. For another biography of Smith see, for example, Fawn M. Brodie's classic *No Man Knows My History: The Life of Joseph Smith, the Mormon Prophet*, New York: Knopf, 1971.

2   For 'preaccumulation', see Patrick Wolfe, 'Purchase by Other Means: The Palestine Nakba and Zionism's Conquest of Economics', *Settler Colonial Studies*, 2: 1, 2012, 133–71. See also Patrick Wolfe, 'Recuperating Binarism: A Heretical Introduction', *Settler Colonial Studies*, 3: 3–4, 2013, 257–79, at 266.

the 'world turned inside out': the attempt to reconstitute political regimes elsewhere as a response to growing revolutionary tensions.[3]

The 'world turned inside out' and its political traditions envisage the constitution of heterotopias. They are not utopian.[4] Jonathan Hughes defines Brigham Young a 'practical utopian', a thoroughly pragmatic leader, desiring exclusiveness and self-sufficiency.[5] But all world-turned-inside-out projects are about 'practical' utopianism rather than utopianism. After all, the *imagination* of alternative 'worlds' elsewhere as a *contribution* to revolution, what utopian projects propose, is not the *population* of 'worlds' elsewhere as an *alternative* to revolution (revolution is here understood flexibly to identify all processes that fundamentally disrupt a specific social formation). Besides, a global rather than a US or North American perspective in the study of Mormon history has also historicist roots. The early Mormons thought globally – indeed, universally.

And yet Mormon nineteenth-century history has generally been seen in relation to American history, either as an exception or as an epitome, rarely in a global context. A recent reading that cast Mormons as typical rather than atypical American settlers is Jared Farmer's *On Zion's Mount*.[6]

---

3   The 'world turned inside out' is related to (and yet crucially distinct from) the revolutionary traditions that Christopher Hill seminally called the 'world turned upside down', and emphasizes the separation between an 'inside' and an 'outside', and between metropole and settler periphery. On the world turned upside down, see Christopher Hill, *The World Turned Upside-Down: Radical Ideas During the English Revolution*, London: Penguin, 1972. On the world turned inside out, see James Livingston, *The World Turned Inside Out: American Thought and Culture at the End of the 20th Century*, New York: Rowman and Littlefield Publishers, 2010; Lorenzo Veracini, 'Suburbia, Settler Colonialism and the World Turned Inside Out', *Housing, Theory and Society*, 29: 4, 2012, 339–57; Gabriel Piterberg, Lorenzo Veracini, 'Wakefield, Marx, and the World Turned Inside Out', *The Journal of Global History*, 10: 3, 2015, 457–78; Lorenzo Veracini, *The World Turned Inside Out*, London: Verso, 2021.

4   For a discussion of the distinction between utopian and 'heterotopian' spaces, see Michel Foucault, *Heterotopia and the City: Public Space in a Postcivil Society*, London: Taylor & Francis, 2008 [1967]), 13–30. Foucault argues that utopias and heterotopias are profoundly dissimilar. For him, utopias are primarily imagined locations; heterotopias actually exist.

5   Jonathan Hughes, *The Vital Few: The Entrepreneur and American Economic Progress*, Oxford: Oxford University Press, 1986, 105. For another entry point to Mormon history, see John G. Turner, *Brigham Young, Pioneer Prophet*, Cambridge: Harvard University Press, 2012.

6   Jared Farmer, *On Zion's Mount: Mormons, Indians, and the American Landscape*, Cambridge: Harvard University Press, 2008.

Farmer draws attention to the construction of a settler-indigenized landscape, and demonstrates that Mormons took their 'indigenization' seriously. He focuses on landscape and on a determination to belong in it as putative Indigenous peoples. Settler indigenization – the process through which a collective that originates somewhere else becomes indigenous to the new locale – turns a historical relation to the land ('we arrived here at a particular time') into an ontological one ('we were constituted here'), something all settler-colonial projects aspire to (settler indigenization sustains claims to legitimacy and represses actual indigeneity). However, while Farmer argues that a similar inclination can be seen operating in much of the US, processes of settler indigenization similar to those that he charts in Provo, Utah fundamentally characterize the settler-colonial situation globally.[7] Exceptionalism has indeed had several critics. Klaus Hansen's *Mormonism and the American Experience* persuasively argued that Mormon theology and the 'doctrine of eternal progression' in particular should be seen as quintessentially American.[8] Walter Nugent outlined the consistent convergence of American and Mormon imperialisms.[9] Konden Smith Hansen revisited the question of the Mormon American 'frontier'.[10]

---

7   On the settler-colonial 'situation', see Lorenzo Veracini, *Settler Colonialism: A Theoretical Overview*, Houndmills: Palgrave, 2010.

8   Klaus Hansen, *Mormonism and the American Experience*, Chicago: University of Chicago Press, 1981. On Mormon exceptionalism see, for example, Leonard J. Arrington, Davis Bitton, *The Mormon Experience: A History of the Latter-Day Saints*, Urbana, IL: University of Illinois Press, 1992, especially 109–84. For an historical geography of the Mormon West, see Ethan R. Yorgason, *Transformation of the Mormon Culture Region*, Urbana, IL: University of Illinois Press, 2003.

9   Walter Nugent, 'The Mormons and America's Empires', *Journal of Mormon History*, 36: 2, 2010, 1–28. On the convergence of Mormonism and settler colonialism specifically, see Elise Boxer, '"This is the Place!" Disrupting Mormon Settler Colonialism', in Gina Colvin, Joanna Brooks (eds), *Decolonizing Mormonism: Approaching a Postcolonial Zion*, Salt Lake City: University of Utah Press, 2019, 77–100; Elise Boxer, 'The Book of Mormon as Mormon Settler Colonialism', in P. Jane Hafen, Brenden Rensink (eds), *Essays on American Indian and Mormon History*, Salt Lake City: University of Utah Press, 2019, 3–22; Thomas W. Murphy, 'Views from Turtle Island: Settler Colonialism and Indigenous Mormon Entanglements', in R. Gordon Shepherd, A. Gary Shepherd, Ryan T. Cragun (eds), *The Palgrave Handbook of Global Mormonism*, Houndmills: Palgrave, 2020, 751–79.

10   Konden Smith Hansen, *Frontier Religion: Mormons and America, 1857–1907*, Salt Lake City: University of Utah Press, 2019.

Conversely, Wallace Stegner's *Mormon Country* (1942), and *The Gathering of Zion* (1964) highlighted the Mormon collectivist ethos and read it as atypical *vis-a-vis* American frontier individualism.[11] Likewise, global analyses of settlement processes typically refer to Mormon history to emphasize exceptionalism. In his global survey, John Weaver compares the Mormon and Boer unique capacity to move across the land in an organized fashion. 'Factionalism' caused the expeditions of other settlers to 'splinter', he notes, 'but the amount of planning and co-ordination by Boers was perhaps equalled only by the Mormon exodus from Missouri to Utah'.[12] Equally, Jacob Metzer juxtaposes the Mormon settlement with settlements in what would become Liberia and pre-state Israel to emphasize uniqueness.[13] He is not the first one to compare the metaphorical 'Israel' of the Mormon Saints and the literal one.[14] A comparative approach, Metzer argues, is definitely justified: these are the colonial settlements of 'others'. There are two ideal types, he suggests: the exclusive settler-colonial model, characterized by Indigenous disappearance; and the 'African' settler model, characterized by Indigenous exploitation. The Mormon, the Americo-Liberian, and the Zionist enterprises, however, conform to neither type. He emphasizes the inherent 'otherness' of these colonizers and the push factors, but he also emphasizes that they were all preconstituted peoples (like – as he admits, in a way that diminishes his argument about 'atypicality' – the New England Pilgrims and the Pennsylvania Quakers).[15] But Metzer's African model of settler-colonization

11   Wallace Stegner, *Mormon Country*, Lincoln, NE: University of Nebraska Press, 2003 [1942]; Wallace Stegner, *The Gathering of Zion: The Story of the Mormon Trail*, New York: McGraw-Hill, 1964.

12   John C. Weaver, *The Great Land Rush and the Making of the Modern World, 1650–1900*, Montreal: McGill-Queen's University Press, 2003, 282.

13   Jacob Metzer, 'Jews in Mandatory Palestine and Additional Phenomena of *Atypical* Settler Colonization in Modern Time', in Christopher Lloyd, Jacob Metzer, Richard Sutch (eds), *Settler Economies in World History*, Leiden: Brill, 2013, 171.

14   For a comparative approach to the study of Mormon settlement practices, see Arnon Soffer, 'The Settlement Process of the Mormons in Utah and the Jews in Israel', *Comparative Social Research*, 9, 1986, 197–229.

15   Jacob Metzer, 'Jews in Mandatory Palestine and Additional Phenomena of *Atypical* Settler Colonization in Modern Time', 171, note 1. Using entirely different terms but reaching a similar conclusion, Patricia Nelson Limerick argues that Mormons constitute a separate 'ethnicity'. See Patricia Nelson Limerick, 'Peace Initiative: Using the Mormons to Rethink Culture and Ethnicity in

is essentially a straw man in this analysis, and in important ways most settler collectives are pre-emptively constituted as a people before they depart: the worried perception of rising contradictions and impending social upheaval, and their subsequent decision to collectively displace are *constitutive* experiences.[16] Pre-emption begets pre-constitution. Besides, the very notion of a Promised Land constitutes a specific collective before the land. Before can mean prior and beside: the settler collective is before it is before the land. This is the Mormon experience.

Serial Primitive Accumulations

I will begin with an originary event. As an originary event, what Marx called 'so-called primitive accumulation' remains unrivalled (originary is as good a translation of *ursprünglich* as primitive). In Marxist theory, it is the process that leads to capitalism where there was none. Richard Lyman Bushman notes how in 1803 the Smiths had crossed the 'boundary dividing independent ownership from tenancy and day labor'.[17] They had entered the wage economy. This is a crucial event in this story; the Smiths saw it as a crucial event. Joseph's mother, Lucy, referred to the 'embarrassment of poverty' and the 'embarrassment of debt'.[18] Debt is rent, and rent extraction inevitably carries significant social implications. In a 'frontier' setting, however, debt assumes a very specific meaning (my definition of frontier is a place where land is bloody cheap – where 'bloody' is not unnecessary swearing but a literal descriptor). As Edward Gibbon Wakefield understood while thinking about North America, the availability of 'free' land imperils the normal operation of what he defined as 'capitalist civilization' and Karl Marx would describe as 'capitalism'. Wakefield was the discoverer of primitive accumulation; he had detected it by looking at its dissolution in the settler

---

American History', in Patricia Nelson Limerick, *Something in the Soil: Legacies and Reckonings in the New West*, New York: Norton, 2000, 245–55.

16   On Mormon self-constitution, see Charles L. Cohen, 'The Construction of the Mormon People', in Matthew J. Grow, Reid L. Neilson (eds), *From the Outside Looking In: Essays on Mormon History, Theology, and Culture*, New York: Oxford University Press, 2016, 135–69.

17   Bushman, *Joseph Smith*, 19.

18   Ibid.

colonies.[19] But the Smiths discovered it the other way: they witnessed its reconstitution after its previous dissolution in the frontier of settlement. Debt marked their separation from their means of subsistence.

Subsequently, the Smiths moved repeatedly but remained in New England. Eventually, they 'broke entirely free of the network of family and friends and in 1816 migrated to upstate New York'.[20] This is a second foundational event in this story. According to Massimo De Angelis, one of the most eminent contemporary scholars of primitive accumulation, 'separation' is its defining characteristic: separation from specific locales, expulsion; separation from means of subsistence, dispossession; and separation from networks of support, isolation.[21] A familial network had protected the Smiths from the upheavals brought about by a raging 'Market Revolution'.[22] This network's disappearance was underscored by ultimate separation: physical displacement. Except that, while normally primitive accumulation results in wage labour, where 'free' land remains available, what Wakefield called 'dispersion' undoes primitive accumulation.[23] In frontier settings, or in areas where the social memory of settlement is still prominent, it produces some wage labour *and* a further escape from it. The Smiths opted for the latter. Their choice was shaped by a long-lasting tradition of settler-colonial displacement towards sparsely settled areas. If Methodism, as E.P. Thompson famously demonstrated in *The Making of The English Working Class*, can be seen as the religious sensibility of the wage relation, a religion of accommodation, Mormonism can be seen as the religion of an escape.[24]

---

19   Piterberg, Veracini, 'Wakefield, Marx, and the World Turned Inside Out'.

20   Bushman, *Joseph Smith*, 19.

21   See Massimo De Angelis, 'Separating the Doing and the Deed: Capital and the Continuous Character of Enclosures', *Historical Materialism*, 12: 2, 2004, 57–87; Massimo De Angelis, *The Beginnings of History: Value Struggles and Global Capital*, London: Pluto Press, 2007.

22   On the 'Market Revolution', see Charles Sellers, *The Market Revolution: Jacksonian America, 1815–1846*, New York: Oxford University Press, 1991; Harry L. Watson, *Liberty and Power: The Politics of Jacksonian America*, New York: Hill and Wang, 1990. Watson argues that there *was* a 'Market Revolution': everywhere at some point in time 'the balance between household and market production tipped in favor of the latter' (262). On the historiography of the 'Market Revolution', see Watson, *Liberty and Power*, 255–79.

23   See Piterberg, Veracini, 'Wakefield, Marx and the World Turned Inside Out'.

24   E.P. Thompson, *The Making of the English Working Class*, New York: Pantheon Books, 1964.

Upstate New York was in social upheaval and the Smiths arrived at a very special time. It was a setting where 'Moderate Light', 'New Light' and other revivals fought especially bitter culture wars, and where an agrarian crisis was acutely felt.[25] The Smiths had been tenants and had moved from farm to farm. What Sellers defines as the 'stem-family matrix' of subsistence reproduction had been violently disrupted in their case.[26] Rural people, he notes, had attempted to survive capitalist dislocations through enhanced familism. They were developing new forms of religious sensibility as well, and whereas a genuinely apocalyptic imagination had become 'epidemic' in this particular region and milieu by the 1820s, Methodists and Baptists were struggling to compete with a variety of revivals.[27] Organized religion was unable to meet the needs of a particularly unsettled population. A generalized perception of losing control was one result of social upheaval: belief in magic, money-digging, and blaming Masons were some of the collective responses.[28] Occult beliefs and practices had circulated widely in New England since the seventeenth century and were revitalized.[29] But the inability to sustain a traditional family-centred life in the face of revolutionary crisis meant that fathers more than others were losing control. Attempts to reinstate patriarchal authority in the face of a variety of challenges should be seen in this context: a generation of young fathers saw their 'manhood' threatened by their inability to meet traditional familial obligations.[30]

---

25   On religious revivals in upstate New York and their connection to social dislocations, see Paul E. Johnson, *Shopkeeper's Millennium: Society and Revivals in Rochester, New York, 1815–1837*, New York: Hill & Wang, 2004 [1975].

26   Sellers, *The Market Revolution*, 219.

27   See Alan Taylor, 'The Free Seekers: Religious Culture in Upstate New York, 1790–1835', in Matthew J. Grow, Reid L. Neilson (eds), *From the Outside Looking In: Essays on Mormon History, Theology, and Culture*, New York: Oxford University Press, 2016, 13–33.

28   See D. Michael Quinn, *Early Mormonism and the Magic World View*, Salt Lake City: Signature Books, 1987.

29   See John Brooke, *Refiners' Fire: The Making of Mormon Cosmology, 1644–1844*, Cambridge: Cambridge University Press, 1994.

30   On this dynamic in a frontier context, see Honor Sachs, *Home Rule: Manhood and National Expansion on the Eighteenth Century Kentucky Frontier*, New Haven, CT: Yale University Press, 2015; for this dynamic in a related cultural setting, a setting where many of those who were moving to the frontier were coming from, see Stephanie McCurry, *Masters of Small Worlds: Yeoman Households, Gender Relations and the Political Culture of the Antebellum South Carolina Low Country*, New York: Oxford University Press, 1995.

A patriarchal heterotopian project would make sense to them, and the Mormon movement was not the only collective displacement across North America that sought to reinstate the traditional agrarian settler family challenged by a market-driven economy.[31]

However, and very importantly, in North America, being subjected to a process of primitive accumulation cannot fail to make one feel like an Indian. Debt, conversely, as anyone who is failing to service an overburdening mortgage may confirm, can make one see angels. If processes of primitive accumulation relate to both you and Indians, an angel may end up telling you that your ancestors have Indian descendants and that you are *related* to them; that they are distant relations (relation should be here understood literally, and in a context fundamentally shaped by familial forms, and it is this relation that produces a type of settler indigenization).[32] Whether there actually was an angel is ultimately a moot question. Joseph Smith was ready to receive a message.

In turn, indigenization, like in other settler-colonial contexts, sustains a prior and superior claim. The *Book of Mormon* tells the story of a Jewish clan that populated America. The 'original' Mormon mission was to convert and assimilate the 'red Israelites'. Settler indigenization was a response to primitive accumulation in a settler-colonial context. But it was a peculiar type of primitive accumulation. It was actually *a series* of repeated dispossessions. One thing is to lose a farm; another is to lose a succession of farms like the Smiths had. Seriality is crucial here.[33] Primitive accumulation is ongoing but should be something a

---

31 Thomas Richard suggests that one of the drivers of the overland migration to Oregon was a desire to return to the 'so-called "patrimonial family"' and the 'traditional agrarian family' (120), which was premised on the settlers' ability to bestow land to their sons and provide for their wives and daughters. See Thomas Richard, '"Farewell to America": The Expatriation Politics of Overland Migration, 1841–1846', *Pacific Historical Review*, 86: 1, 114–52, and Kathleen Neils Conzen, 'A Saga of Families', in Clyde A. Milner, Carol A. O'Conner, Martha A. Sandweiss (eds), *The Oxford History of the American West*, New York: Oxford University Press, 1994, 315–58. Sellers also makes this argument. See Sellers, *The Market Revolution*, 225.

32 On settler 'indigenization', the ubiquitous settler desire to turn an historical claim into an ontological one, see Veracini, *Settler Colonialism*.

33 For an argument highlighting the importance of seriality in frontier settings, see Ed White, *The Backcountry and the City: Colonization and Conflict in Early America*, Minneapolis: University of Minnesota Press, 2005.

specific individual or family has to go through only once; this is why it has 'primitive' in it. Afterwards, one has capitalist exploitation. For the Smiths, however, primitive was also recurrent.

Palmyra, New York: the Smiths' wagon brings them there, and, at first, they rent land, but then they purchase a farm and settle. They do not own it outright and need to build everything. But they eventually lose it (in 1825). Instead of paying their mortgage, they had built a house.[34] So, primitive accumulation catches up despite repeated escapes: it is a repeated trauma. This is a third foundational event in this story. While, conceptually and etymologically, there is a close link associating vision and trauma (from *traum* in German), an emphasis on serial primitive accumulation can contribute to explaining why Smith's visions would be appealing to people who had in their living memory a direct experience of the enclosures – many went to 'Zion' from Britain's northern industrial districts – and why his visions were appalling to the anti-Mormon settlers who had successfully avoided primitive accumulations through a pre-emptive movement to the American mid-Western frontiers.[35] The latter felt secure in their escape, property and status, and were interested in taking advantage of the accumulative possibilities that they enabled.[36] Mormonism was originally about a failed escape, but many had successfully escaped.

Separation, repeated trauma, primitive accumulation: Smith goes to pray in the woods – the home was overcrowded – and specifically to a place where he had left his axe on a stump in a clearing, a suggestive reference to the Smiths' failed attempt to retain unmediated

---

34   See Bushman, *Joseph Smith*, 42.
35   See Grant Underwood, 'The Religious Milieu of English Mormonism' in Richard L. Jensen, Malcolm R. Thorpe (eds), *Mormons in Early Victorian Britain*, Salt Lake City: University of Utah Press, 1989, 31–48.
36   On the role of anti-Mormonism in shaping US settler traditions, see Sarah Barringer Gordon, *The Mormon Question: Polygamy and Constitutional Conflict in Nineteenth-Century America*, Chapel Hill, NC: University of North Carolina Press, 2002; Bruce Burgett, 'On the Mormon Question: Race, Sex, and Polygamy in the 1850s and the 1990s', *American Quarterly*, 57: 1, 2005, 86–94; J. Spencer Fluhman, *A Peculiar People: Anti-Mormonism and the Making of Religion in Nineteenth-Century America*, Chapel Hill: NC, University of North Carolina Press, 2012; Christine Talbot, *A Foreign Kingdom: Mormons and Polygamy in American Political Culture, 1852–1890*, Urbana, IL: University of Illinois Press, 2013.

access to their means of subsistence. There he has a revelation. That is where Mormonism begins, as settler-colonial a setting as can be possibly imagined. The angel Moroni tells Smith about a book containing 'an account of the former inhabitants of this continent' and the 'fullness of the everlasting Gospel' as it had been revealed to the ancient inhabitants of the land. This is also crucial: having lost his land yet again, Smith now identified with the Indigenous vanquished. Bushman concludes that the book was the work of a 'rural visionary'.[37] I agree: it was the work of a *settler* rural visionary facing an existential crisis.

The vision was clear and clarifying: the Indigenous peoples of the past (and therefore the Indigenous peoples of the present) are not indigenous – they were Israelites who migrated from Jerusalem and practised their religion in the New World. As the city was doomed on the eve of the Babylonian captivity, they had left in a pre-emptive move. Their civilization had subsequently died because of internal strife. That is how the logic went: social strife – revolutionary upheaval – is the destroyer of civilizations; against strife, better to seek out a new settlement and better to do so pre-emptively. Fragments of American Protestant culture, theological opinions and politics, anti-Masonic agitation, biblical language, and Yankee vernacular all contributed to the vision.[38] But, if the ingredients were indeed composite, as many have noted, the recipe was typically settler-colonial: simultaneously claiming indigeneity against exogenous 'others' (for example, the impersonal forces that were repossessing his farm), and claiming a more authentic legitimacy against 'fallen' Indigenous peoples.

The *Book of Mormon* was indeed promoted at first as a 'history of the origins of the Indians'.[39] The need to craft a superior claim in the face of primitive accumulation processes in a settler-colonial setting should be considered also. The Smiths had lost their land, *like* the Indians, and they saw themselves as descendants of its original possessors, *unlike* the speculators who dispossessed them. Besides, if one's ancestors have Indian descendants one may look at Indian land as one's inheritance, a pretty powerful claim, even if an unenforceable one (inheritance was

---

37 Bushman, *Joseph Smith*, 58, 72, 111, 127, 143.
38 On the biblical text as a political text in the early Republic, see Eran Shalev, *American Zion: The Old Testament as a Political Text from the Revolution to the Civil War*, New Haven: Yale University Press, 2013.
39 Bushman, *Joseph Smith*, 94.

indeed a crucial term in the developing Mormon ideology). Admittedly, the *Book of Mormon* is not interested in Indian anthropology, but this is the point: its Indians are not actual Indians; they are dispossessed proto-Christians, *like* the Mormons at the time. The Lamanites are savages, idle, bloodthirsty, and half-naked; they attack the cities of the civilized Nephites. But they are 'Israel', and they are to be restored: restored to the Holy Land, restored to a specific place. They are to be restored like the farm should be restored to its owners.

That this approach is not exceptional in comparable situations should be emphasized, and settler-colonial projects are routinely framed as a return (that is, a 'restoration'). And they are always ambivalent towards Indigenous peoples, always proposing their relocation somewhere else, and often claiming them in one way or another for settler indigenizing purposes. In the book the dark Lamanites eventually win and the white-skinned Nephites are vanquished, but this is also the point: crafting a superior settler claim requires imagining an Indigenous one that has lapsed. 'Restoration', was indeed a crucial term in the developing language of the Mormon faith: restoration promised the continent to the native people only in the context of the indigenization of the settler – in their raptures, the early Mormons were said to speak Indian languages – and of the parallel deindigenization of really existing Indians.[40] Enoch's people were seen, after all, as 'strangers and pilgrims on the earth', not as Indigenous people.[41] A repeated process of primitive accumulation in a settler-colonial context shaped an ideology that responded to revolutionary upheaval with reference to Indigenous peoples and their dispossession.

The *Book of Mormon* gave some American settlers a deep past in the New World when they most needed it.[42] The *Book of Mormon* can be read as a 'document of profound social protest', a book specifically documenting the social protest of a settler-colonial constituency, a type of social protest that embraces displacement rather than contestation over

---

40 See Bushman, *Joseph Smith*, 150.
41 Cited in ibid., 106.
42 For an argument regarding the settler need to construct a 'long memory on the basis of a short history', see Gérard Bouchard, *The Making of the Nations and Cultures of the New World: An Essay in Comparative History*, Montreal: McGill-Queen's University Press, 2008, at 22.

a geography that they have in some way already vacated.[43] The possibility and advisability of political contestation is not part of this tradition; in the *Book of Mormon*, for example, monarchy *is* terminated, but through abdication, not via a violent political upheaval.[44] This social protest changes worlds rather than change the world; it turns the world inside out rather than upside down. To do so, it crafts a sovereignty that is inherently mobile and envisages a displacement that produces a settlement that cannot be undone. They constitute a portable endowment – a type of preaccumulation. The next section briefly outlines the latter; the subsequent section addresses the former.

A Settlement that Cannot Be Undone

Mormonism succeeded because of the institutional mechanisms that Smith set up. He was an extraordinary creator of governance mechanisms, a clear indication of the arrogation of sovereign capabilities that characterizes all settler-colonial projects. This ability was part of what Patrick Wolfe defined as 'preaccumulation'.[45] Preaccumulation is crucial to settler colonialism as a mode of domination; it endows settler colonists – founders of political orders that carry their sovereignty with them – with significant advantages in their struggle to settle the land and against Indigenous peoples. Already the ancient Greek settlers could rely on vessels, weapons, tools, food, and seed they knew how to cultivate, while their successful expeditions, when they were successful, could also rely on superior weapons, navigational capabilities, and on the institution of their *poleis* to come. Wolfe refers to

> the historical preconditions that had equipped the invaders for settlement before they first set foot in Native country. These preconditions, a kind of historical capital, brought together a range of economic, technological, military, cultural and moral attributes that were the combined outcome of centuries of Eurocolonial history.[46]

---

43   Bushman, *Joseph Smith*, 104.
44   See ibid., 102.
45   Wolfe, 'Purchase by Other Means', especially 136–40.
46   Ibid., 137.

This 'aggregate historical endowment that settlers brought with them', was part of 'an invasive inheritance that had been forged through centuries of colonial expansion and associated class struggle'.[47] The endowment had a technological component, for example, what historian of settler-colonial New England Jeremy Belknap called in his *History of New Hampshire* (1784, 1791, 1792) the 'literall advantage', the ability and determination with which settlers would record transactions,[48] but was not limited to superior know-how. It included history itself. In the specific case of the Mormon settlement, primitive accumulation and preaccumulation are closely related because the *experience* of serial primitive accumulation had constituted the Mormon project and would form part of its inheritance. In their case, this experience would contribute to preaccumulation and chase the spectre of possible new primitive accumulations. While related, therefore, these two concepts are crucially distinct:

> in contrast to the tortuous, centuries-long domestic development of industrial capitalism and its associated social relations, Eurocolonial society arrived in Native country *ex nihilo* (or perhaps *ex machina*) and ready-made, condensing the power and violence of the long run. This pre-formedness, a plenitude that is independent of local determinations, is preaccumulation's central characteristic.[49]

Serial primitive accumulation, dispossession, had pre-formed the Mormon collective. In this sense too it was before the land: expulsion and exile had prompted collective self-constitution, a sequence that reverses the narrative structure that is inherent in all stories about 'promised lands'. Crucially, the Mormon preaccumulated endowment included an understanding of capitalism as unsettlement. It had to be brought under control: preaccumulation would undo primitive accumulation, and preemptive displacement would enable preaccumulation. Displacement must precede a social dislocation that is coming.

---

47 Ibid., 'Purchase by Other Means', 138.
48 See Agnes Delahaye, 'Jeremy Belknap's *History of New Hampshire* in context: Settler Colonialism and the Historiography of New England', *Journal of Early American History*, 8: 1, 2018. Belknap explicitly links 'literall advantage' and Indigenous loss of title.
49 Wolfe, 'Purchase by Other Means', 139.

As for the socialist Zionist settler colonialists Wolfe was analysing, the Mormon settlement came before capitalism, even if capitalism in the guise of the market revolution had actually come first. 'The capital that Zionists garnered for investment in Palestine', he noted, 'was not conditional on the return of a financial profit'.[50] Capital in that extraordinary instance would not behave like capital; this was for Wolfe the most crucial feature of the Zionist preaccumulation. It is important to note that the Mormon 'consecrated properties' were likewise tampering with capital behaving as capital. They were designed to provide an 'inheritance' for Mormon families on arrival, but as many anxious contemporary observers of Mormon ways frequently remarked, these demands were fundamentally upturning the ways capital accumulation was to normally proceed.

If settlers typically move with their possessions (they are otherwise mere refugees), the 'law of consecrated properties' was designed to instantly turn migrants into settlers (that is, people who move with a specific sovereign capacity). Moreover, 'inheritance' implies a return (inherit, inherent, and heritage all share the same etymology). The Mormon families would move endowed with a sovereign capacity and towards their inheritance: it was to be a movement forward through space and backward in time towards a restoration – only this double movement would undo the trauma of an original dispossession. As a result, displacement would undo primitive accumulations once and for all.

But, if moving towards an inheritance is construed as a return, the market revolution's attack against the stability of familial networks had to be countered also. The Mormons had to 'keep track' of their children; it was the best way the 'Saints could be growing in glory and intelligence'.[51] Fathers had to reacquire control over social reproduction; this would also be a return. So, Joseph's father, defeated by 'the rigors of the economic order', would become a 'prince over his posterity'.[52] 'Inheritance' as a term describing properties in 'Zion' was all about a 'father's wish to bestow a legacy on his children'. Bushman concludes: in 'restoring priesthood, Smith restored fatherhood'.[53] But it was the modern economy that had deconstructed it in the first place; Mormonism had a prehistory.

---

50   Ibid., 140.
51   See Bushman, *Joseph Smith*, 210.
52   See ibid., 262.
53   Ibid., 263.

In this context, polygamy was a logical conclusion: dispersed families lost farms; embedded networks of multiple families would not.[54] Smith was a polygamist since 1835. Polygamy would maximize the reproduction of a specific socio-political body, a reproductive capacity that would further chase the spectre of renewed primitive accumulation away: 'The Lord has revealed to me that it is his will that righteous men shall take Righteous women [sic] even a plurality of Wives that a Righteous race may be sent forth upon the Earth preparatory to the ushering in of the Millennial Reign of our Redeemer', Smith concluded.[55] Binding families together through plural marriage and baptizing the dead would strengthen a forming socio-political collective's resilience.[56] It was a kind of preaccumulation – the settler collective would travel in a cohesive fashion – the bonds that would ensure its cohesiveness would not need to develop in the new locale.

A revelation promised Smith a 'hundred fold in this world, of fathers and mothers, brothers and sisters, *houses and lands, wives and children*, and crowns of eternal lives in the eternal worlds.'[57] Plural marriage was about 'binding' families by covenant; adultery, a typically settler-colonial concern, remained a deadly sin (if reproducing one particular collective *in the place of another* is what settler-colonial projects are about, adultery is for them especially damaging and therefore a capital sin).[58] Family was everything in this context; even the 'ultimate social order of heaven was familial'.[59] Familism and a patriarchal reflex had been

---

54 See William R. Handley, *Marriage, Violence, and the Nation in the American Literary West*, Cambridge: Cambridge University Press, 2002.

55 Cited in Bushman, *Joseph Smith*, 326.

56 See Laurel Thatcher Ulrich, *A House Full of Females: Plural Marriage and Women's Rights in Early Mormonism, 1835–1870*, New York: Knopf, 2017.

57 Cited in Bushman, *Joseph Smith*, 440 (my emphasis).

58 Settlers during the 'settler revolution' frequently considered amending marriage as an institution. Charles Wentworth Dilke (the ideologist of a settler 'Greater Britannia') was somewhat appreciative of Mormon polygamy. For him the Mormons expressed 'the religious and social system of the most successful of all pioneers in English civilization'. Charles Wentworth Dilke, *Greater Britain: A Record of Travel in English-Speaking Countries During 1866 and 1867*, London: Macmillan 1868, 179. It wasn't polygamy, but Australian and British authorities contested at the end of the nineteenth century the right of Australian settlers to legally marry the sisters of their deceased wife.

59 Bushman, *Joseph Smith*, 444.

common responses to primitive and other accumulations; the Mormon family was a response to serial primitive accumulation.

Consecrated properties, Mormon universal priesthood, and polygamy were designed to maximize the human material available for a settlement that could not be undone. If primitive accumulation was moving fast, the new socio-political collective had to move even faster through space and time. A fierce growth rate would compress time. The very poor could not normally displace on their own, but a properly organized settlement could now rely on them. Mobilizing the poor required 'caring' for them, and this entailed the creation of 'a radical new economic order'.[60] But this was not a redistribution of privatized assets, what would have amounted to a revolutionary move; this was a reallocation predicated on displacement, a move aimed at ensuring that the fast-moving market revolution could not catch up. Settlement itself – that is, each settlement at any specific site – was to care for the poor. The faithful were to 'consecrate' their properties and surpluses were to be distributed. It was a system where immigrants would 'deed their property to the Church and receive back a "stewardship" proportionate to their needs and talents'.[61] This maximized the reproductive capabilities of the settlements. The early Mormon economic order was a settlement-maximizing order.[62] As a result, Mormon communities were able to effectively settle marginal lands. It is important to stress that it was unequally distributed property, not property itself, that prevented 'Zion' from becoming actualized, and that the law of consecrated property did not abolish property and only envisaged individual stewards operating autonomously in a market economy. To some, it looked like a revolution, but it was rather an escape from the growing revolutionary tensions that Smith forecasted. He saw future social upheaval as inevitable. The economic order he devised was indeed an alternative to all revolutions.

If speculation produced the unsettlement of primitive accumulation, the Mormon land regime must be primarily anti-speculative. Brigham Young would confirm it:

---

60 Ibid., 154.
61 Ibid., 236.
62 See Robert Christian Kahlert, *Salvation and Solvency: The Socio-Economic Policies of Early Mormonism*, Berlin: De Gruyter, 2016.

> No man should buy or sell land. Every man should have his land measured off to him for city and farming purposes, what he could till. He might till as he pleased, but he should be industrious and take care of it.[63]

The Mormon settlers would thus be protected from all monopolies, from any private party controlling natural resources, from merchants and credit providers that would profit from a capacity to link the settlers with wider circuits of trade, and from inflation, one of the typical scourges of the market revolution (the Mormon Church controlled prices and charges in the 'Great Basin Kingdom').

Leonard Arrington offered that the Mormons saw property in land as a 'life-lease subject to beneficial use and social direction'.[64] The most important principle informing Mormon notions of 'stewardship' was indeed that in no case a speculative monopoly could be obtained and exploited. Brigham Young said he 'would disfellowship a man who had received liberally from the Lord, and refused to put it out to usury', and while this applied to Mormons, it also referred to Indigenous and exogenous owners.[65] It is significant that banning land speculation was associated with an explicit repudiation of prior occupation as a legitimating claim. The Mormons claimed a superior title to land simultaneously against Indigenous and exogenous others.

The Mormon settlers would thus be protected from all monopolies, from any private party controlling natural resources, from inflation, one of the typical scourges of the market revolution, the Mormon Church controlled prices and charges in the 'Great Basin Kingdom', and from merchants and credit providers that would profit from a capacity to link the settlers with wider circuits of trade. This is why the Church established a monopoly of its own: the Zion's Cooperative Mercantile Institution. This amounts, Arrington concludes, to a 'group limitation of the rights of private property'.[66] The aim was to establish settlements

---

63   Cited in Metzer, 'Jews in Mandatory Palestine', 191.
64   Leonard J. Arrington, 'Property Among the Mormons', *Rural Sociology*, 16, 1951, 339–52, at 344. On the ways in which this notion reproduced Calvin's, see ibid., 344, note 18.
65   Arrington, 'Property Among the Mormons', 346.
66   Ibid., 351.

that could not be undone by market forces. Smith had finally realized that insulation from market forces, preaccumulation, could only be premised on an exclusive sovereign capacity.

A Settler Radical Sovereignty

Mormonism was to be a rhizomatic religion – no professional clergy, egalitarian participation, every male was an 'elder' – and a religion of familial networks.[67] Families, extended families, many extended families converted. They were the constituent units of a rapidly expanding movement (movement here is indeed an appropriate term). A programmatic decentralization made it the religion of pre-emptive displacement. The 'New Jerusalem' was to be a refuge against the coming calamities. As calamities would concentrate on the cities and the East, the Saints would move in the other direction. A revelation commanded: 'Go to the Ohio'.[68] The same revelation said: 'I will give unto you my law, and *there* you shall be endowed with power from on high'.[69] A sovereign capacity, 'law', is therefore only validated through movement: 'there', of course, means 'not here'. Accordingly, sovereignty became place-specific (where 'the place' is not a locale of origin but a locale of an arrival that is construed as a return). And so the 'Book of Abraham' begins with a matter-of-fact reference to the need to displace: 'In the land of the Chaldeans, at the residence of my father, I, Abraham, saw that it was needful for me to obtain *another place* of residence'.[70] Abraham, like the Mormons, escapes the authority of a sovereign that cannot be challenged.

The book said that Enoch's people lived in 'a city called Zion'. In Zion there can be no strife and 'there was no poor among them'.[71] The Mormon Zion was primarily a refuge, and Smith's geopolitical vision was indeed apocalyptic. He saw

---

67 See D. Michael Quinn, *The Mormon Hierarchy: Origins of Power*, Salt Lake City: Signature Books, 1994.
68 Cited in Bushman, *Joseph Smith*, 124.
69 Cited in ibid., 156.
70 Cited in ibid., 132.
71 Cited in ibid., 141.

a series of wars unfolding out of one another – North versus South, Great Britain and the nations, *slaves* rising up, then *Indians*, 'will marshall themselves and shall become exceeding angry' – until 'the consumption decreed, hath made a full end of all nations'.[72]

But, *before* the Indigenous and the exogenous 'Others' of a population economy that is recognizably settler-colonial would run amok, the Saints would return to 'Zion'. The Priesthood doctrines deliberately replicated the rituals of ancient Israel, and Mormonism was literally about *returning*. If the filo-Semitic Puritans who had gone to New England had seen themselves *like* the ancient Israelites, the Mormons *were* the ancient Israelites, returning to the temples, not the churches, returning to their actual inheritance, not to a providential gift, and returning, physically removing ('gathering') to 'Zion', Old Testament style. In their case, it was not metaphorical identification; it was literal.[73]

Independence, Jackson County, Missouri, was the 'land of promise, and the place for the city of Zion'.[74] There, the Mormon settlers were asked to pledge in a compact 'to keep the laws of god *on this land*, which you have never … kept in your own land'. The site-specific nature of this claim to sovereignty could not be more explicit: 'on this land' and 'your own land' are not the same, and only in the former the settler collective can be legitimately sovereign. All settlers know about this distinction, that is why they move.[75] They inherited the land from God, but Smith talked about Independence as a realtor would. This was to be a model city, a genuine New Jerusalem, and a positive message was associated with a negative one: imminent calamity – the world had gone horribly wrong and would get worse – urged a fast 'ingathering'. The prospect of imminent upheaval, a series of upheavals, demanded displacement, and so geography itself was turned inside out. Bushman concludes that 'New York, Washington and London combined did not outweigh Zion in the geography of Joseph Smith's revelations'.[76] But 'Zion' was not exactly a

---

72   Ibid., 192 (emphasis added).
73   On return as a fundamental trait of settler colonialism, see Gabriel Piterberg, *Returns of Zionism: Myths, Politics and Scholarship in Israel*, London: Verso, 2008.
74   Cited in Bushman, *Joseph Smith*, 163.
75   Cited in ibid., 163.
76   Ibid., 168.

place; it was a series of transitions. Seriality again: from upstate New York to Kirtland, Ohio, and then to Independence, Missouri, Nauvoo, Illinois, and – after sectional splitting following Smith's assassination – to what would become Utah.

If 'Zion' was not a specific locale, sovereignty would travel with the Mormons. But joining someone else's settlement would expose the Saints to the possibility of further unsettlement, and only a capacity to shape the institutions of a destination locale would protect the Saints from repeated trauma. This localized constituent charge was especially problematic, because what looks like a harmless exodus to some can look like a dangerous invasion to others. It all crucially depends on *where* you are: 'ingathering' and 'exodus' only look the same if you are on the move.

Smith planned cities: 'Zion' was to be a mixed urban/rural type of settlement.[77] It was designed to reduce interaction to a minimum, and the long blocks that filled his plot faced other lots' back gardens, not each other. Zion was a special type of town, where 'neither commerce nor civil government is given architectural form'.[78] Smith envisaged an expandable network of urban locations, a 'church of cities, rather than a church of congregations'.[79] This was, in ideological terms, a crucial turning point: cities are territorial institutions, congregations merely self-rule. Smith therefore envisaged an explicitly territorializing and sovereign act: each new city was to be 'a stake of Zion'.[80] This was where the Mormon project encountered its utter limit before relocating to the west.

The non-Mormon Jackson County settlers immediately sensed and resented the Mormon claim to sovereign territoriality. You do not do that to settlers because this is precisely what *they* are doing. They asked that the Mormons leave. They did not really ask. Faced with Mormon territorial sovereign self-constitution, the settlers counter-constituted themselves as a sovereign political body. Spencer Fluhman perceptively concludes that 'Mormonism functioned like a screen upon which Americans could project their crises'.[81] In this case, it was a crisis that prompted self-constitution. War followed, and it is significant that the Jackson County settler 'mob' understood the Mormon collective as comprised

---

77 See ibid., 219–22.
78 Ibid., 220.
79 Ibid., 221–2.
80 Cited in ibid., 254.
81 Fluhman, '*A Peculiar People*', 104.

of non-sovereign migrants and not as settlers. They saw the Mormons as "'the very dregs" of society without property or education, elevated but little "above the condition of our blacks'" (in North America a collective that is perceived as eminently deprived of any sovereign capacity would indeed look like a group of Black people).[82] The Mormons could be welcome only as sovereignty-deprived individuals, but certainly not as a sovereignty-endowed collective. At first, the Mormons responded to the settler ultimatum by thinking about another home – 'an other place of beginning will be no injury to Zion in the end', then they attempted to coexist and to self-defend.[83] They were treated slightly better than Black people, but the non-Mormon settlers ended up treating the Saints 'like Indians and drove them out as if they were wartime foes'.[84] They enacted a familiar mode of settler-colonial ethnic cleansing. It was so familiar, that 'Mormonize' even became a general term indicating violent expulsion. Talking about Kansas and about yet another group claiming a superior sovereignty, a Missouri senator would eventually proclaim that his movement's intention was to 'Mormonize' the abolitionists.[85]

The Mormons tried to organize militarily. Their armed military expedition to Jackson County was a serious attempt, and it is important that Smith thought that 'the camp' was actually the rehearsal for the future journey to 'Zion'. The expedition was an early attempt to establish a travelling Mormon self-defending sovereign polity. For the moment, however, the Mormons focused on shifting the narrative register and began telling 'their story not as a narrative of revelations, but as one of persecutions'.[86] This shift is crucial in the process of collective self-constitution because persecution in one place begets sovereignty in another.

Far West, Missouri was a successful Mormon town erected in accordance with Smith's template. Caldwell County was almost exclusively

---

82   Cited in Bushman, *Joseph Smith*, 224. On the racialization of Mormons, see Paul Reeve, *Religion of a Different Color: Race and the Mormon Struggle for Whiteness*, New York: Oxford University Press, 2015. On the other hand, Reeve's book is also useful to explore the shift in Mormon thinking about race from the Smith era to the era of Young. The shift reflects the distinction between a collective seeking to establish a sovereign polity and one seeking to defend it.
83   Cited in Bushman, *Joseph Smith*, 225.
84   Cited in ibid., 235.
85   Cited in W.H. Brands, *The Age of Gold: The California Gold Rush and the New American Dream*, New York: Anchor Books, 2003, 337.
86   Bushman, *Joseph Smith*, 226.

populated by Mormons. Mormons would settle marginal lands, and not even unsuitable environments would undo their settlement – preaccumulation worked. But if a localized settler Mormon sovereignty had now been asserted at the county level, the irreconcilable contradiction pitting different settler collective sovereign claims would eventually re-emerge at state level. Settlers in surrounding locations still saw the Mormons as an existential danger to their project because they actually were. In a settler-colonial context, if one is not recognized as a settler, one is either an Indigenous or an exogenous 'other' (or their 'friend'). The Missouri governor noted: 'Your neighbors accuse your people, of holding illicit communications with the Indians and of being opposed to slavery'.[87] Indeed, rumours repeatedly insisted that the Mormons were in league with the Indians. In these rhetorical stances, the Mormons, like the Indians and the 'blacks', were marking the outer limit of the sovereign settler body politic. Yet again, the Mormons actually declared themselves above settler law and could decide elections. One of their leaders famously noted: 'neither will we permit any man or set of men to institute vexatious law-suits against us, to cheat us out of our just rights; if they do, woe be unto them'.[88] We now know that there was no way out of this contradiction except the way out, and the Missourians forcibly and mercilessly drove the Mormons out of the state – this dynamic would later recur at the intrastate level, only to be resolved by a prolonged federal occupation of Utah and a renewed trek.[89]

Then the Mormons went to Illinois and eastern Iowa. This time they moved as refugees; the story of their persecution had to be told to ensure that they would be received as non-sovereign migrants that were expressing no collective sovereign claims. And yet, even if the experience of the exile from Missouri would produce a theology of suffering and the historiography of a persecuted minority, a new revelation from God still insisted on the need to 'build up a city & call my saints to this place!'[90]

---

87 Cited in ibid., 344.

88 Cited in ibid., 254.

89 See Brent M. Rogers, *Unpopular Sovereignty: Mormons and the Federal Management of Early Utah Territory*, Lincoln, NE: University of Nebraska Press, 2017. On the 'second great trek' to Alberta following 1887, see Roy A. Prete, Carma T. Prete, *Canadian Mormons: History of the Church of Jesus Christ of Latter-day Saints*, Salt Lake City: Deseret Book Company, 2017.

90 Cited in Bushman, *Joseph Smith*, 382.

Commerce, Illinois: the original purchase was on easy terms, but the movement was burdened by the prospect of increasing debt. Only sustained immigration would enable the Church to meet the repayments. Missionary activity would need to convince people to migrate, and fast. On the other hand, this landscape was no longer invested with religious meaning. The accent shifted: now the whole of North and South America were designated as 'Zion', and the restoration of Israel would target many more beside the Lamanites. For all that commerce had done to unleash the market revolution and associated primitive accumulations in the first place, 'Commerce' was obviously inappropriate. The Indian-sounding 'Nauvoo' sounded much better.

Nauvoo, Illinois had a charter aimed at maximizing self-governance and local control. It also had *a militia*. Enhanced local control and an external network of support were the response to strategic defeat in Missouri. The law of consecration was suspended and did not apply in Nauvoo. Internal cohesion would be assured instead by enlisting the support of the richer Mormons. The emphasis on refuge from impending calamities was also dropped; people would come to Nauvoo to prosper. Nonetheless, eventually, the local non-Mormon settlers, again, became concerned that the Mormons were becoming a 'political body'.[91] That is because, again, they were. The existence of a militia controlled directly by the Church raised anxieties and became a particular point of contention. Anti-Mormon committees in surrounding areas were promptly formed and the prospect of expulsion was raised again. As both mainstream national parties in a consolidating party system began collaborating locally on anti-Mormon agendas, plans for a further move to Texas, Oregon, or California were laid and Smith told 'the Twelve' (the Church's governing committee) to send exploring expeditions and search for locations 'where we can remove after the Temple is completed and build a city in a day and have a government of our own in a healthy climate'.[92] Immediate sovereignty – in a day – and a recognizable autonomous government were now explicit aims. Smith proposed that the new move west be supported by a Mormon militia authorized by the US government to protect the settlers. He was proposing the institution of a genuine marching republic.

---

91   Ibid., 428.
92   Cited in ibid., 518–19.

It was to be one of his last contributions. After he was lynched, the Mormons were expelled and set out. Their trek was actually a filibustering expedition, and only the Mexican–American War would turn it into something different. They got to the Great Basin and then Brigham Young said: 'this is the place'.

Conclusion

Richard Brodhead has linked John Wesley Emerson, Nat Turner, and Joseph Smith for their ability to engage with an American prophetic tradition.[93] I would like to associate Edward Gibbon Wakefield, who was not American but was thinking about America when pretending to be writing from Sydney, Joseph Smith, and Henry George: they all dealt with the issue of primitive accumulation in frontier contexts – even if they did not use the term – they were all disappointed at the way the new societies had developed, and they all forecasted that social peace would be disrupted unless something was done, and fast. They all had vivid 'visions' following personally traumatic experiences, and they all came up with what they believed to be viable solutions for enabling a *return* to a status quo ante they imagined had existed before degeneration had set in. These solutions all relied in one way or another on preaccumulation: preaccumulation would provide an endowment that would enable a new type of settlement. Each of them also had difficulty seeing really existing Indigenous peoples.[94]

In very different ways, they all invoked a 'group limitation of the rights of private property'. Even if Wakefield's 'sufficient price' of land was aimed at introducing primitive accumulation for the sake of what he called

---

93 Richard H. Brodhead, 'Prophets in America ca. 1830: Emerson, Nat Turner, Joseph Smith', in Matthew J. Grow, Reid L. Neilson (eds), *From the Outside Looking In: Essays on Mormon History, Theology, and Culture*, New York: Oxford University Press, 2016, 34–54.

94 On Wakefield's contribution to shaping political traditions, see Bernard Semmel's classic 'The Philosophic Radicals and Colonialism', *The Journal of Economic History*, 21: 4, 1961, 513–25. On Henry George, see Charles A. Barker's equally classic *Henry George*, New York: Oxford University Press, 1955; John L. Thomas, *Alternative America: Edward Bellamy, Henry George, Henry Demarest Lloyd, and the Adversary Tradition*, Cambridge: Harvard University Press, 1987.

'capitalist civilization', the notion that the government should tamper with the price of land horrified the orthodox political economists. They shunned him afterwards. And, if Smith's law of consecration established an inheritance that would protect families from primitive accumulation's further encroachment, George attempted to reverse primitive accumulation's surreptitious introduction with a 'single tax' that targeted the concentration of landed property. One wanted to introduce primitive accumulation where there could be none, the other wanted to disallow its introduction where there should be none, the last one wanted to reverse its introduction where there should have been none. These devices were never seriously tried, they may have been unworkable, but they nonetheless carried momentous consequences.

4

J.G.A. Pocock's Antipodean Gaze from the Standpoint of a Fellow Colonist

Gabriel Piterberg

In the opening page of his *The Discovery of Islands* (2005), historian of political thought J.G.A. Pocock declares: 'I am a fourth-generation colonist'. I too belong to a settler-colonizing nation whose dominant ideology, unlike Pocock with regard to New Zealand, I disavow. In this chapter I argue that Pocock's colonist-perspective is a lens that affords a fresh reading of his magnificent oeuvre, which adds to, rather than excludes, the vast commentary it has elicited. The chapter unfolds in three steps. First, I explain what Pocock meant by the antipodean condition and show that Pocock's New British History, which he conceived in the early 1970s in response to Britain's turn to Europe, was in fact the reaction of an indignant colonist, whose mother country had discarded his nation and had left its history in abeyance. In the second step I position my own colonist-perspective vis-à-vis Pocock's, thereby clarifying the utterance 'standpoint of a fellow colonist' in the title. In the final step, I make the comparative discussion wider and add themes that pertain to settler colonial nationalism. In the Conclusion – admittedly in a speculative manner – I propose that what I call Pocock's antipodean gaze might retrospectively illuminate his special oeuvre in stimulating ways. For this purpose, I focus on the middle part of Pocock's magnum opus, *The Machiavellian Moment* (1975); and on Volume 4 of his extensive commentary upon Edward Gibbon, *Barbarians, Savages and Empires* (2005), paying special attention to what Pocock has termed 'Enlightenment anthropology'.[1]

There is no anniversary that compels one to reflect at this time on the magnificent corpus of writing J.G.A. Pocock's mighty mind and pen produced.[2] However, given E.H. Carr's dictum that history is a dialogue between present and past, there is Brexit. The mostly English about-face towards Europe in 2016 sent me scurrying to re-read Pocock's *The Discovery of Islands: Essays in British History* (2005). Most of the volume's essays were written in the 1990s and early 2000s, with a highly significant exception: Pocock's manifesto of a new British history, which had been delivered and published in 1973–74. Palpably, what prompted Pocock to propose a new British history was indignation – the indignation of a colonist, I shall argue – at that towards which Brexit is an about-face. Britain's turn to Europe in the early 1970s was for Pocock tantamount to discarding the shared history of 'the Atlantic archipelago' and its white settler dominions across the globe. The concomitant was resentment of the problematic construction of a certain Europe, a notable expression of which had appeared in *London Review of Books* ('Deconstructing Europe', 1991) and was included in *Discovery*. The mood that pervades *Discovery* may be captured by reference to the colonists in Thomas More's *Utopia*.[3] The Utopian colonists are docile and voiceless in the face of the mother country's demographic needs: they are planted on the island's adjacent mainland if the former becomes overpopulated and seeks to acquire *Lebensraum*, and their colony may be dismantled if the island faces population-contraction. In More's ideal commonwealth,

---

1   The series' overall title is *Barbarism and Religion* (Cambridge University Press, 1999).

2   Writing this chapter fondly reminded me of the single malt Patrick Wolfe and I had consumed during long conversations. I sorely and lovingly miss him. Emblematic of Patrick's generosity of spirit, as well as of his Althusserian predilection for structures, he wrote in the copy of *Settler Colonialism and the Transformation of Anthropology* he gave me: 'Friendship is a structure not an event'.

3   The passage on colonization in *Utopia* has received some attention. In the book I am currently writing, *From Thomas More to Theodor Herzl: On Ideal Commonwealths and Settler Colonies*, I examine that passage in a Talmudic fashion.

mother country trumps colonies.[4] Several of *Discovery*'s essays feel like an attempt to furnish the silently obedient Utopian colonists with an indignant voice; to furnish them with a history that is autonomous, but simultaneously partakes in the shared history of mother country and its colonies, a history they are entitled to write and interpret.

Brexit aside, the other reason to reflect on Pocock's work is a conspicuous lacuna in the scholarly examination of this towering historian. The best analyses of Pocock's historical writing have failed to address this question: is there a connection between Pocock's declared colonist's heritage and his historiography? And if there is such a connection, what is its nature?[5] Even in discussions on Pocock's proposed new British history, the author's statement that his colonist descent was central to his formation as a historian has not elicited serious probing into the significance of that descent; the focus has been the extent to which Pocock's programme is helpful, valid and may propel forward the study of British history.[6] It is noteworthy that Pocock himself, twenty-five years after he had unearthed the call for a new British history, continued to impress upon those who addressed his programme in one of the historical profession's most central venues, that he had a perspective and that that perspective was his colonist heritage and experience.[7]

Clearly to state what I do and do not wish to do in this chapter, I do not wish to discuss the merits and demerits of Pocock's programme of a new British history, which other scholars have done voluminously. I am interested in the manifestations of Pocock's declared colonist heritage in his writing. Using the framework of comparative settler colonial

---

4   For the passage on colonization in More's *Utopia* see Paul Turner's translation for the Penguin Classics edition of 1965, 60.

5   In what is in my view the most insightful volume of commentary on Pocock's oeuvre there is no reference to this question. The word colony – or any of its cognates – does not appear in the index. See D.N. DeLuna (ed.), assisted by P. Anderson and G. Burgess, *The Political Imagination in History: Essays Concerning J.G.A. Pocock*, Baltimore: Owlworks, 2006.

6   A notable example is R. Bourke, 'Pocock and the Presuppositions of the New British History', *The Historical Journal*, 53: 3, 2010, 747–70. To be sure, the commentary on the programme itself is perceptive, but the significance of what the programme's author has to say about himself is largely unexamined.

7   J.G.A. Pocock, 'The New British History in Atlantic Perspective: An Antipodean Commentary', *The American Historical Review*, 104: 2, 1999, 490–500 (emphasis added).

studies, I shall argue that while Pocock is a settler-thinker, he is also a unique one. The uniqueness – in addition to Pocock's intellectual prowess and originality – is a deep-seated sense of vulnerability and dependence, which stems from New Zealand's peculiarity as a settler-colonial case: the unparalleled presence and self-assertion of the Indigenous community; and the distance from the mother country and its increasing aloofness. Exacerbated by the threat of the global capitalist market, this sense of vulnerability leads Pocock to search for a settler–indigene dialogue in order to achieve common and equitable nationhood and to preserve national sovereignty.

To accentuate Pocock's singularity as a settler-writer, one could invoke Albert Memmi's memorable type of 'le colon de bonne volonté' (the well-intentioned settler).[8] Using that type, I wrote an article comparing Albert Camus and the remarkable Israeli writer S. Yizhar (1916–2006).[9] There is a visceral difference between Camus, and Pocock and Yizhar. The latter two had genuine compassion for the natives and indignation at what their fellow settlers did to them; the former was an abashed apologist of the *Pied-Noir* community and any compunctions he had were directed at the metropolitan power. This difference might be explained, at least in part, by class affiliation. Pocock's was the professional middle class, and Yizhar belonged to the Mayflower elite of the pre-state Zionist Yishuv; more elevated classes are more prone to produce the odd moral individual because they can afford it. Camus might have been hardened by the rough realities of the Belcourt working-class neighbourhood of Algiers in which he grew up. However, Pocock is unique in that he appreciates the Maori relationship with the land no less than he values his own and his fellow colonists'.

The second part of the chapter's title, 'from the standpoint of a fellow colonist', warrants a comment, for I am the fellow colonist. I shall later elaborate that standpoint, as well as the thoughts stimulated by Pocock's Antipodean perception in a fellow colonist who is the product of and has written about another settler-colonial case. The gist of these thoughts is that, whereas the Pacific archipelago has become Aotearoa as much as

---

8   Albert Memmi, *Portrait du Colonisé* précédé de *Portrait du Colonisateur*, Paris: Gallimard, 1957. Memmi also uses 'colonizateur' and 'petit Blanc'; these are not interchangeable, but I cannot discuss the subtle differences here.

9   Gabriel Piterberg, 'Literature of Settler Societies: Albert Camus, S. Yizhar and Amos Oz', *Settler Colonial Studies*, 2: 1, 2011, 1–45.

it is New Zealand, Palestine/Israel is alarmingly becoming Jewish (Land of) Israel while the erasure of Arab Palestine continues apace. It is an interesting exercise, because the hefty commentary on Pocock's call for a new British history has invariably issued from scholars of British history. This, however, should not be misconstrued as a presumptuous attempt to imply scholarly parity. I am a lesser historian than Pocock.

On the Standpoint of a Colonist

One of many contributions Patrick Wolfe made to our understanding of the clash between invading white settlers and Indigenous people lay in his insightful notion of preaccumulation.[10] That he paid heed to the concept of accumulation was indebted to Marxian thought, in which primitive accumulation and mature capitalist accumulation had played a central role. In his application of the Marxian concept specifically to the settler–indigene strife, Wolfe pointed out an inherent advantage that the settlers, as a social body exogenous to the geography marked for colonization, possessed, whereas the natives, by dint of being indigenous to the same geography and having no hinterland or mother country, perforce did not. The preaccumulated capital the settlers had possessed was latent; it became manifest in the process of colonization and dispossession of the native community. The settler preaccumulation essentially consisted of two major components. The first was latent human capital, which became manifest through immigration. Much attention has been paid to the depletion of Indigenous societies caused by settler violence, which, at times, amounted to genocides of people and animals and lethal diseases against which the Indigenous population had no immune systems. But immigration has tilted the demographic balance in favour of the settlers no less effectively than violence and disease did simply because no society, however naturally reproductive, can outpace demographic growth through massive immigration. The second component was financial capital. The impact of this component is obvious, but Wolfe offered a corrective to the distorting lens of Anglo settlerism. In the traditional model, colonial companies and other entrepreneurial schemes

---

10 Patrick Wolfe, 'Purchase by Other Means: The Palestine Nakba and Zionism's Conquest of Economics', *Settler Colonial Studies*, 2: 1, 2012.

that financed settlements in the colonies demanded profitability or the plug would be pulled and the settlement fall apart. This model was pivotal to the history of settler colonialism, but there were other models which are significant for this chapter. The German colonization of the eastern Prussian march in the late nineteenth century and the Labour Zionist colonization of Palestine after the First World War were connected (the former informed the latter) and had this in common: the financiers were not private enterprises of some sort, but ideologically committed collective bodies – the German state and the World Zionist Organization respectively. It meant that, although German settlers in the Prussian march and Labour Zionist settlers in Palestine were beholden by respective financiers to productive labour, they were crucially *not* beholden to profitability.

In this chapter, I suggest an addition to Wolfe's description of pre-accumulation: ideational preaccumulation should be considered beside human and financial capital. In Wolfe's notion of preaccumulation, possible preaccumulated assets possessed by the natives are conspicuously absent. I would venture that the pre-contact relationship with the land and non-Western forms of land ownership were preaccumulated native assets; and that the retrospective knowledge of the eventual defeat of alas too many native societies by their settler foes should not preclude consideration of these as preaccumulation. There is a certain structural similarity between settler and Indigenous preaccumulation, for, in both cases, the distinction of the latent and the manifest obtains. The Indigenous relationship with and ownership of the land had of course existed prior to the arrival of the colonial power and the white settlers brought in the wake of conquest; but these became manifest – that is, politically deployed as a collective action – when the metropolitan power and its settlers challenged them. This point is not just a play with the originally Freudian latent/manifest idea (in *The Interpretation of Dreams*). It is related to the underlying argument of this chapter: that what has primarily shaped both native and settler communities in recent centuries is the encounter between them, not the separate historical trajectory of each prior to and during that encounter.

The ideational dimension of preaccumulation I present here entirely emanates from essays by Pocock who, needless to say, never used the notion. Two essays Pocock wrote in the 1990s excavate, in effect though not by intention, the ideational capital the British settlers had preaccumulated, brought to New Zealand, and subsequently deployed in the colony. The first essay was on what Pocock called Enlightenment anthropology (1992). In Pocock's intellectual trajectory, that excellent essay was the spark that ignited the writing of a fourth volume of commentary on Gibbon, as I shall later show. For this discussion, the essay brings to the fore the pivotal importance of the two ideational and legal pillars the Crown and settlers had preaccumulated in Britain: the Western concepts of private property and sovereignty. In the second essay, on the contested interpretations of the Treaty of Waitangi (1840), New Zealand's foundational event and document, Pocock in effect demonstrates how the preaccumulated ideational baggage of metropole and settlers was deployed in the colony and later the settler state of New Zealand. In terms of the present discussion, the latently preaccumulated concepts of private property and sovereignty became manifest in the colony because they were challenged by the Maori preaccumulated concepts of property and sovereignty. It is the nasty encounter between natives and settler that collapses the separate preaccumulated histories of these two communities into one – however brutal, violent, and acrimonious – shared history that has shaped both of them.

I focus here on *Discovery*'s opening essay, 'The Antipodean Perception (2003)',[11] which Pocock wrote especially for that volume. If 'British history: a plea for a new subject (1973/1974)' is the manifesto of Pocock's new British history, 'The Antipodean Perception' is the manifesto's retrospective preamble. Four components are discernible in this personal account: Pocock the colonist-by-descent, the islander, the Antipodean and the historian. Pocock enunciates the purpose at the outset: 'to explain what it is to write history from New Zealand and how I came to do it, and place myself in context as a transitory figure in the history of historiography. It is relevant to what I have to say in these essays that I am of settler descent in the fourth generation, and relevant also that, although I write as a New Zealander, I write as that not uncommon phenomenon, a New Zealand expatriate. It would take a long time to explain why this is one way of being a New Zealander'.[12] It is important for what follows to bear in mind the significance Pocock attributes to being an expatriate. This

---

11   J.G.A. Pocock, 'The Antipodean Perception', in J.G.A. Pocock, *The Discovery of Islands*, Cambridge: Cambridge University Press, 2005, 3–24.

12   Ibid., 3.

stage-setting essay is an interplay between the New Zealand of the 1930s and 1940s, in which Pocock was formed as a young person and which he remembers, and later developments in that country of which he is well informed but from afar.

The details Pocock offers next are relevant to not only his formation and essays, but also the present discussion:

> My great-grandfather, Lewis Greville Pocock (1823–88), joined his brother John Thomas (1814–1876) in the Cape Colony of South Africa in the year 1842, and my father, also Lewis Greville (1890–1975), after wartime service in the Royal Field Artillery, took a degree in classics at University College, London, and was appointed professor at what was then Canterbury University College in New Zealand, to which country we moved at the end of 1927, when I was three years old. I am reciting what Maori term *whakapapa*, a record of one's ancestors and the voyages by which they arrived, and it is part of this statement that his sister, Mary Agard Pocock (1886–1977), became professor of botany in what was then Rhodes University College in Grahamstown, Cape Province, so that the move from middle-class business to middle-class professional life was made by both genders in the generation before my own. If I am a fourth-generation colonist, I am a second-generation academic.[13]

If the paternal side of Pocock's formation accounts for the colonist-heritage, academic path and acquisition of Latin at an early age, the maternal influence accounts for his chosen discipline, history, as well as the consciousness of being an islander. Noting that he studied the classics – 'my father's subject' – 'since I was of the last generation to learn Latin because that was the way to become educated and had been for a thousand years'[14], he credits his mother for the fact that he became a historian rather than classicist: 'but of history, which was to be my main subject, I learned more than any school was able to teach me from my mother, born Antoinette Le Gros (1889–1976), who continued as a teacher after she moved to New Zealand'. The formative impact of the maternal side does not end there: 'It is relevant to the theme of these

---

13 Ibid.
14 Ibid., 3–4.

essays that she was by birth a Channel Islander, the daughter of a French-speaking Methodist minister; how there came to be such people is an episode in 'British history' as I suggest it should be studied. Of settler descent on my father's side, I am on hers descended from an island people on the seas between the Atlantic archipelago and the peninsula of Europe'. Recalling a visit to St Heliers (an affluent suburb of Auckland) with his mother and sister in 1950, Pocock reports that he noticed a couplet engraved on a public building's wall by the Norman chronicler Wace. In it the writer had identified himself as 'Wace de l'isle de Gersui [Jersey]'. 'By that time', Pocock intimates, 'I knew about islands and the need to proclaim oneself from them. It was a lesson I had learned in the Antipodes'.[15]

Pocock's presentation of his formation warrants commentary. Although not directly related to the subject of this chapter, the significance of Pocock's disciplinary choice is deeper than the mere fact that he became a historian, because his interest in the history of historical writing and consciousness has been as avid as that in the history of political thought. To put it more precisely, in Pocock's oeuvre, the history of historiography is an integral part of the history of political thought in the period 1500–1800. This is self-evident in Pocock's multi-volume study of Edward Gibbon; it may also explain, at least in part, the extraordinary scholarly energy he spent on James Harrington, the most history-driven political theorist of the generation of English Civil War thinkers.

Then there is Pocock's declared identity of islander and Antipodean, an identity that in my view is inextricable from being of colonist's descent. Pocock's intimation quoted above might unwittingly create the impression that islander and Antipodean amount to the same thing, but they do not. Pocock is, of course, aware that they do not, but he does not attribute much significance to the difference: '[New Zealand] consisted of a small and fairly recent human population and their cultures, occupying an archipelago of two major islands and many lesser islands situated on the globe at a point nearly but not quite the antipodes of the Atlantic archipelago with which most of these essays deal'.[16]

The ostensibly seamless passage from archipelago to antipodes in this geographical description occludes the fact that the passage is

---

15 Ibid., 4.
16 Ibid.

ideologically rapturous. The ostensible seamlessness is achieved by a descriptive register applied to both New Zealand being an archipelago, and its *global positioning*. However, as Gramsci taught us, an ideology is most effectively uncovered by looking at utterances that seem innocuously self-evident, a matter of common sense. An island (or an archipelago) requires only the ocean as its referent; Antipodes require, in this case, the Atlantic archipelago as theirs. Islander is a marker of identity Pocock the New Zealander might share, at least to a certain extent, with his fellow citizens of Maori descent; Antipodean sets him apart from them, and brings to the fore his being a colonist of British descent for it demarcates the settler–indigene fault line. An island is a geographical designation that, comparatively, is less perspectival than antipodes. The *sine qua non* of antipodes is that the centre of gravity, relative to which an antipode can be one, exists elsewhere. The 'anti' in antipode requires a 'pode'; to designate one archipelago (in the Pacific) as Antipodes and another archipelago (in the Atlantic) as 'pode' is, to use the title of an Alan Bennett play, a question of attribution, which is to say an utterly perspectival action. Maoris could presumably share Pocock's consciousness of being an islander, though linguistic and cultural differences in expressing that consciousness matter a great deal; but they would not share his consciousness of being Antipodean, and would reject it as a component of their collective identity.

Antipodean identity was an Australasian colonist-trait, of which Pocock's history from the Antipodes is possibly the most sophisticated articulation. The Antipodean perspective is not a simple and straightforward de-centring of Britain; it is more complicated than that. In Part II of *Leviathan* ('Of Common-wealth'), Chapter 24 ('Of the Nutrition, and Procreation of a Common-wealth'), there is a remarkable section entitled 'The Children of a Common-wealth – Colonies'. Hobbes opened that section thus: 'The Procreation, or Children of a Common-wealth, are those we call *Plantations*, or *Colonies*; which are numbers of men sent out from the Common-wealth, under a Conductor, or Governour, to inhabit a forraign Country, either formerly voyd of Inhabitants, or made voyd then, by warre'.[17] I comment elsewhere on the significance of this section in the context in which Hobbes wrote it. For the present

---

17 T. Hobbes, *Leviathan*, 1651, C.B. Macpherson (ed.), London: Penguin Books, 1985, 301. Emphases are Hobbes's.

discussion, Hobbes's metaphor of the reproductive and parental relationship between a commonwealth and the colonies it spawns is apt in that it illuminates the gist of the Antipodean gaze upon the mother country. Whereas Hobbes emphasized the obligation of those colonists who had formed 'a Common-wealth of themselves' to show 'Honour' and 'Friendship' to the Fathers who had made them 'free from their domestique government', in the Antipodean perspective the former remind the latter of their parental duties, of the fact that the parents and 'the Children, whom they emancipate', share a history.[18] Those who are de-centred by the Antipodean gaze are neither the colonists nor the commonwealth that planted them, but the 'Inhabitants' of the 'forraign Country' which had *not* been 'made voyd then, by warre', like New Zealand's Maoris.

An illustration of a nineteenth-century antipodean perspective, different than Pocock's but antipodean nonetheless, is a shift in the spatial imagination of Edward Gibbon Wakefield (b. 1796 in London, d. 1862 in New Zealand), the English entrepreneur and theoretician of colonization.[19] Wakefield's life was dedicated to settler colonies and to the relationship between Britain and its white settler colonies, and he showed little interest in other types of colonies. He emigrated from Britain to New Zealand towards the end of his life. Much of his writing, though not all of it, was the product of mental exertion and reading rather than travelling or literally having been a colonist, and the inspiration for this endeavour came from his formidable Quaker paternal grandmother, Priscilla.[20] *A letter from Sydney* (1829) was the first expression of Wakefield's interest in settler colonization. He composed an epistolary conversation between a colonist in Australia (the author) and a statesman in England. A passage in that text, whose significance has gone unnoticed, suggests that the embryo of gazing at Britain from the Antipodes, a gaze Pocock would fully develop a century and a half later, had been present in Wakefield's imagination. Wakefield envisioned a farewell from his grandmother upon setting off to Australia. She had noticed how marginal Australia and New Zealand were on the map she held. In response, the author

---

18   The references to Hobbes's terms and phrases are to Hobbes, *Leviathan*, 301.

19   See Gabriel Piterberg, Lorenzo Veracini, 'Wakefield, Marx, and the World Turned Inside Out', *Journal of Global History*, 10: 3, 2015, 457–78. Interest in Wakefield has grown in the past decade.

20   Ibid., 463.

tore Australasia off the map, reattached it at the opposite margin, and turned the map upside down.[21] The effect of this act was not to nullify the mother country, but to look at it from the Antipodes rather than to look at the Antipodes from the mother country, as the grandmother had done. Wakefield's imaginary act, with the benefit of hindsight, foregrounded not only Pocock's history from the Antipodes, but also James Belich's (another New Zealander) grand thesis of the nineteenth-century settler revolution.[22] In a different way, whose register is radically critical, Wakefield's tampering with his grandmother's map may have also foregrounded the budding field of settler colonial studies; that field has become global but its hub is Australasian.[23]

As Pocock continues to set the stage for *Discovery*'s essays in his opening 'The antipodean perspective', so he continues to reaffirm and reproduce the colonist's consciousness, and simultaneously to ossify the settler–indigene fault line. Importantly, Pocock continues to evince the bifurcated historical consciousness of a colonist: the history of the Australasian settler communities, which for Pocock is the history of the attainment of autonomy and subsequently full sovereignty within the British Empire,[24] is itself autonomous of the history of interaction with Aboriginal and Maori societies. Provocatively put, it is remarkable that Pocock considers the removal of Indigenous peoples and seizure of their land extrinsic to the attainment of sovereignty. At best the settler/indigene interaction's history is tangential to the history of settler sovereignty, and even that only up to the point where the land, upon which sovereignty was established, had been seized from the natives. I shall return to this point, because it is pivotal to understanding settler historical consciousness.

---

21 Ibid., 472.
22 James Belich, *Replenishing the Earth: The Settler Revolution and the Rise of the Anglo World, 1783–1939*, New York: Oxford University Press, 2009.
23 See for example: the journal *Settler Colonial Studies* as a whole; Alex Calder, *The Settler's Plot: How Stories Take Place in New Zealand*, Auckland: Auckland University Press, 2011. For the globalization of the field, see Fiona Bateman and L. Pilkington (eds), *Studies in Settler Colonialism: Politics, Identity and Culture*, New York: Palgrave Macmillan, 2011; Lisa Ford and Tim Rowse (eds), *Between Indigenous and Settler Governance*, Abingdon: Routledge, 2012.
24 In the nineteenth century the term was '[settler] responsible government'; in Hobbes's language it would be the colonists becoming 'a Common-wealth of themselves' with the approval of the commonwealth whence they came.

Let me illustrate these determinations. Pocock describes both Maori and *pakeha* as immigrant-settler communities that changed the environment they had found; but his description – regardless of whether one wishes to define one as community as Indigenous and the other settler or refer to both as settler communities – buttresses, again, the fault line between them. Emphasizing the relative aloofness of the archipelago from neighbouring ecosystems, Pocock uses an odd register:

> [The archipelago that became New Zealand] was colonized from the central Pacific; that is, the first terrestrial mammals, who were members of the human species, arrived from that quarter a thousand years ago or less, in ocean-going galleys called *waka*, and found the islands populated by large birds, of whom many species had become flightless in the absence of predators. The humans rapidly exterminated most of these, imposing on themselves changes in economy and culture which archaeology does more than tradition to recapture. These occurred in the course of settlement and colonization, in an environment radically unlike that of the central Pacific's island systems.[25]

I say an odd register because of the mélange of straightforward scholarly terminology (migration, colonization, settlement) on the one hand, and David Attenborough-esque language ('the first terrestrial mammals, who were members of the human species', and the like) on the other. The resort to the latter to describe a historical process that took place as late as the early second millennium AD – roughly contemporaneous with, say, the migration of Turkish tribes to Asia Minor and settlement there – is striking. Pocock was obviously eager to depict the central Pacific migrants as colonizers, but the fact that they had colonized a literally empty land (of humans and other predators, that is) rather than an ideological *terra nullius* must have seemed a problem; and hence the terrestrial mammals who colonize naked nature and rapidly exterminate flightless birds.

Pocock's explanation of the essence of the difference between Maori and *pakeha* is ontological. Ontology and its cognates are bandied about too liberally, but, here, the explanation truly is of opposite ways of being in the world. According to Pocock, these two communities were formed by migration and colonization, and the ontological difference hinges

---

25 Ibid., 5.

on how voyaging was imagined and practised: formative and singularly unrepeatable for the *tangata whenua* (Maori); formative and infinitely repeatable for the *pakeha*.

With all these environments [of the archipelago] the Polynesian settlers had to establish a relationship, constructing and imagining systems of animism and ancestry which permitted them to call themselves *tangata whenua*, or people of the land. In this imagery it is noteworthy that *te whenua* – the placenta, the birthplace, the land of the ancestors – is more prominent than *te moana*, the great ocean across which the ancestors came, without as far as we know establishing two-way systems of travel or commerce. *Whakapapa* [ancestral voyages] commonly end by naming the *waka* in which the ancestors arrived, but the *tangata whenua*, though descended from great navigators, seem not to think of themselves as a people of seafarers whose culture is shaped by recurrent voyaging. The migration has happened once, and ended at the *whenua*.[26]

In proceeding to describe his own specific community, colonists 'overwhelmingly British and Irish in both birth and conscious identity', Pocock immediately determines: 'In this [voyaging] – if described correctly – the *tangata whenua* differ from the *pakeha*'.[27] He continues to adumbrate the ontological chasm:

The voyages that brought [the *pakeha*] to their archipelago committed them, before the voyages were made, to a global system of commerce moving in many directions. Every voyage, therefore, was remembered, repeatable, and might in other circumstances not have been made; identity was optional and in that sense fragile. It has yet to appear whether the voyagers in the *waka* knew that feeling. The *pakeha* were not merely capable of the two-way voyage: they were in New Zealand to engage in a two-way commerce, which did, has done and does much to make them what they are. They have remained the people of a dependent economy, exporting products in exchange for the capital they do not generate themselves; and the markets on which they depend are

26 Ibid.
27 Ibid.

situated at global distances, and have until very recently indeed been the homelands of a particular culture which the *pakeha* have inherited and imported, while wondering how far they can generate culture of their own. This in brief is the antipodean condition.[28]

The antipodean condition, then, is for Pocock the defining feature of what the *pakeha* are in the world. Although already mentioned, it is important to emphasize the two components that for Pocock comprise this ontology: voyage (or voyaging) and the land. For the *tangata whenua*, in Pocock's understanding, the formative and unrepeatable voyage is subjected to the land; more precisely, the singular voyage facilitates attachment to the land – even for the memory of the ancestors, the land of birth as placenta had been more important than the ocean these ancestors traversed – as the primary condition of being in the world. In stark contrast, for the *pakeha* voyaging stands in the way of attachment to the land. Pocock explains the crucial impact upon him, when he was an undergraduate in the early 1940s, of a group of New Zealand poets known as the Caxton poets, most notably Allen Curnow. In this context, he writes:

> The Caxton poets … had much to say about the encounter between the human and a land which resisted all attempts to imagine it, and made it their business to present this encounter as itself imaginatively exciting; it is this paradox which we have yet to locate in the imagination of the *tangata whenua*. The *pakeha*, as I have said, remember a voyage before they imagine a land, and *the tension between the two is very strong* [emphasis added].[29]

The contrast between Pocock's rendering of *pakeha* consciousness in the 1940s, in which the tension between remembering a voyage and imagining a land led to a fragile collective identity, and his memory of himself at the same period is noteworthy:

> At this point I should revert to the study of history as it was when I was a schoolboy and undergraduate in the 1930s and 1940s. I do not think of the view of history it implied as 'colonial', but others do and

---

28 Ibid., 6.
29 Ibid., 10–11.

it is desirable to see why; part of the story may be that as a fourth-generation colonist but first-generation New Zealander, I was less troubled by the thought of being 'colonial' than those whose fathers and grandfathers were New Zealand born often were. I valued the voyage as well as the land.[30]

The voyage/land tension is conspicuously absent; instead, there is straightforward embracing of both. In the next section I shall address the pivotal question of whether or not the history to which Pocock refers here was colonial, and why for him it was not. At this point I only wish to concur with Pocock's own explanation for the discrepancy between his unproblematic valuing both voyage and land, and the *pakeha* finding that the former impedes the latter: he had a longer colonist heritage in the British Empire's white dominions but was a fresher New Zealander.

To this point, I have shown in what ways Pocock, one of the most outstanding historians of his generation, is also a settler-thinker. In the following sections, aided by a comparative approach among other things, I shall argue that as a settler-thinker he is unique. That uniqueness is objective and subjective: objectively, New Zealand is a peculiar settler case, which has made the *pakeha*, certainly Pocock, vulnerable and dependent; subjectively, Pocock's intellectual prowess and originality defy simple categorizations, and his ethical insistence on settler–indigene equality and dialogue is a very rare commodity indeed.

On the Standpoint of a Fellow Colonist

I am Pocock's junior by three decades, but share with him certain biographical features. Like Pocock, I am the product of settler nations and spent a significant stint at *the* commonwealth that spawned much of settler colonialism. I was born in Argentina (a settler nation) and my family immigrated to Israel (another settler nation) when I was seven years old; I did my doctorate in the history of the Ottoman Empire at – from Pocock's Cambridge vantage point – the unmentionable Other Place; I spent much of my academic career in the United States (the most powerful settler nation on earth) and I am an expatriate Israeli. Not to

---

30 Ibid., 9.

feign naivety, many would deem unacceptable the premise that Israel is a settler nation state in its history, ideology, institutions, and praxis, and others would pronounce it treasonous. But many others share this premise and have shown that Israel is a settler-colonial case, and I have made my modest contribution to establishing that the premise is correct and truthful.[31] This means that as settler-colonial cases New Zealand and Israel are comparable.

A word on the comparative aspect of the field of settler colonial studies is necessary. Here, as on many other occasions, the impact of Patrick Wolfe's interventions has been momentous. I shall allude to these interventions when I discuss Pocock's view on the colonial question. That field emerged from three assumptions. The first is that settler colonies and colonies of exploitation (or settler and metropole colonialisms) are not only discrete formations of colonial domination but also antithetical ones. In this sense, settler colonial studies have reasserted a vital distinction that had been clear to nineteenth-century thinkers like Marx, Wakefield and John Stuart Mill, but that distinction was detrimentally dulled in the twentieth century. The second assumption is that, from the English (re)colonization of Ireland in the late sixteenth century forward,[32] and especially in the nineteenth century, settler–creole[33] colonialism became

---

31 See Gabriel Piterberg, *The Returns of Zionism: Myths, Politics and Scholarship in Israel*, London: Verso, 2008, Chapter 2.

32 Pocock is well aware of Ireland's place in the history of settler colonialism (*Discovery*, 92–3). In a succinct formulation he also manifests awareness of the creole nature of settler nationalism in Ireland: 'By the year 1698 the theses of settler nationalism were beginning to pass – not without vigorous countermoves – into the discourse of a "Protestant nation" claiming to be at the point of absorbing what remained of its Old Irish and Old English predecessors, so that all Irish could be said to be English. This was no less a nationalism than a colonialism; colonists … have their quarrels with the authority that sent them out and seeks to pursue them, and may base claims to autonomy on their wars and treaties with the Indigenous peoples preceding them. Thus Peruvian creoles claimed to be the heirs of the Inca, and an Irish Protestant nationalism sought to base itself in a Catholic, Norman and Milesian past'. Ibid., 103.

33 For a recent, fruitfully comparative, deployment of the notion of 'Creole', see J. Simon, *The Ideology of Creole Revolution*, Cambridge: Cambridge University Press, 2017. The way Simon builds on Benedict Anderson's observations on 'Creolism' (in *Imagined Communities*) as well as Marx–Engels's on ideology (in *The German Ideology*) is noteworthy.

a global phenomenon. The third is that the global phenomenon's component parts, which is to say settler colonies and settler-colonial nation states, are comparable; but, crucially, comparable does not mean identical, and comparisons underscore differences as much as they reveal similarities. Wolfe could not have been more brilliantly concise: 'National histories are unique but unexceptional'.[34] His final study is a masterful exhibition of comparative history at its best, one that both identifies comparable structures and is attuned to the significance of differences.[35]

I would like, briefly, to create a comparative framework, within which I proceed to place Pocock's antipodean perception and the reading of that perception by the fellow colonist. This settler-colonial comparison consists of three cases: Argentina, Israel, and New Zealand; it looks at the fateful triangle of natives – mother country – settlers.[36] New Zealand and Israel share the fact that the settlers have been unsuccessful in irrevocably and completely removing the indigenes, who have endured severe blows but whose continued presence is politically consequential. Anyone who ever seriously looked into a settler–indigene conflict would concur that the most effective resistance Indigenous peoples can mount is simply – needless to say, it is anything but simple – to stay put. The notable difference is of course the explosiveness and ferocity of that type of conflict in Israel/Palestine and its centrality in world and regional politics. This does not require much elaboration, except for drawing attention to realities that have either gone unnoticed or been suppressed. The presence and citizenship of New Zealand's Maori community is not in question or under threat. In stark contrast, the inferior citizenship of the Palestinians who have been Israelis since the 1948 war and its aftermath is continually being eroded formally and informally, and may be revoked altogether in the future;[37] and the mere existence

---

34 Patrick Wolfe, 'Purchase by Other Means', 135.

35 Patrick Wolfe, *Traces of History: Elementary Structures of Race*, London: Verso, 2016.

36 For Argentina, see Belich, *Replenishing*, 518–47; D. Rock, *Argentina: 1516–1987*, Berkeley and Los Angeles: University of California Press, 1987 [1985], 1–199; K. Gallo, *The Struggle for an Enlightened Republic: Buenos Aires and Rivadavia*, London: Institute for the Study of the Americas, 2006. For New Zealand, see J. Belich, *Replenishing*, relevant sections; and several of Pocock's essays in *Discovery*.

37 Given the new Jewish Nation-State Law (*Hok ha-Le'om* in Hebrew)

of the Palestinians in the Occupied Territories is under imminent threat of what amounts to collective strangulation. It might be charged that I exaggerate, but such a charge would be based on an underestimation of this particular settler–indigene conflict's volatility as well as on a misplaced faith in the international community. Another reality, which the comparative approach brings to the fore, is that not only in New Zealand, but also in more aggressively eliminatory cases like Argentina and the US, the settlers recognize the nativeness of the natives. I know not of any other settler colonial situation – Afrikaner ideology came close but was not as effective – in which the natives' nativeness is as thoroughly and vehemently denied as it is in Zionist Israel.[38] Moreover, the exponential intensification of this denial has been congruous with the unassailable ascendancy of the messianic right among the country's Jewish majority and the governments this majority consistently votes into power.

In Argentina the native Indians, unlike the Maori and Palestinians, were obliterated in military campaigns meant to facilitate what Belich calls hyper-colonization[39] in the pampas and Patagonia, in the second half of the nineteenth century. This marked the end of a complicated history, which I cannot present here. To expand the comparative framework, the structural and temporal similarity of Argentina and the US is considerable. In both cases the removal of the metropolitan mother country, even if this is not the only explanatory factor, enabled the subsequent removal of the indigenous Indians; in both cases the Indigenous communities had significantly figured in the mother country's colonial economy, albeit in very different ways (trade in British North America, forced labour in Spanish South America, including parts of what became Argentina), but became superfluous to the settlers' economy once the mother country had been expelled; in both cases this process occurred roughly at the same time – the settlers' riddance of the mother country in the late eighteenth/early nineteenth centuries, and the removal of the native Indians throughout the nineteenth century; in both cases,

---

passed by the Knesset in July 2018, that future might be ominously around the corner.

38   See L. Thompson, *The Political Mythology of Apartheid*, New Haven and London: Yale University Press, Chapter 3, especially 70.

39   This is a concept he uses throughout *Replenishing* in the analysis of settler colonialism in general.

elimination of the Indigenous society coincided, not coincidentally, with hyper-colonization and massive immigration.

If New Zealand and Israel are distinct from Argentina in terms of the consequential presence of Indigenous communities, the three countries differ in terms of their relations with a mother country: these relations place Zionist Israel on one extreme, New Zealand on the other, and Argentina betwixt and between. To begin with the extremes, in the Zionist Israeli case there is no mother country[40] or, more subtly and accurately, in the settlers' ideological perception the geography designated for 'return' and attainment of sovereignty *is* inseparably the mother country and hence the singular denial of the natives' nativeness. It is imperative to distinguish between mother country and international patron, for the settlers would not have survived without the latter but have done quite well without the former. The Zionist project would have been nipped in the bud without the British Empire (for instance, during the 1936–9 Indigenous uprising in Palestine, which the British crushed with ruthlessness insufficiently noticed in the annals of global colonial counter-insurgency); and the state of Israel, cautiously put, would be an altogether different kettle of fish without the unconditional American embrace. The enormous importance of an international patron for the politics of the settler–indigene demographic battle is underappreciated. In native–settler conflicts, much attention is paid – rightly so – to the diminishment of the Indigenous population through settler violence. In addition, settlers possess a preaccumulated human capital, which natives perforce do not. This capital actualizes in immigration, which has altered the demographic balance no less than violence. However fertile a society might be, natural reproduction cannot rival incessant waves of immigration; in settler colonization, demography, together with the cycles of boom-and-bust Belich analyses so effectively, is the least stable variable. The pre-state Zionist Yishuv grew exponentially relative to the Arab majority under the British Mandate. Despite Zionist lachrymose moaning to the contrary, that growth would have been impossible if the British had not allowed it to happen. In a similar vein, the massive immigration of non-Arabs[41] from the ex-Soviet Union

---

40 Patrick Wolfe once remarked that the Diaspora is a 'diffused' metropole. The heavy involvement of American Jewry in Israel/Palestine makes this remark not implausible. Patrick Wolfe, 'Purchase by Other Means', 136.

41 I use the term non-Arabs advisedly. According to rabbinical *Halakha*,

in the 1990s, which altered yet again Israel/Palestine's demography in the settlers' favour, would have been impossible without substantial US involvement.

New Zealand represents the other extreme, certainly in Pocock's consciousness, because the dependence on the mother country has been overwhelming. Paradoxically perhaps, the distance of the Pacific archipelago from the Atlantic one enhanced the sense of dependence and, for Pocock, the sense of isolation. Britain's turn to Europe in the 1970s exacerbated the sense of isolation, even if by then Pocock had already relocated to the US. The dependence upon the mother country tangibly comes to the fore in Pocock's emphasis, alluded to earlier, on multiple voyaging – imagined as well as real, cultural no less than economic – as the centrepiece of the New Zealand colonist's Antipodean condition. The Indigenous community's strength and self-assertion compounds the colonist's sense of vulnerability. In the final section, we shall see how vulnerability, aggravated by the global market, leads Pocock in the 1990s to a search for *pakeha-tangata whenua* dialogue, which would emanate from the ongoing contestation and re-interpretation of New Zealand's founding event, the 1840 Treaty of Waitangi. For the fellow colonist, the thought of such dialogue would be no more than a pathetic fantasy, which doesn't merit even the adjective utopian.

Unlike Israel and like New Zealand, Argentina did have a mother country; unlike New Zealand, to use a colloquial, the Argentine creoles – both Buenos Aires Unitarists and provincial Federalists, who otherwise fought each other tooth and nail until the 1860s – dropped Bourbon Spain like it's hot early in the nineteenth century. Moreover, in a process Belich examines with much insight, Britain became – though not as a source of immigrant-settlers – Argentina's surrogate mother country. It is perhaps not by coincidence that not only Belich but also Wakefield before him 'coopted' Argentina into an Anglo framework of global settlerism.

---

which in Israel has exclusive power to determine who is a kosher Jew (and therefore a fully accredited citizen), many of these immigrants were not Jewish. What mattered for the political calculus of this conflict's demography was that the immigrants were exogenous non-Arabs, who for obvious reasons became part and parcel of the Jewish majority, not their Jewishness according to rabbinical criteria. For the immigrants this was a viable way to exit the crumbling Soviet Union; but had they been afforded choice, Israel would not have been the preferred destination for many of them.

As if Belich was whispering in his ear 'hyper-colonization', Juan Bautista Alberdi, of the famous 1837 generation of notable Argentine creoles, coined in the early 1850s a dictum which is a possible way to encapsulate settler colonialism: *'Gobernar es poblar'* (To govern is to populate).[42] Cultural ties with Spain did re-emerge in the twentieth century, and there was substantial immigration – Galician and Basque rather than Castilian – at the end of the nineteenth and early twentieth centuries; but once removed, Spain never was Argentina's mother country in the way Britain was for its settler colonies or even settler nation states. I would go so far as to argue that Britain was more significant even for the US in the nineteenth century than Spain was for Argentina. As Belich points out, it is meaningful that Argentina in the early twentieth century, for commercial reasons, tried to become Britain's additional Dominion. The attempt failed for cultural rather than economic reasons, vindicating the Greater Britain instinct of an organic bond between Britain and its white settler colonies. The attempt, however, was neither implausible nor devoid of context.[43]

This abrupt discarding of a mother country by settlers is partly explicable by the demise of Spain as a colonial power and the unrivalled ascendancy of Britain. Another part of the explication is the historical marginality of Buenos Aires – the uncontested centre of the Republic since the 1860s at the latest – in the Habsburg colonial architecture of South America. If one observed Habsburg Spanish South America and forfeited the benefit of hindsight, one would be justified in predicting that the north-west of what became Argentina – areas around towns like Jujuy, Salta, and Tucumán – would be part of an entity whose centre was Potosí or Lima, and one would be reluctant to predict the fate of the Upper Paraná. Buenos Aires became central only in the second half of the eighteenth century. As part of Bourbon colonial reforms, which inter alia created in 1776 the Viceroyalty of the River Plate, severing large chunks of Spanish South America from the Viceroyalty of Lima, Buenos Aires's growing centrality was recognized. However, this was a dialectical recognition, familiar in the history of settler colonialism and colonialism more broadly: metropolitan colonial powers sow the seeds of their expulsion. True, the fantasy of the Buenos Aires elite to possess the entire

---

42 Rock, *Argentina*, 114.
43 Belich, *Replenishing*, 538–40.

Viceroyalty of the River Plate was swiftly shattered: it almost instantly lost Upper Peru (Bolivia), the north of the Upper Paraná (Paraguay) and the eastern estuary of the River Plate (Uruguay). Even the imposition of Buenos Aires's domination over what became Argentina's provinces required a series of seemingly interminable wars. Ultimately, the Buenos Aires–oriented elite prevailed and established a settler republic. Economically, the growth of Buenos Aires and its pampas hinterland occurred despite Spanish colonial rule, and much of it – illegal regional and international trade and contraband or expansion of de facto land ownership in the pampas – undermined the colonial economy. The bottom line is that Argentina represents a settler-colonial case, which in a sense ran against the grain of its colonial master. The peremptory riddance of Spain was therefore not just creole bravado, but the culmination of a long historical process.

To place the individuals within the comparative exercise, Pocock and his fellow colonist obviously share the settler-colonial framework but differ significantly in terms of settler assertion vis-à-vis both native communities and mother country. Summarily put, the vulnerability of the *pakeha* relative to the Argentine creoles and Israeli Zionists are pertinent to Pocock's ultimate identification with his settler community and the fellow colonist's disavowal of his, even if individuals cannot be reduced to their nations' history and present circumstance. The other shared feature is the condition of existing as expatriates. Pocock chooses to describe his condition by invoking the previously mentioned notion of voyaging (more precisely, of the *pakeha* defined by multiple voyaging), and one wonders whether his view of history 'as never quite at home' might imply that he too has never been quite at home:

> My own career in these decades ... continued to be a story of voyagings. I spent several years in England ... [and] subsequently moved more than once between England and New Zealand, but in 1966 departed from that pattern by accepting an offer from Washington University in St Louis – thus moving from the distance between antipodean archipelagos to the junction of two rivers in the heartland of a continent. Since then, I have continued to live in the forty-eight contiguous states, but still regard the world as an archipelago of histories rather than a tectonic of continents. I see histories as both transplanted by voyagings and generated by settlements and contacts, and consequently as never

quite at home. In this I claim to have anticipated and accommodated some part at least of the post-modern stress on fictiveness and momentariness (just as the 'linguistic turn' was not altogether astonishing to one who had studied texts and their contexts with [Herbert] Butterfield and [Peter] Laslett in Cambridge before and after 1950).[44]

Within the broad category of expatriates, Pocock and his fellow colonist belong in that peculiar phenomenon of nomadic academics.

Where Pocock and I not so much disagree but diverge is in our visceral positions on sovereignty, and the divergence is interesting because we share the circumstance of expatriate colonists. The theme of sovereignty is central to understanding settlerism, even if this theme is of course not exclusively settler colonial.[45] It would be grossly impoverishing to reduce a corpus of historical work as rich as Pocock's to one theme, but it is also undeniable that the attainment of sovereignty is thematically significant in his writing, certainly in *Discovery*. Examples abound; I choose one which is not only poignant but also shows that Pocock's motivation to write on sovereignty in this particular context is defensive; that is, he feels that it is under threat. In the introductory essay (2003) to *Discovery*'s Part IV ('New Zealand in the Strange Multiplicity'), Pocock engages with the outstanding intellectual historian James Tully. Comparing the sovereignties of Canada and New Zealand, he observes:

> The question [concerning a figure in a sculpture by the First Nation sculptor Bill Reid] – no doubt an answerable one – presented itself because Reid and Tully were western Canadians, and Tully sees Canada as a texture of sovereignties, British, French and First Nation, relations between which must remain fluid and historical. The First Nations therefore negotiate a number of treaties with a number of treaty partners. New Zealand, by comparison, a unitary state rather than federation, has redefined its sovereignty as an ongoing debate over the treaty, between the *tangata whenua* and the Crown, by which that sovereignty was established [the 1840 Treaty of Waitangi]. The relations between sovereignty and history are therefore different here, and give

---

44 Pocock, *Discovery*, 19.
45 On settler sovereignty see Lorenzo Veracini, *Settler Colonialism: A Theoretical Overview*, Basingstoke: Palgrave Macmillan, 2010.

rise to histories differently written from those to be found or expected in the Canadian case, or perhaps in James Tully's philosophy.[46]

This comparison, via Tully's 1993 Seeley Lectures at Cambridge, and the aforementioned sense of threat, lead Pocock to choose sovereignty as the underlying thread that runs through Part IV's essays:

> These are narratives of sovereignty, and I have chosen throughout these essays to make sovereignty, *imperium* and 'empire' keys to the diversity of British history, and history itself a product of the political associations which have possessed sovereignty enough to make it. There are many ways of conceiving history, and all should enjoy parity of esteem; I choose this one because it is under threat and there are ways of being that are threatened with it. In the essays making up this section, I try to show how New Zealand history may be written into the context of history I know how to write.[47]

As settler-colonial projects, New Zealand and Israel diverge on the theme of sovereignty. New Zealand's sovereignty fundamentally emanates from the Treaty of Waitangi (1840), contestation and re-interpretation of that Treaty notwithstanding. Israeli sovereignty within the Green Line emanates from the comprehensive defeat of its foes in 1947–8, and from the Rhodes Armistice Agreement of 1949. Interestingly, neither country has a formal constitution. To speak of threat and ways of being that are threatened in Israel/Palestine is to speak of an Indigenous society threatened by the settler state's overdose of sovereignty; one, moreover, that from its victims' perspective is insidious because, paradoxically, it is so ill-defined that its application makes Jesuit casuistry look benign. My take on settler sovereignty, as distinguished from Pocock's and Tully's, is subversive. I am informed by the original work of a like-minded Israeli scholar, Amnon Raz-Krakotzkin. In a way, the title of Raz-Krakotzkin's short essay on the problematic notion of Israeli secularity retrospectively captures the essence of his more substantial earlier work. The ironic, or dialectical, wit of that title encapsulates the secular settlers' claim for sovereignty: 'There is no God but He promised us the

---

46 Pocock, *Discovery*, 198.
47 Ibid.

land'.⁴⁸ A decade earlier Raz-Krakotzkin penned a seminal essay whose title was as telling as the one just quoted: 'Exile within Sovereignty: Towards a Critique of the "Negation of Exile" in Israeli Culture'.⁴⁹ I wrote lengthily on Raz-Krakotzkin's exilic critique of Zionist Israeli sovereignty and on the manner it informed my own examination of Israel/Palestine as a settler-colonial situation; I am not going to repeat that exposition here, but will base on it comments which are pertinent to this discussion.⁵⁰

If I was inspired by Raz-Krakotzkin's essay, he in turn had been inspired by Walter Benjamin's *Theses on the Concept of History*. If there is a more Benjaminian reading, in its ethical and political insights, of a triumphantly sovereign historiography than Raz-Krakotzkin's I have yet to encounter it. As an ideology, Zionism is premised on a principle that consists in three inextricably entwined expressions: the negation of exile, the return to the land of Israel, and the return to history. The presupposition underlying this principle is that from the mists of time, Jews have constituted a territorial nation, whose existence sans sovereignty over the land of Israel was/is inauthentic and abnormal, as was exile as a way of being in the world. In a complementary formulation, that existence was history-less or outside of history, within which realm only sovereign (and European, it might be added) nations reside and hence sovereignty equals a return to history. Summarily put, Raz-Krakotzkin proposes to insert into sovereignty a political and ethical stance that is exilic, one that defiantly invokes those whose historical experiences are negated by a sovereign culture and those whose humanity is denied in the present by a sovereign state. Being in exile within sovereignty, in other words, is for him the politics of solidarity with sovereignty's downtrodden. Although Raz-Krakotzkin is part of a modern, progressive, and secular (alas vanishing) Jewish genealogy, there is something discrete about his circumstance. The distancing, or existential sense of exile, of individuals such as Hannah Arendt, Bernard Lazare, and of course Benjamin inhered in their historical situation. Raz-Krakotzkin, by default, belongs to the privileged sovereign majority, in opposition to which he deploys the ethics and politics of exile; the locational preposition 'within' in the title

---

48 A. Raz-Krakotzkin, 'There is no God but He promised us the land', (Hebrew), *Mitaam*, 3, September 2005, 71–7.

49 This essay appeared in Hebrew and it is regrettable that an English translation is yet to be furnished.

50 Piterberg, *Returns of Zionism*, Chapter 3.

of his essay, 'Exile *within* Sovereignty', is singularly significant. Whereas Pocock and, more relatedly, I are expatriates, Raz-Krakotzkin, in order to sense the solidarity with those whom sovereignty has marginalized and oppressed, needs to live within that sovereignty.

In my writing on Zionism and Israel/Palestine in the context of comparative settler colonialism, I developed and emphasized the extent to which the couplet negation of exile/return to the land of Israel is in fact a double negation centred on exile. The negation of exile negates the infinite variety of the histories Jews experienced in exile by ideologically ascribing them a uniform territorial urge to return to the land of Israel; the religious ritual of longing to the land, which was part of the exilic way of being, is retrospectively portrayed – falsified, some would say – as an urge for sovereignty. The return to the land of Israel completes the negation for it asserts that not only the land's custodians were in exile but also the land itself. The land of Israel was suspended from history as long as it was not under Jewish sovereignty. The Jewish nation *and* its biblically endowed land were outside or without history; both of these abstractions (the Jewish nation and the biblically constructed land of Israel) return to history – according to Raz-Krakotzkin, enter the fold of the West's colonial history – with the reassertion of Jewish sovereignty over the land. For those who would counter-argue that I describe the right-wing messianic version of Zionism but ignore liberal and labourite Zionism, I submit Gershom Scholem's monumental Zionist project, upon which Raz-Krakotzkin and I have separately commented.[51]

The prefix *re* in words such as reassertion, restoration (of the Jewish people to its land) and return have in this context a meaningful history, which was Protestant, especially English, and subsequently Zionist, but not immanently Jewish.[52] In the comparative language of settler colonialism, this is an extreme case of denying the post–second century AD and pre-contact historical worthiness of the territory over which sovereignty

---

51 A. Raz-Krakotzkin, 'The Golem of Scholem: Messianism and Zionism in the Writings of Rabbi Avraham Isaac HaKohen Kook and Gershom Scholem', in C. Miething (ed.), *Politik und Religion im Judentum*, Tübingen: Max Niemeyer Verlag, 1999, 223–9; Piterberg, '"But Was I Really Primed": Gershom Scholem's Zionist Project', in H. Trüper, D. Chakrabarty and S. Subrahmanyam (eds), *Historical Teleologies in the Modern World*, London: Bloomsbury Press, 2015, 275–301.

52 Piterberg, *Returns of Zionism*, Chapter 7.

is sought, and of the worthiness – or historicity – of the Indigenous relationship with the land. To reiterate a point I made earlier, I do not know of another settler case in which the very nativeness of the natives is so fundamentally and with such political effectiveness denied. It is chiefly for this reason that, whereas Pocock chooses to write narratives of sovereignty and, moreover, feels that sovereignty and ways of being that it entails are threatened, I – relating to a palpably more vigorous sovereignty – choose to underscore the consequential attempt to erase the non-Jewish history of the land, and of the native, this sovereignty effects. It is telling that historians such as Pocock and James Belich begin their historical narratives of the archipelago that became New Zealand from the Polynesian migration and settlement.[53] No Zionist historian would begin a history of the land of Israel from the Arab conquest in the 630s AD and subsequent settlement.[54] More poignantly, no Zionist historian would begin a history of the land/nation from – contrary to the biblical narrative – the ethno-religious fusion of various Canaanite 'peoples' in the Iron Age, out of which fusion some sort of monotheistic community likely emerged (that is, there was not an Exodus from Egypt, Mount Sinai spectacle, invasion, conquest, and so on).[55]

This brings me to the heart of the fellow colonist's standpoint more broadly. Ever since I started writing on settler colonialism, I have been

---

53 J. Belich, *Making Peoples: A History of the New Zealanders from Polynesian Settlement to the End of the Nineteenth Century*, London: Penguin, 2007.

54 There is an exception, which proves the same point as the rule. Ben-Zion Dinur (1884–1973), one of the most effective Zionist historians thanks to his successful political career rather than scholarly prowess, averred that the period of Exile had commenced not with the loss of formal sovereignty but with the Arab conquest, because the latter had brought to an end Jewish grip on and tillage of the land. Although Dinur painted his determination in Zionist colours, the tillage-argument is as old as the beginning of settler colonialism in Ireland, perhaps even as old as Virgil's *The Georgics*. For Dinur, see U. Ram, 'Zionist Historiography and the Invention of Modern Jewish Nationhood', *History and Memory*, 7: 1, 1995, 91–125, and Piterberg, *Returns of Zionism*, Chapter 4. For Ireland see J.P. Montaño, *The Roots of English Colonialism in Ireland*, Cambridge: Cambridge University Press, 2011.

55 On the refutation of the biblical narrative by critical Israeli archaeologists and the alternative theses they propose, as well as the tradition of the critical-philological study of the Old Testament, see Piterberg, *Returns of Zionism*, Chapter 7.

bothered by this question: does not the focus on settlers' consciousness, their ideology, literature, and scholarship, unwittingly but inevitably result in asserting their world, even if the starting point is critical? For a long time, I found solace and reassurance in Edward Said's (for me) consciousness-changing chapter 'Zionism from the Standpoint of Its Victims' (in *The Question of Palestine*, 1979). In that chapter, Said did not directly engage with the colonized Palestinians, but with the consequences for them of texts by Moses Hess, George Eliot, and Herzl. This is precisely what I have done, perhaps more thoroughly and contextually than Said did in that essay. I have read the settler material not only in terms of the writers' contextual intentions but also, pointedly, of what the structural consequences were for the colonized. However, reading the settlers against the grain of their ideology, from the perspective of what that ideology meant for the natives, is not the same as actually reading the natives, which I have not done. Writing a review of an excellent volume,[56] I became somewhat disconcerted by the complacency of my position because I realized that, whereas in Said's case the victims' perspective was in the authorial voice, it perforce could not be in mine.

At that point, I happened to read a compelling essay by Carlo Ginzburg on 'the historian's craft, today'. It felt like an invitation further to contemplate one's standpoint, which I accepted with alacrity.[57] As the title suggests, Ginzburg's essay is informed, indeed inspired, by Marc Bloch. In a section in which he reflects on his extensive research on inquisitorial trials, witchcraft, and peasant culture in the sixteenth century, Ginzburg intimates that 'With some embarrassment I discovered, apart from my emotional identification with the victims, a troubling intellectual contiguity with the persecutors: a condition that I sought to analyse in an essay titled "The Inquisitor as Anthropologist"'. Slightly later, he adds: 'Emotional identification with the victims, intellectual contiguity with the inquisitors: we are far removed from the elements which, in the model of historical research described by Bloch, look closer to positivism'.[58] Adapting Ginzburg's statement to this author is the closest

---

56 Gabriel Piterberg, 'Review of L. Ford and T. Rowse (eds.), *Between Indigenous and Settler Governance* (2012)', *Journal of Global History*, 9, 2014, 171–4.

57 Carlo Ginzburg, 'Our Words, and Theirs: A Reflection on the Historian's Craft, Today', in S. Fellman and M. Rahikainen (eds), *In Quest of Theory, Method and Evidence*, Cambridge: Cambridge Publishing Scholars, 2012, 97–119.

58 Ibid., 106.

I can come to a definition of the fellow colonist's standpoint: emotional and political identification with the indigenous Palestinians, intellectual and cultural contiguity with the Zionist Israeli settlers, far removed from the sovereign positivism Benjamin and Raz-Krakotzkin subverted. The tension that inheres in this position is productive, and needn't be allayed or resolved.

National History and Settler Colonialism

I should like to discuss in some detail two related observations Pocock makes. One is concerned with the understanding of the land/labour formation in a settler situation; or, in a negative formulation, with the insistence that seizure of land from and subjugation of native peoples, but avoidance of exploiting native labour, do not constitute a discrete form of colonial domination. The other is the construction of a settler history to which the presence of indigenes is at best tangential. Here, too, the discussion is meant to look at Pocock from the standpoint of a fellow colonist, who is the product of and has written about another settler-colonial situation; a fellow colonist, who is also interested in settler colonialism as a global and comparative field of study. I submit two passages from *Discovery* and closely scrutinize them.

After commenting on the confusion that has arisen from the replacement of the term 'imperialism' by 'colonialism' and the subsequent introduction of 'post-colonialism', Pocock makes a comparative observation:

> Colonists, meaning settlers, are involved in what is now called colonialism to the extent to which they are settled among previous or indigenous populations whom they reduce to political and cultural subjection. The South African English-speakers who are among my forebears settled among both Africans and Afrikaners (a settler people of a very different type) by whom they were outnumbered, and it can be said that they never attained political or perhaps cultural autonomy. British policy in South Africa was made in London, or on the Rand, and not by them. In Australia and New Zealand, colonies were established among, and expropriated, Aboriginals and Maori. These peoples, their responses to colonization, and what it did to them, differed so greatly as

to give Australian and New Zealand history radically different characters; but in neither case were relations between settlers and indigenous peoples so dominant or obsessive as to be central to the self-formation of the former. Having seized the land of the *tangata whenua*, they did not need their labour, or think about them very much, but set about the importation of a white working class, relations with whom dominated their subsequent politics and history. The New Zealand in which I grew up was able to construct a historical narrative in which Maori played no independent part after about 1870; that people has spent the last fifty years asserting itself in politics and compelling a new historiography.[59]

Much later in *Discovery*, Pocock adumbrates that observation in an essay titled 'The Neo-Britains and the Three Empires' (2003, written for the volume). In this reiteration, Pocock adds to the land/labour theme features that form *Discovery*'s essence: settler history is the history of national sovereignty (as quoted earlier, the kind of history Pocock knows how to write); to that history the Indigenous people are tangential at best; although that history is nationally sovereign, it is simultaneously an integral part of British history.

> The settlements in western Australia, eastern Australia and New Zealand ... were met by indigenous populations whose land they needed more than they did their labour. They therefore engaged in expropriation more than domination, and were more inclined to ignore, even to forget and deny, the indigenous presence than to become obsessed by it. The profound differences between the Maori and Aboriginal societies and their responses to colonization gives New Zealand history a character unlike Australian; in New Zealand there are wars, but no genocide, in Australia no wars but micro-genocides in some number. But the two are deeply alike, and at times hard to distinguish, in that they are from an early date marked by the presence of a settler, 'white', working class, whose relations with other classes make both Australian and New Zealand politics for a long time a politics of labour and capital. They develop increasingly sovereign parliamentary governments within which these conflicts are fought out, and it is this, among other things, which makes them nations writing histories of

---

59   Pocock, *Discovery of Islands*, 7.

their own. These are, however, British histories in the sense that nearly all their determinants (including the Irish presence) are the product of British expansion, and this is why these national cultures must be considered part of 'British history' and empowered to engage in its interpretation.[60]

To address the land/labour formation first: what Pocock describes, though he seems unaware of it, is precisely the formation that makes Australasia, and several other cases, a settler colonial form of domination rather than a colonial one; more specifically, in the taxonomy of settler colonies, this land/labour formation is what makes New Zealand and Australia *pure settlement colonies*.[61] Pocock is unaware of the basic and crucial material distinction between settler (especially pure settlement) colonies on the one hand, and metropole or exploitation colonies on the other, as different, Lorenzo Veracini would say antithetical kinds of colonial domination.[62] His unawareness is clearly indicated by his use of 'colonialism' in general, and by the fact that this leads him to ascribe colonialism only to conquest and subjugation as originary events, but to discard its validity for what subsequently transpired because the exploitation of native labour had been eschewed. In a memorable and appreciative critique of Franz Fanon and Amílcar Cabral, Patrick Wolfe observed that 'for all the homage paid to heterogeneity and difference, the bulk of "'post'"-colonial theorizing is disabled by a monolithic, and surprisingly unexamined, notion of colonialism'. One reason for this, he continued,

> consists in the historical accident (or is it?) that the native founders of the post-colonial canon came from franchise or dependent – as opposed to settler or creole – colonies. This gave these guerrilla theoreticians the advantage of speaking to an oppressed majority, on whose labour a colonizing minority was vulnerably dependent … But what if

---

60   Ibid., 189.
61   Notable scholars who developed the taxonomy of settler colonies are D.K. Fieldhouse, G. Fredrickson and G. Shafir. For a summary of this taxonomy see Piterberg, *Returns of Zionsim*, Chapter 2.
62   See especially Lorenzo Veracini 'Understanding Colonialism and Settler Colonialism as Distinct Formations', *Interventions: International Journal of Postcolonial Studies*, 16: 5, 2014, 615–33.

the colonizers are not dependent on native labour? – indeed, what if the natives themselves have been reduced to a small minority whose survival can hardly be seen to furnish the colonizing society with more than a remission from ideological embarrassment?[63]

This is what happens when 'the colonizers are not dependent on native labour'. In a pure settlement colony, the settlers covet the natives' land but none – with momentary exceptions – of their labour. From the settlers' perspective, in this land/labour formation the indigenes become superfluous, not needed for the formation's socio-economic reproduction. What settlers ideally desire from Indigenous peoples is disappearance, not necessarily individually but as a political collective that stands between the settlers and the land. As Wolfe perceptively noticed, '[In a pure settlement colony] it is difficult to speak of an articulation between colonizer and native since the determinate articulation is not to a society but directly to the land, a precondition of social organization. Since it is incoherent to talk of an articulation between humans and things, this social relationship can be conceived as a negative articulation.'[64] Exploitation of forced labour did exist in pure settler colonies: white convicts in Australia, white working class in Australia and New Zealand (as Pocock points out), and African slaves in the southern colonies/states of the US. However, that exploited labour was, crucially, exogenous not Indigenous, which is to say that those whose labour was extracted did not have a pre-contact relationship with the land. In settler colonial cases, but *not* pure settlement ones, where native labour was critical for the formation's reproduction, like the *Pieds-Noirs* in French Algeria and Afrikaners in South Africa, settler sovereignty was vulnerable and in the final analysis did not survive the challenges it faced. There were, of course, other reasons for the dispersion of the *Pied-Noir* community in the early 1960s and the defeat of Afrikaner South Africa three decades later, but the dependence of these settler-formations on native labour did not help their endurance.

In short, the simultaneous avoidance of native labour and covetousness of native land bespeak a discrete form of colonial domination, not

---

63 Patrick Wolfe, *Settler Colonialism and the Transformation of Anthropology: The Politics and Poetics of an Ethnographic Event*, London: Cassell, 1999, 1.
64 Ibid., 2.

absence thereof. The other point raised above is the construction of a history, of which interaction with the natives is independent, except for the originary event of conquest and seizure of land. This is common to all national settler histories. It is helpful to start from the event – structure opposition in the settler-colonial context. This is probably Wolfe's most oft-cited observation:

> Settler colonies were (are) premised on the elimination of native societies. The split tensing reflects a determinate feature of settler colonization. The colonizers come to stay – invasion is a structure not an event. In contrast [in metropole colonies without settlers], for all the hollow formality of decolonization, at least the legislators generally change colour.[65]

In a settler-colonial situation where the settlers have won sovereignty and established a state, there is no post-colonialism or post of any sort. That settler nations call their riddance of the metropolitan power that planted them and their overwhelming the native society war of independence attests to their material and ideological triumph, not to independence being a universal enfranchisement: 'We the People' equals 'We the Colonists'; or, to take a cue from Joshua Simon,[66] 'We the Creoles'. Similarly, try telling Palestinian Israelis that since 1948 they have experienced life as citizens of a post-colonial, independent state rather than an ethnocratically sovereign, settler one that has been looting their land and demolishing homes, and Judaizing the landscape: you'd elicit a baffled look in response.

In short (again), settlerism is a persistent structure, which does not go away after the initial shock and awe of invasion, seizure of land, and frontier violence as events of origination. Settlerism underlies not only settler colonies but also sovereign settler states in ways that are tangibly consequential for both natives and settlers, even if settlers construct

---

65 Ibid. Probably unaware, Wolfe elaborates in this statement Hobbes's assertion, quoted earlier, that commonwealths, in order to procreate, plant colonies in foreign lands either 'voyd of former Inhabitants or made voyd then, by warre'. For the question of elimination see Patrick Wolfe, 'Settler Colonialism and the Elimination of the Native', *Journal of Genocide Research*, 8: 4, 2006, 387–409.

66 See his comparative *Ideology of Creole Revolutions*, Cambridge: Cambridge University Press, 2017.

narratives of self-formation – and they invariably do – in which the presence of natives ostensibly looks immaterial. The reason this matter is complicated, which is reflected in the quotations of Pocock above, is that the asymmetry of power between settlers and natives makes murky, or confusing, the relationship between objective reality, and ideology and consciousness. The land/labour formation called pure settlement colony is an objective reality: it really exists because the settlers have the power to impose it upon the natives. In this formation the settlers materially and discursively construct a rigid and rationalized fault line between themselves and the natives, which with the passage of time the settlers further ossify. On this basis, it is possible to see how Pocock could make the utterances quoted above. The native and settler communities, on the basis of domains of reality that really exist, are hell bent on constructing narratives of self-formation that are autonomous of each other. The nasty interaction between these two communities is not ignored, but the argument that the interaction has shaped both communities is ideologically not permitted. Writers such as Wolfe and I obdurately insist that it is the encounter that has formed and shaped – the present perfect tense is not coincidental – both communities. Politically, recognition that the horrid and acrimonious history of settlers and natives is nonetheless a shared history, rather than two bifurcated histories autonomous of each other, might be a necessary – albeit far from sufficient – condition for shared citizenship and governance.

The standpoint of the fellow colonist throws additional light on the conundrum that is the settler–indigene encounter. I focus on a foremost instance of the pure settlement colony, namely, the kibbutz. It is dusk and Minerva's Owl may spread its wings because kibbutzim no longer exist as kibbutzim; they are suburbia in an advanced, extremely unequal, capitalist economy. I would like to begin from a telling anecdote, which my late mother recounted to me in great detail long after it had taken place. Upon immigration to Israel in 1963, my family first settled in a kibbutz, on the far left of Labour Zionism's ideological spectrum; my late father was offered a job as the kibbutz's doctor. My mother, also a physician, worked in a hospital at the nearby town of Hadera. An opinionated, intelligent, and occasionally provocative individual, she plucked up the courage to raise a question, in broken Hebrew, at a social gathering in the kibbutz. Her question was this: 'Where are the Arabs?' There was, she reported, an eerie silence, until one of the comrades kindly encouraged her to explain what she meant. My mother said that in Buenos Aires the Israeli ambassador, a distant family relative aware of her communist filiation, had told her about the kibbutz as an experiment in socialist utopia and the prospective thrill of participating in its realization. Socialism, she continued, was internationalist and she had been told that the kibbutz movement was about Zionism and the fraternity of workers and nations. She had seen Arabs at the hospital, so they must be somewhere, but none in the kibbutz. The result of all this was that my mother, for a while, rendered medical services to Palestinian communities in the Wadi Ara area, a fifteen-minute drive east of the kibbutz. When my mother told this episode, retrospection was at play, her naivety was simultaneously genuine[67] and feigned, and as a raconteur she could be a tad self-congratulatory. I tell this anecdote for a simple reason: it illustrates how, in as tiny a geography as Israel/Palestine, in the formation of a pure settlement colony/state, the natives can be made near-invisible, savage foes who dwell 'Where the Jackals Howl',[68] and have nothing to do with 'who we are', even when they are present at such proximity.

That is why I think it would be simplistic to dismiss Pocock's observation – that settlers construct narratives of self-formation to which the encounter with and presence of natives is either immaterial or tangential – as ideological false consciousness. That Tel Aviv, one of the whitest cities in the urban landscape of the Mediterranean, Western Europe, and Scandinavia, can celebrate beach life, night life, and gay life, while in Qalqilya, a mere twenty-four kilometres to the north-east, 100,000 Palestinians exist in an open air prison (never mind the Gaza Strip), is reality; an horrific reality, but real nonetheless. Tel Aviv can celebrate its alleged liberal openness and market it as a tourist attraction, and the incarceration and isolation of entire Palestinian communities can continue apace, as if the two occurred on different planets, unrelated to one another. The problem is that in a terribly twisted way, the asymmetry of power is real and they do seem to occur on different planets. In a sense, while the reality of the pure settlement colony is real for both settlers and natives, it is also a secondary reality. Underneath it is how that pure settlement

---

67 She was at the time unaware of the Nakba and the military government imposed on the Palestinian citizens (1949–66).

68 This is the English title of Amos Oz's collection of stories (New York, Harcourt Brace Jovanovich, 1975). The title of the Hebrew original (1965, first edition) is, literally, 'in the Jackals' lands'.

colony came to be, what was it that made settlers discard native labour, not only to covet native land. The kibbutz is an excellent example, with its specific but comparable history. We move from the anecdotal to the structural, and from the idealist view of the kibbutz as an attempt to realize a socialist utopia to a materialist examination of the kibbutz as a major colonizing method, which pivoted on the exclusion of Arab labour and exclusion of Arabs from the land.

In 1981 George Fredrickson published his path-breaking *White Supremacy* (1981), which wrought havoc with the bifurcation of settler historical consciousness into a narrative of self-formation ('who we are') and a narrative of interaction with natives and imported slaves ('what we did but that's not who we are'). Treading the path Fredrickson had blazed, two notable studies appeared: Gershon Shafir's on Israel/Palestine, and two decades later Aziz Rana's on the US.[69] Crudely put, for the sake of brevity, my writing on the subject is complementary to Shafir's, in the sense that I have added an analysis of the ideological and literary superstructure to his original examination of the material and institutional base. This is obviously not the venue for extensive commentary on Shafir's work; I did that elsewhere.[70] Its pertinence to this discussion is that through a hard-nosed materialist investigation and matter-of-fact register, Shafir's work deals a lethal blow to what I call above bifurcated settler historical consciousness, whereby the formation of settler nation states on the one hand, and the settler–indigene conflict on the other, are two discrete and impregnable stories. Uninterested in themes such as historical consciousness (at least not directly), Shafir shows that, from its inception, that is 1882–1914, the process of the formation of the Israeli state and society and the Israeli–Palestinian conflict constitute a single historical-sociological narrative, in which the latter shaped the former.

Shafir applies this overarching argument to the kibbutz. In the earliest Zionist wave of immigration and settlement, known in that parlance as the First Aliya (1880s and 1890s), the prevailing land/labour formation

---

69 G. Shafir, *Land, Labour and the Origins of the Israeli-Palestinian Conflict, 1882–1914*, Cambridge: Cambridge University Press, 1989; A. Rana, *The Two Faces of American Freedom*, Cambridge: Harvard University Press, 2010.

70 For extended commentary, on which I base this passage, see Gabriel Piterberg, 'Israeli Sociology's Young Hegelian: Gershon Shafir and the Settler-Colonial Framework', *Journal of Palestine Studies*, 44: 3, 2015, 17–38.

was the ethnic plantation. This formation was dependent on cheap Arab labour. Informed by the French Algerian model, the technocrats of Baron Edmond de Rothschild, who sponsored the project, designed the ethnic plantations and oversaw their operation. Come 1904 and the second wave of Zionist immigration, the famed Second Aliya that would produce the state's founding elite, presented a sociologically different kettle of fish: essentially a group of unattached youth in dire need of wage-labour. This vaguely socialist group of colonists organized a campaign under the loftily ideological slogan of the Conquest of Labour,[71] more mundanely a campaign to oust the native Palestinians from employment in the ethnic plantations, by putting pressure on the plantations' owners exclusively to employ white settlers, to unite 'Hebrew land' with 'Hebrew labour'. The Conquest of Labour campaign failed miserably, because in an open labour market the young settlers could not compete with native labour. They were less effective workers, and to make themselves even less competitive demanded higher wages. Additionally, the Palestinian peasants had a fall-back economy in their villages, to which seasonal employment in the ethnic plantations was supplemental, whereas the settlers entirely depended on wage-labour. The failure produced a crucial turning point in the annals of Zionist settlerism.

Inspired by Bismarck's (unsuccessful) project of the settler colonization of the eastern Prussian march (Ostmark), whose purpose was to germanize a predominantly Polish region, two highly gifted German-Jewish experts of colonization and settlement, Franz Oppenheimer and Arthur Ruppin, fundamentally transformed the method of Zionist colonization from the French Algerian model of the ethnic plantation to the German-inspired model of cooperative settlements, of which the kibbutz was the jewel in the crown (there were other forms). These cooperative settlements were pure settlement colonies which, to make a long story short, made labour and land exclusive settler domains, and exclusive of natives. The settlers concomitantly benefited from the fact that, importantly, the World Zionist Organization, rather than wealthy philanthropists, had begun to acquire land on which the cooperative settlements were established. The pure settlement colony formation now had the three vital resources for its development: land and labour that

---

71 It is significant that conquest, intuitively associated with land, was applied to labour.

are exclusive of natives, and immigration from explosively anti-Semitic Europe. The settler–indigene fault line, which in the ethnic plantation was murky and porous because labour made natives visible, became rationalized and rigid in the pure settlement formation. My mother's question, 'Where are the Arabs?', had a structural context which has not vanished with the passage of time. That the kibbutzim, from their inception until today, have been Arabrein is a structure not an event of origination. The structure is chiefly explicable by the settler–native encounter rather than socialist utopias. Ruppin, the chief architect of Labour Zionism's cooperative settlements, had been as fond of utopian socialism as Margaret Thatcher was of trade unionism.

Shafir perceptively posits that the early transformation from ethnic plantation to pure settlement colony, coupled with Labour Zionism's hegemony roughly from 1930 to 1980, has created not only material reality but also what can be loosely termed a pure settlement state of mind. This explains Labour's adherence to partition, and in its later iteration the two-state solution: short of irrevocable elimination, strict separation of natives and settlers is the *sine qua non* of this type of settlerism. The Oslo Accords were a shrewdly devised plan to confine the Palestinians to well-guarded reservations in which they would police themselves. They were not a fit of settler magnanimity that offered sovereignty to the native community. This is worth repeating: the kind of plan that Oslo was, is conceivable because, from a very early stage, Palestinian labour has been superfluous to the Zionist and then Israeli economy; it is all about land – which is still coveted in its entirety – and the articulation, to re-invoke Wolfe, is still not to the colonized native but directly to the land. True, especially after 1967, Palestinian labour was exploited in certain sectors of the economy, but harsh as it may sound, I would insist that this labour is crucial for the survival in extremely difficult circumstances of Palestinians thereby employed more than it is vital for the Israeli economy.

To conclude this section, I return to Pocock. The threat he senses is that the Britishness of New Zealand is on the cusp of oblivion. Three sources feed it: the mother country discarding its former white settler colonies, of which the turn to Europe was emblematic; New Zealand's transformed demography; and New Zealand's transformed culture, especially the ascendancy of a historiography that acutely undermines the narratives of self-formation, which formed the young Pocock in the

1930s and 1940s. In the next section, we shall see a fourth source, which threatens both *pakeha* and Maori: the global market. Pocock writes: 'Any narrative of autonomy must instantly be rewritten from the point of view of those it fails to include; it is right to do this, but wrong to suppose that the alienation of the excluded automatically deprives the history of the included of its substance'.[72] Pocock's assertion is poorly worded. To write a narrative of autonomy, and then magnanimously to allow those excluded from the autonomy's narrative to write another from their alienated point of view is the easy – and the liberal, I dare say – way out. The real question is whether those who have determined whom the autonomy – and autonomy here is a softer way of saying sovereignty – should include and whom it should exclude are willing to recognize that the act of exclusion is constitutive of who they collectively are. To use Pocock's own language, that the act of exclusion is pivotal to the substance of the history of the included.

To recapture a point made earlier, I strongly believe that it is necessary for native and settler communities to recognize that they share a history of violent conflict and acrimony, a shared history, which collectively shaped both of them, in order to hope to share a land equitably. In settler-colonial situations, in which the settlers have not eliminated the Indigenous society as a political collective, the unbending insistence of the conflict's sides that each community should have its own impermeable telos, to which the encounter with the other community is essentially irrelevant, is not just intellectually wrong; it is politically unhelpful. This might be true, more broadly, for the neoliberal global world we inhabit: the ruling classes should be satisfied to afford subalterns a celebration of identity-narratives, if they judge that the celebration makes subalterns obsequiously content. Narratives of identity obtain neither equal citizenship nor equal access to resources. Moreover, narratives of identity affect societal fragmentation, which helps to perpetuate the unequitable status quo. A mosaic of atomized communities, which are different in a uniformly modular manner and consume the same commodities and the same stupefying culture, could not suit global capital better.

---

72   Pocock, *Discovery of Islands*, 8–9.

Is a Settler–Native Dialogue Possible?

I would finally like to mention two remarkable essays, in which Pocock explores the possibility of a dialogue between *tangata whenua* and *pakeha*, a dialogue which in Israel within its 1949 borders, where the *tangata whenua*'s citizenship (never mind an equal one) is an open question, would be in the realm of the imponderable. It is of course worse with regard to the Palestinian *tangata whenua* in the West Bank and Gaza, whose humanity the Jewish *pakeha* deny. Pocock delivered and subsequently published the essays in the 1990s, and they appear sequentially in *Discovery*. The first, '*Tangata Whenua* and Enlightenment Anthropology', reconstructs the history of the theorization of the two communities, *tangata whenua* and *pakeha*. The second essay, 'Law, Sovereignty and History in a Divided Culture: The Case of New Zealand and the Treaty of Waitangi', asks whether the unceasing interpretation of and contestation over New Zealand's foundational treaty might not in fact be the basis for a native–settler dialogue, the basis for common nationhood. These essays are sufficiently remarkable to merit discussion in their own right. The relevance to this chapter is invaluable: what ultimately enables Pocock even to contemplate a dialogue is the *encounter* of the two communities as a structure, their shared history in other words, not two teloi that are independent of one another.

If we take these two essays as a unit – and their sequential placement in *Discovery* is not merely chronological – it is interesting to dwell on Pocock's telling conclusion of the second essay ('Law, Sovereignty'). Pocock's mood when he had unearthed the call for a new British history in the 1970s was indignant. When he proposed a *tangata whenua–pakeha* dialogue in the 1990s, essentially a search for common nationhood and sovereignty, he seems to have been pessimistic and fatigued. The new British history and attendant Antipodean perception had been an exclusively *pakeha* preserve, an assertion of their right to partake in writing and interpreting British – archipelagic actually – history. So, what made Pocock appeal to the *tangata whenua* in the 1990s in his quest of a history, which perforce would be more Aotearoan and less New Zealandic? The answer is twofold. One part of it was the onslaught of the neoliberal global market at that period, an onslaught that threatened (still does) to undermine political communities. The other part of the answer is Pocock's fatigue of being an expatriate colonist, a desire of obtaining a figurative pied-à-terre. 'I confess myself tired of being deconstructed', Pocock remarks, 'and in search of *turangawaewae* [a place to stand], not so much a place to stand as a means of standing somewhere'.[73]

It is interesting that Pocock, who could not be accused of sympathy to Marxism, is nonetheless informed by Marxist thought in observing that the market threatens to pulverize national sovereignty, and that this predicament may be what Maori and *pakeha* share. He explicitly says so:

> The criticism here outlined has a good deal of substance; it is put forward by surviving Marxists among others. As Marxism recedes into the past as either a system or a programme, we may pick its bones and find there some important critical perceptions. Let me conclude by examining some of its predictions as they may affect the *pakeha*, rather than the *tangata whenua*, in the historical context shared by both.[74]

Especially insightful is Pocock's observation – Marxism is probably to blame for its dialectical nature – that the most open-minded government as far as the Maori were concerned was also the one that did most to surrender national sovereignty to global capital:

> As a New Zealander, I find it significant that the debate over the Treaty of Waitangi [1840], an investigation and redefinition of the foundations of national sovereignty, was initiated under the fourth Labour government of 1984–90, which will be remembered in the national history – if the nation survives to have one – as a unique blend of the creative and the radically destructive. I use the adverb to give emphasis to the latter adjective because the other politics initiated by that government are reducible to the rapid and often the forced sale of national assets – those owned by the state, and then more and more of those which might constitute a national economy – into hands so widely dispersed that their sale amounted to a radical … abdication by the state to a market international or extra-national in character.[75]

---

73 Ibid., 255.
74 Ibid., 253.
75 Ibid.

Pocock then proceeds to explain why the 'radically destructive' negates the 'creative', and to assert that this puts Maori and *pakeha* in the same boat:

> It is no accident that the Waitangi Tribunal [the body tasked with reinterpreting the Treaty] owes much of its authority to an appeal to the Treaty against a decision to transfer lands acquired by the crown to state-owned enterprises over which the market was to have an authority which the crown has abdicated; or that it could be asked what meaning there would be to Maori re-acquisition of ancestral *mana* [authority] over off-shore fishing grounds if all that could be done with it was to negotiate the sale of fishing rights to operations based in Korea and Taiwan. The *iwi* [tribes] found themselves in a world where sovereignty might mean mostly the right to dispose of sovereignty ... This time the *pakeha* – or quite a number of them – shared the same predicament [as the *iwi*'s since 1840].[76]

To be sure, Pocock is as far as he can be from deifying the sovereign state, as evinced by his warning of 'the disastrous German idealist conviction that the state (even the state at war) was the highest expression of freedom of the personality', although I am not sure that the warning ought to be confined to German idealism. Yet, ultimately, the loss of the sovereign political community amounts to the loss of personality:

> Instead of living in political communities where we were – supposedly – members as individuals of the sovereign which determined its role in history, we are to live in economic communities where our role as self-enacting individuals has yet to be defined as other than that of the consumer. And it is hard to say that consumers determine their own destiny. We may all have to go and live where the market has most need of us – as consumers, by the way, more than as producers. I have heard Sir Tipene O'Regan observe that the problem before both *tangata waka* [literally: people of a canoe; by 'both' Pocock means Maori and European colonists as peoples who came from the sea] is how to avoid becoming boat people.[77]

---

76 Ibid., 253–4.
77 Ibid., 254.

The uniqueness of Pocock as a settler-thinker is embodied in the final sentences of the 'Law, Sovereignty' essay. I have not encountered a thinker, certainly not one of Pocock's magnitude, for whom a dialogue that leads to common nationhood is the only way to preserve national sovereignty. Patrick Wolfe emphasized on several occasions the extent to which settlers deny both the historicity and value of the Indigenous relationship with the land. When settlers notice natives not as mere foes, as some Zionist writers did, they deem them part of the land's fauna and flora. Compared to other settler thinkers, Pocock appreciates the value of the *tangata whenua*'s relationship with and attachment to the land no less than he does his own or the *pakeha*'s. This partly stems from New Zealand's distinctiveness as a settler colonial case; at the same time, I think it also stems from Pocock's republican commitment, which is sufficiently large equitably to include *tangata whenua* and *pakeha*:

> Political community therefore matters, and so does sovereignty. In the case I have been reviewing, Maori and *pakeha* have been renegotiating sovereignty even as it is being sold out from under them, and I can imagine conditions in which they both want their *rangatiratanga* [literally: chieftainship, lordship] and *turangawaewae* [a place to stand] back again, and have to begin by deciding whether they are still there to demand them.[78]

Conclusion

I raise this concluding thought in a perfunctory fashion. This chapter is a reading of *Discovery*; but what if we were to read *Discovery* as a chapter of a book whose first chapter was 'The Ancient Constitution', followed by 'The Machiavellian Moment' and 'Barbarians, Savages and Empires' (Volume 4 of the commentary on Gibbon) as further chapters?[79] Three

---

78　Ibid., 255.
79　J.G.A. Pocock, *The Ancient Constitution and the Feudal Law*, Cambridge: Cambridge University Press, 1957; J.G.A. Pocock, *The Machiavellian Moment: Florentine Political Thought and the Atlantic Republican Tradition*, Princeton: Princeton University Press, 1975; J.G.A. Pocock, *Barbarism and Religion, Volume 4: Barbarians, Savages and Empire*, Cambridge: Cambridge University Press, 2005.

questions subsequently arise. The first is why had Pocock delayed – the verb is not unproblematic – revealing the connection between his make-up, specifically the colonist heritage, and his historiography until he made it explicit in *Discovery*? The second question is whether Pocock thought that the connection was relevant for not only *Discovery*'s essays, but also other studies such as *Barbarians, Savages and Empires*, a work for which the opening section in the 'Enlightenment Anthropology' essay in *Discovery* was a starting point?[80] The third question is whether *Discovery*, independently of Pocock's contextual intentions when he wrote other studies, affords us a retrospective view of these other studies, such as his interpretation of James Harrington?

I read Quentin Skinner's seminal 'Meaning and Understanding in the History of Ideas' for the first time as an undergraduate at Tel Aviv University and many times since. Consequently, I am immune from the peril of applying the mythologies Skinner enumerates to Pocock's oeuvre, especially those of coherence and prolepsis. As a result, while seeking neither coherence nor early works whose meaning had to await later ones to be fully revealed, I do wish to raise the possibility that Pocock's colonist heritage may be pertinent beyond *Discovery*. The initial stimulus for the thought with which I conclude is a compellingly incisive passage Pocock wrote on Harrington. It had first appeared in *The Ancient Constitution*, and reappeared, more elegantly in my view, in *The Machiavellian Moment*:

> It was not new to suggest that the decline of military power in the hands of the nobility had led to important changes in political power, or that it had left the king face to face with his commons. Harrington's crucial innovation – which makes him the true pioneer of civic humanist thought in England – was to erect these perceptions into a general history of political power in both Europe and England, founded on the Machiavellian theory of the possession of arms as necessary to political personality. The Florentines had stressed that if a man bore arms not for himself but for another, he was incapable of citizenship, since the use of arms – the crucial act in asserting both power and virtue – must be at his command if he was to be at the republic's; and they had

---

80 Pocock explicitly says it was a starting point; see *Discovery of Islands*, 201, note 3.

perceived the transition from Roman republic to empire in terms of the rise and fall of armed individuality. Harrington's acquaintance with English legal antiquarianism permitted him at this point to add a further dimension – one which, as he put it, Machiavelli had very narrowly missed: the bearing of arms, once it was seen as a function of feudal tenure, proved to be based upon the possession of property. The crucial distinction was that between vassalage and freehold; it determined whether a man's sword was his lord's or his own and the commonwealth's; and the function of free proprietorship became the liberation of arms, and consequently of the personality, for free public action and civic virtue. The politicization of the human person had now attained full expression in the language of English political thought; God's Englishman was now *zōon politikon* in virtue of his sword and his freehold.[81]

One wonders if the portrayal in Pocock's hand of Harrington's fully politicized republican citizen might not be, concomitantly, the portrayal of a republican colonist, who with his sword and freehold would help to carry Harrington's Oceana[82] to its millennial destiny as an ideal commonwealth for expansion.

---

81 Pocock, *Machiavellian Moment*, 386. For the earlier formulation see Pocock, *Ancient Constitution*, 129.
82 See also J.G.A. Pocock (ed.), *Harrington: Commonwealth of Oceana and A System of Politics*, Cambridge: Cambridge University Press, 1992.

Conclusion

'They Are in Our Town but Not of It' – Patrick Wolfe and Belonging

Lynette Russell

With Patrick Wolfe's death in 2016 we sadly lost one of the most original, committed, and generous historians of colonialism.[1] Patrick's intellectual influence was immense; he was read by historians, anthropologists, archaeologists, cultural theorists and Indigenous scholars the world over. Among his many achievements was a contribution to developing a much-cited, oft-subjected to critique, and hugely influential theory of settler colonialism. As a politically engaged scholar and an impassioned champion for Indigenous rights, Patrick drew heavily on the scholarly

---

1   This exploration of Patrick's career was greatly enhanced by the work of David Haworth who shared with me the task of documenting Patrick's impact. I am pleased to note that in 2019 I established the annual Patrick Wolfe bursary for the Australian Historical Association – sincere thanks to Zora Simic, Mike Wolfe and Maeve Williams for all their assistance, and to Ben Silberstein for helping me untangle some of my ideas. To Myles Russell-Cook whose memories of Patrick were pertinent and textured I am grateful. Ultimately my greatest thanks go to my mentor, supervisor, and friend, Patrick, who is forever missed.

and activist analytical work and research conducted by Indigenous people both Australian and international. This was a debt he never failed to acknowledge. Patrick's scholarship has been pivotal to my intellectual development, it has provided a foundation, and a structure. Even decades after my first encounter, Patrick's influence continues. In this essay I do not attempt even the pretence of objectivity; such a position would be impossible and indeed disingenuous. Eschewing objectivity seems highly appropriate in this context – as the Aboriginal scholar Tony Birch noted in the obituary he wrote for *Aboriginal History*, Patrick was 'an openly emotional thinker' who 'strongly felt that [Indigenous] subjectivity, rather than being a dirty word, was an intellectual asset'.[2] Patrick, while an ally and 'comrade' of Indigenous people never failed to identify himself as a newcomer, a settler, an immigrant. When describing his hometown Healesville, which was home to the Coranderrk Aboriginal Station, he noted:

> Terrible things were done at Coranderrk. When I go to the supermarket or the post office, I see descendants of people to whom these things were done. They generally keep themselves to themselves. They are in our town but not of it. They are of Wurundjeri country, which I am in but not of.[3]

He understood the complexity of settler-colonial relations, he knew where he 'belonged', and he trod carefully but defiantly.

In these concluding pages, I want to consider three aspects of Patrick's work: interdisciplinarity and impact; settler and postcolonialism, and his multisite analysis. All of these are aspects that relate to one of Patrick's main motivations which was to understand and interrogate the various locations in which race and colonialism and settler colonialism plays out. Patrick was one of the very few people who did multisite research and comparative research on this level and this depth characterizes his work.

---

2   Tony Birch, 'Good Patrick', *Aboriginal History*, 40, 2016, 225–6.
3   Patrick Wolfe, *Traces of History: Elementary Structures of Race*, London: Verso, 2016, 80.

Interdisciplinarity and Impact

While Patrick is usually described as an historian, and much of his writing is historical, it is also much more than that. As an activist scholar, he was an anthropologist, an ethnographer, and a political agent. His final monograph, *Traces of History: Elementary Structures of Race*, is a culmination of the intellectual work that can be found in each of those areas. From my perspective, Patrick was one of the most important theorists of racial formation over the past three decades.

When taken as a whole, Patrick's output was by no means voluminous.[4] On the contrary, it was modest and certainly would not be considered adequate by the bean-counters who currently police university academics and their research 'products'. However, his work has been cited nearly 4,000 times, a figure that puts him as one of Australia's most highly cited humanities scholars.[5] His influence on a generation of scholars is enormous. My connection to his intellectual project emerged from his supervising my doctoral research. I approached him with an anthropology and archaeology background with the idea that I might research for a PhD in history, and, as he recognized the value of interdisciplinarity, he enthusiastically agreed. Through him I learned of Edward Said and the critique of orientalism, I was exposed to the (at that stage) crude attempts others had made at creating an intellectual school of Aboriginalism. From here, we began to engage with and interrogate settler colonialism. It is a direct segue, that settler-colonial theory became a framework from which I started to conduct my own analyses. For most of my academic career, I have been concerned with Aboriginal agency – the ways in which Aboriginal people have responded and reacted to various components and aspects of colonialism.[6] The doctoral thesis became my first book, *Savage Imaginings*, in which I explored the ways

---

4 I include a bibliography of his work for anyone interested in following up his ideas.

5 I had to recreate this figure by systematically working through various Google Scholar citations. As anyone who knew Patrick would attest, he cared little for the number crunching of referencing or citation games. I suspect he would find it amusing to have someone work through his publications looking for 'impact'.

6 I have not (yet) worked with Torres Strait Islanders so I am using the term Aboriginal here and not Indigenous deliberately and consciously.

in which public discourses of aboriginality and Aboriginal identity had been shaped by colonial powers rather than by Aboriginal people themselves.[7] Across a range of genres, popular culture, museums, and academic writing I attempted to show how Aboriginal people responded, and continue to respond, to the ways that they are framed, and subjected to the colonial gaze.

Settler and Postcolonialism

As already noted, Patrick was crucial to my intellectual development perhaps most importantly via his first book *Settler Colonialism and the Transformation of Anthropology*. The idea of settler colonialism as a structure and not an event was radical and paradigm changing. Over the next two decades we can see how that thought (event versus structure) became an essential part of his legacy as a scholar. In *Traces of History*, it is evident that he is trying to make this premise more complex, more nuanced, and to work through some of the implications within that idea. He is both responding to critique but also demonstrating how his own intellectual work had morphed. When first published, *Settler Colonialism and the Transformation of Anthropology* was part of three different dominant political and scholarly conversations that were taking place in the 1990s around how to think about and theorize colonialism.

The first of these conversations attempted to configure the idea of 'postcolonialism' and the questioning of the politics of independence. In the Australian context, it was the emergence of a Federated Nation State and the formal transfer of colonial power to elites which was regarded as ending the colonial period. Of course, for Indigenous people, this is a postcolonialism that stands in contrast to their ongoing experience of being colonized. Australia, like New Zealand, is both colony and colonizer. The notion that the transfer of power and the establishment of self-governance leads to the postcolonial era, is shown to be spurious at best.

The second discourse was concerned with language and terminology and how this dominated conversations about race – especially in the

---

7   Lynette Russell, *Savage Imaginings: Historical and Contemporary Constructions of Australian Aboriginalities*, Melbourne: Australian Scholarly Publications, 2001.

settler societies of the United States, Canada, Australia, and New Zealand. There were frequent references to a language of diversity and multiculturalism and the special place of Indigenous people as First Nations and Traditional Owners was subsumed by the shift to a multicultural framework. As a result, for a time, many considered the relevant way of thinking about race was through politics of difference and the capacity of cultural difference to be reconciled through within global values.

The final conversation that I regard as pivotal was within the history discipline itself. History in the 1990s became more political, more radical, and more presentist than it had previously been. Using the term colonial in settler-invader settings was now a conscious and overtly political statement. While in America this idea that colonial/colonialism referred to the present has only really taken hold with Native American scholars rather than the history discipline as a whole, what emerged out of this period was the sense that all histories are connected to the dominant politics at large, all settler-colonial states have their own exceptional histories, giving us opportunities to see both similarities and patterns as well as the unique and site-specific. However, Patrick challenged this by arguing for appraising a structure not an event. Suddenly, here was the paradigm that said there is something that links all of these different communities and it is the effort of particular settlers to remove and eliminate the Native.

In *Settler Colonialism*, we can see the development of his theoretical premise of the 'logic of elimination', which he followed up in several seminal publications.[8] Patrick's argument, which is much cited, is that settler colonialism operates through and indeed is dependent on a 'logic of elimination'. Settler-colonial power both requires and emerges out of the destruction of native peoples, their social and political groups, and their culture, if not their literal eradication.[9] Accordingly, the iterative process of eliminating Indigenous peoples is a feature of settler societies,

---

8   See Patrick Wolfe, *Logics of Elimination: Colonial Policies on Indigenous Peoples in Australia and the United States*, University of Nebraska Human Rights and Human Diversity Initiative Monograph Series, 2000; Patrick Wolfe, 'Settler Colonialism and the Elimination of the Native', *Journal of Genocide Research*, 8: 4, 2006, 387–409. For a precursor, see Patrick Wolfe, 'Nation and MiscegeNation: Discursive Continuity in the Post-Mabo Era', *Social Analysis*, 36, 1994, 93–152.

9   Although I prefer the term 'Indigenous', Wolfe prefers the nineteenth-century phrase of 'native' in this context.

both historically and into the future. This 'elimination' is often construed to be equivalent to genocide, but it is not – settler colonialism needs to destroy Indigenous societies *only* to the extent that this is required for dispossession and the subsequent repossession of the land. This is Patrick's most important point, which clarifies both the why and the how settler societies based on the logic of elimination also protect and argue for restrictive rights for Indigenous people via political recognition, cultural heritage protections, and even native titles rights as long as these stand in opposition to native sovereignty. The creation of welfare dependency is therefore seen as both a form of control and elimination, as a minority people who depend on the state for their physical survival are unlikely to challenge for control of the land.

In his book *Red Skin, White Masks*, Native American scholar Glen Coulthard builds on Patrick's work as he explores, expands, and then challenges the elimination of the native within a framework of critiquing the politics of recognition.[10] Patrick's most significant contribution was the assertion that settler-colonial power requires destruction of Indigenous people and colonies. He argues that, in fact, the elimination of Indigenous people is a continuous feature of settler societies both in Australia and America, and elsewhere. Through countless examples, he demonstrates that this is not merely something that happened in the past, but that it continues to the current moment. To understand this, we must look beyond historical texts and consider cultural and Indigenous studies, anthropology and politics. One thing about Patrick was that he was never interested in an apolitical past, he was really interested in contemporary politics, and how the historical trajectory of what he identified in the past played out today. He was an activist at heart.

Multisite Analysis

Criticisms of Patrick's work were varied and many.[11] One aspect of this criticism, which became a persistent critique of both Patrick's work and

---

10   Glen Coulthard, *Red Skin, White Masks: Rejecting the Colonial Politics of Recognition*, Minneapolis: University of Minnesota Press, 2014.

11   Antipathy for his work is found in Tim Rowse, 'Rethinking Indigenous Histories', Australian Historical Association Plenary Panel, 2013, and Lisa Ford, 'Locating Indigenous Self-Determination in the Margins of Settler Sovereignty:

the field in general, was that this structure was monocausal, that it was a sort of self-fulfilling prophesy: if it is structure, not event, then everything is covered, and it is very difficult to be able to make sense of historical shifts and changes. I think this charge was inappropriately levelled at Patrick's work as he was developing a sophisticated concept at the time, a concept that was indebted to Marx and in its own way not dissimilar to other über concepts that we use, often as a kind of intellectual shorthand, like capitalism, liberalism, or white supremacy. None of which would be regarded as absolute, monolithic or monocausal. Conceptually, *structure* allows us to politically understand what types of agency are available, to see reactions as both contained and unpredictable. In a way, the whole point is to narrow the field through specific conceptual tools. The title of his last book, *Traces of History*, is evidence of the extent to which Patrick acknowledged this criticism. By focusing on the interconnected concepts of race and colonialism as literally the book's data, he was able to infuse the discourse that had previously been about settler colonialism with a great deal of multisite work that demonstrated the relationship between contingency and structure.

Multisite analyses have, for the most part, fallen out of favour. Instead, many historians focus on detailed and empirically rich case studies. Patrick chose to do something both radical and introspective. Over the course of more than a decade of thinking deeply about these issues, he explored and interrogated how he might hold on to the arguments about structure, but also how to develop a model that allows scholars and activists to make broad historical claims that are not merely reduced to micro histories while at the same time incorporating contingencies. *Traces of History* provides for this contingency through the differences in the multisite case studies. He draws links between southern hemisphere Antipodean contexts, along with North America and Palestine. He convincingly argues that the different ways that racialized subjects and indeed racial categories are constructed in these places can be read against each other in similar settler-colonial contexts and structures.

An Introduction', in Lisa Ford and Tim Rowse (eds), *Between Indigenous and Settler Governance*, Abingdon: Routledge, 2013, 1–11.

Conclusion

If Patrick's career is bookended by *Settler Colonialism* and *Traces of History* it is worthwhile seeing these two books in their evolution. In *Traces of History*, he pushes us to reconsider what we might think of settler colonization and the specific locations where we might find it. This is a conceptually masterful book, but it rests on his earlier work, as he delves into a politics that allows us to see structure; to see competing narratives, contingent against political circumstances operating in site-specific ways. Underpinning this is his anthropologist's lens, the biologically decried but socially apt question of race. He argues that racial formations are always incomplete. It is this incompleteness that gives us a glimmer of hope. When he notes that 'the incompleteness of racial domination is the trace and the achievement of resistance, a space of hope',[12] Patrick is effectively saying that if race is historical, it has a beginning – and then perhaps it might also have an ending.

This concluding chapter has been hard to write, much harder than I anticipated. One of the many reasons why I wish Patrick was still here would be to work through his writings and discuss his ideas. It is ironic that his death meant I immersed myself in the entire gamut of his work more completely than ever before. In creating a bibliography of his work, I could see the way his ideas developed, shifted, and morphed. Politically, Patrick and I were very similar, though he was vastly more driven to activism than I am. As I prepared this discussion of his work, I began to see the difference between the experience of writing between race and colonialism in the 1990s and the experience of writing about it today. It is not merely that there has been a transformation in his scholarship; rather that I now see a set of fascinating political formations that have emerged allowing the scholarship to connect to contemporary conversations in a way that was not necessarily the case twenty years ago.

Patrick's work is and will always be of the left – he was ultimately a Marxist. His work has relevance particularly for those of us who are still interested in seeing how Marx might play out with the historical discourse of contemporary Australia. His work has been taken up by a new generation of people, and his influence is found in the work of

---

12   Wolfe, *Traces of History*, 427.

non-Indigenous and Indigenous scholars and academics.[13] There remain fairly conservative elements within the historical discipline that I think have real difficulties with Patrick's work. But for his intellectual descendants – the students that have come after him that are deeply affected and engaged with this work – he has left a powerful legacy. He listened, he always listened; and he self-reflected, as evidenced by his acceptance of his own naivety when he first came to Australia and was educated by various Aboriginal people, particularly in Melbourne. His naivety was the catalyst for an enormous intellectual legacy.

Bibliography

Books

Wolfe, P., *Settler Colonialism and the Transformation of Anthropology: The Politics and Poetics of an Ethnographic Event*, London: Cassell, 1999.

Wolfe, P., *Traces of History: Elementary Structures of Race*, London: Verso, 2016.

---

13 Of the many scholars who have drawn upon and critically engaged with Patrick's work I note in particular Native Hawaiian scholars Kēhaulani J. Kauanui, '"A Structure, Not an Event": Settler Colonialism and Enduring Indigeneity', *Lateral*, 2016; Noelani Goodyear-Ka'ōpua, *The Seeds We Planted: Portraits of a Native Hawaiian Charter School*, Minneapolis: University of Minnesota Press, 2013; Julie Kaomea, 'Education for Elimination in Nineteenth-Century Hawai'i: Settler Colonialism and the Native Hawaiian Chiefs' Children's Boarding School', *History of Education Quarterly*, 54: 2, 2014, 123–44; Métis scholar Chris Andersen, *Métis: Race, Recognition, and the Struggle for Indigenous Peoplehood*, Vancouver: University of British Columbia Press, 2014; Native American scholar and activist Audra Simpson, *Mohawk Interruptus: Political Life across the Borders of Settler States*, Durham: Duke University Press, 2014; and non-Indigenous writers working in the Australian context including Elizabeth Povinelli, *The Cunning of Recognition: Indigenous Alterities and the Making of Australian Multiculturalism*, Durham: Duke University Press, 2002; Leigh Boucher, 'Masculinity Gone Mad: Settler Colonialism, Medical Discourse and the White Body in Late Nineteenth-century Victoria', *Lilith: A Feminist History Journal*, 13, 2004; Ben Silverstein, 'From Population to Citizen: The Subjects of the 1939 Aboriginal New Deal in Australia's Northern Territory', *KONTUR*, 22, 2011, 17–33.

Articles

Kauanui, J.K. and Patrick Wolfe, 'Settler Colonialism Then and Now', *Politica and Società*, 2, 2012, 235–58.

Lloyd, D. and Patrick Wolfe, 'Settler Colonial Logics and the Neoliberal Regime', *Settler Colonial Studies*, 6: 2, 2016, 109–18.

Wolfe, P., 'Encoding Domination: A Reconsideration of Basil Bernstein's Theory of Codes', *Melbourne Journal of Politics*, 14, 1982, 27–37.

Wolfe, P., 'On Being Woken Up: The Dreamtime in Anthropology and in Australian Settler Culture', *Comparative Studies in Society and History*, 33: 2, 1991, 197–224.

Wolfe, P., 'Reluctant Invaders', Review of *Dark Side of the Dream: Australian Literature and the Postcolonial Mind* by Bob Hodge and Vijay Mishra, *Meanjin*, 51: 2, 1992, 333–8.

Wolfe, P., 'Reply to Bob Hodge and Vijay Mishra', *Meanjin*, 51: 4, 1992, 884–8.

Wolfe, P., 'Nation and MiscegeNation: Discursive Continuity in the Post-Mabo Era', *Social Analysis*, 36, 1994, 93–152.

Wolfe, P., '"White Man's Flour": Doctrines of Virgin Birth in Evolutionist Ethnogenetics and Australian State-Formation', *History and Anthropology*, 8: 1–4, 1994, 165–205.

Wolfe, P., 'History and Imperialism: A Century of Theory, from Marx to Postcolonialism', *American Historical Review*, 102: 2, 1997, 388–420.

Wolfe, P., Review of *Invasion to Embassy: Land in Aboriginal Politics in New South Wales, 1770–1972* by Heather Goodall, *Oceania*, 68: 1, 1997, 73–4.

Wolfe, P., 'Words about Wik: Historian Patrick Wolfe Looks at how Language has Muddied the Wik Debate in this Transcript from Radio National's Lingua Franca', *24 Hours*, June 1998, 64–7.

Wolfe, P., 'The Limits of Native Title', *Meanjin*, 59: 3, 2000, 129–44.

Wolfe, P., 'Land, Labor, and Difference: Elementary Structures of Race', *American Historical Review*, 106: 3, 2001, 866–905.

Wolfe, P., 'Race and Racialisation: Some Thoughts', *Postcolonial Studies*, 5: 1, 2002, 51–62.

Wolfe, P., 'Can the Muslim Speak? An Indebted Critique', *History and Theory*, 41: 3, 2002, 367–80.

Wolfe, P., 'Off-Duty Darwinism', Review of *Disseminating Darwinism: The Role of Place, Race, Religion, and Gender* edited by Ronald L. Numbers and John Stenhouse, *Australian Book Review*, 243, 2002, 47–8.

Wolfe, P., 'Race and Citizenship', *OAH Magazine of History*, 18: 5, 2004, 66–71.

Wolfe, P., Review of *Genocide and Settler Society: Frontier Violence and Stolen Indigenous Children in Australian History* edited by A. Dirk Moses, *Journal of World History*, 16: 4, 2005, 502–5.

Wolfe, P., 'Operation Sandy Track: Michael O'Connor and the War on Australian History', Review of *The Invention of Terra Nullius: Historical and Legal Fictions on the Foundation of Australia* by Michael O'Connor, *Overland*, 183, 2006, 26–31.

Wolfe, P., 'Settler Colonialism and the Elimination of the Native', *Journal of Genocide Research*, 8: 4, 2006, 387–409.

Wolfe, P., 'Corpus Nullius: The Exception of Indians and Other Aliens in US Constitutional Discourse', *Postcolonial Studies*, 10: 2, 2007, 127–51.

Wolfe, P., 'Robert Manne, the Apology and Genocide', *Arena*, 94, 2008, 31–3.

Wolfe, P., Review of *Blood and Soil: A World History of Genocide and Extermination from Sparta to Darfur* by Ben Kiernan, *The Age*, 10 March 2008.

Wolfe, P., 'Universalism and its Discontents: In response to Alastair Davidson', *Thesis Eleven*, 100, 2010, 117–27.

Wolfe, P., 'After the Frontier: Separation and Absorption in US Indian Policy', *Settler Colonial Studies*, 1: 1, 2011, 13–51.

Wolfe, P., Review of *Before Eminent Domain: Toward a History of Expropriation of Land for the Common Good* by Susan Reynolds, *American Historical Review*, 116: 2, 2011, 414–15.

Wolfe, P., 'Purchase by Other Means: The Palestine Nakba and Zionism's Conquest of Economics', *Settler Colonial Studies*, 2: 1, 2012, 133–71.

Wolfe, P., 'New Jews for Old: Settler State Formation and the Impossibility of Zionism: In Memory of Edward W. Said', *Arena*, 37–8, 2012, 285–321.

Wolfe, P., 'Against the Intentional Fallacy: Logocentrism and Continuity in the Rhetoric of Indian Dispossession', *American Indian Culture and Research Journal*, 36: 1, 2012, 3–46.

Wolfe, P., 'The Settler Complex: An Introduction', *American Indian Culture and Research Journal*, 37: 2, 2013, 1–22.

Wolfe, P., 'Recuperating Binarism: A Heretical Introduction', *Settler Colonial Studies*, 3: 3–4, 2013, 257–79.

Book chapters and other essays

Evans, J., Ann Genovese, Alexander Reilly, and Patrick Wolfe, 'Sovereignty: Frontiers of Possibility', in Julie Evans, Ann Genovese, Alexander Reilly, and Patrick Wolfe (eds), *Sovereignty: Frontiers of Possibility*, Honolulu: University of Hawaii Press, 2013, 1–16.

Silverstein, B. and Patrick Wolfe, 'Ideology', in Philippa Levine and John Marriott (eds), *Ashgate Companion to Modern Imperial Histories*, Farnham: Ashgate, 2012, 471–88.

Wolfe, P., 'Logics of Elimination: Colonial Policies on Indigenous Peoples in Australia and the United States', University of Nebraska Human Rights and Human Diversity Initiative, Lincoln: University of Nebraska, 2000.

Wolfe, P., 'The World of History and the World-as-History: Twentieth-Century Theories of Imperialism', in Prasenjit Duara (ed.), *Decolonization: Perspectives from Now and Then*, Rewriting Histories Series, London and New York: Routledge, 2004, 101–17.

Wolfe, P., 'Islam, Europe and Indian Nationalism: Towards a Postcolonial Transnationalism', in Ann Curthoys and Marilyn Lake (eds), *Connected Worlds: History in Transnational Perspective*, Canberra: ANU Press, 2006, 233–65.

Wolfe, P., 'Palestine, Project Europe and the (Un)-Making of the New Jew: In Memory of Edward W. Said', in Ned Curthoys and Debjani Ganguly (eds), *Edward Said: The Legacy of a Public Intellectual*, Melbourne: Melbourne University Press, 2007, 313–37.

Wolfe, P., 'Structure and Event: Settler Colonialism, Time, and the Question of Genocide', in A. Dirk Moses (ed.), *Empire, Colony, Genocide: Conquest, Occupation, and Subaltern Resistance in World History*, New York: Berghahn Books, 2008, 102–32.

Wolfe, P., 'Race and Citizenship', in Gary W. Reichard and Ted Dickson (eds), *America on the World Stage: A Global Approach to US History*, Urbana and Chicago: University of Illinois Press, 2008, 217–28.

Wolfe, P., 'Race and the Trace of History: For Henry Reynolds', in Fiona Bateman and Lionel Pilkington (eds), *Studies in Settler Colonialism: Politics, Identity and Culture*, Basingstoke and New York: Palgrave Macmillan, 2011, 272–96.

Wolfe, P., 'Introduction', in Patrick Wolfe (ed.), *The Settler Complex: Recuperating Binarism in Colonial Studies*, Los Angeles: UCLA American Indian Studies Center, 2016, 1–24.

Edited volumes

Evans, J., Ann Genovese, Alexander Reilly, and Patrick Wolfe (eds), *Sovereignty: Frontiers of Possibility*, Honolulu: University of Hawaii Press, 2013.

Wolfe, P. (ed.), *The Settler Complex: Recuperating Binarism in Colonial Studies*, Los Angeles: UCLA American Indian Studies Center, 2016.

Dissertation

Wolfe, P., 'White Man's Flour: Imperialism and an Appropriated Anthropology', PhD Dissertation, University of Melbourne, 1996.